NOURISH

Also by Isabel Chiara

Eat Your Words

Bod Behavior

Nourish

Beyond Food—
Feeding the Path of Personal Power and Joy

ISABEL CHIARA

Printed in USA.

10 9 8 7 6 5 4 3 2 1

NOURISH:
Beyond Food—Feeding the Path of Personal Power and Joy

ISBN: 978-1-967611-01-0 (paperback)
ISBN: 978-1-967611-00-3 (eBook)
Library of Congress Control Number: 2025908112

Published by Nuclear Healing, Fairfield, CT
Cover design by Olga Plastino
Publication managed by AuthorImprints.com

Learn more at www.isabel-chiara.com

Names have been changed to protect the privacy of clients depicted.

Legal disclaimer: The contents of *Nourish* are not intended as medical advice. Please be aware that, as the author of this book, I am not a medical doctor, nor am I in a position to act as a substitute for medically licensed dietitians or specialists working in the field of eating disorders or any other health condition. While the intention of this book is to offer inspiration for the reader's well-being, please note that by reading this book you agree that your path with nourishment, body connection, and food is determined and best directed by yourself and your personal dietician or medical professional.

For every woman in this world who has searched for the sustenance that feeds her whole system—who longs to ground into her rich roots and expand into her verdant shoots, and turn her seeds of potential into a life in bloom.

Contents

*F*inding and Feeding
the Authentic Self

T he only place to find what is true is inside of ourselves. It's a simple direction; a simple road inward. It can just take what feels like a million lifetimes to finally find the door, the slip-glide-sweep that drops us right into our center, into a place where we can reach into ourselves for truth—where *we know we know*, and that's enough. And the trickiest part about getting the entry ticket—that exclusive pass that allows us VIP access to our own empowered center—is that we can actually believe we have it well before we do. Yes, we can believe we're operating from this inner-truth most of the time, even if, it turns out, we've been hovering outside of ourselves for decades, judging who we think we should be—miles from truly being informed by self.

"Self" is a saucy subject in its own right. The best of both the scientific and the alchemically spiritual worlds all agree that each individual "self" is inextricably interconnected to the whole web of life. That might be why it sometimes feels so hard to tune out the chatter of people sitting next to us in a public space, or not be emotionally impacted by global news. It's interconnectedness that enables us to love, receive, extend ourselves, feel hurt, and make amends. And even in all this inevitable interconnection, at the same time, as twisted as it might sound—we're sorely alone. We're born into one body, and we live life through this sole center of "I." We can make union, commit to marriages or partnerships, incorporate, and more—but at best, through all of this, we're learning the art of compatibility, the art of commitment between self and other; single particles in an ocean of light.

Whatever "self" is, it has a full-on sensory system: tactile, olfactory, oral, aural, visual. We're packed with amazing defenses—systemic immunity, programmed with a complex ability to respond. We drink in the universe; we let it saturate our cells. Our "self" biologically digests life's processes through a body—chews up experience and does its best to synthesize life—like a cow chews grass. Midst taking in sunlight and shadow, experiencing circadian and lunar rhythms, and the elemental energies inherent in our environments, we somehow absorb the outer world while maintaining homeostasis: a range of "self." We live inside an ever-changing cellular situation: a self in a body. And when we can use our faculties—our minds, our breath, and our senses—to dial into our core sense of embodiment, we get to make use of the greatest gift of our design as human beings, namely the ability to harness "identity": a self-awareness that engages with life's opportunities in an ever-changing world, crafting its unique contribution in the tapestry of time.

It is my belief that, especially as women, our "selves" have historically been malnourished. Our decades of obsessive wrestling with diets and attempting to fit into an externally imposed concept of some "perfect physique." Pressures to appear infallibly, agelessly perfect, have distracted us from the true glorious power we can tap into when we accept ourselves; when we choose what nourishes "self" from the inside out. After writing two books that heavily explored themes around food, eating, behavior, and being in a body, I released a first-of-its-kind app—Nourish—which encourages users to explore and transform their under-pinning narratives about food and eating through highly visual active meditations, accessing the deep psyche to acti-vate their most nourished lives. Soon after, the manuscript of this book, *Nourish*, poured through me—a book that would piece together modalities, therapeutic perspectives, anthropological considerations, and my own personal que-ries formed around two central questions: "*Beyond* food and diet, what does it mean to be a woman living a truly nourished life in the twenty-first century? And how do we choose nourishment from the inside out?"

I wanted to write a kind of woman's manual—a wo-manual—that would remind us of our own inner-torchlight. This light guides us to the unique door-way of our own central wisdom, a wisdom that is ours to embody and share as we wish in this world. For me, this book was a personal self-divining tool for creating a pro-foundly nourished life, where nourishment is a term de-fined by our own standards, a way to claim personal sanc-tity, professional triumph, and rich relationships.

And my hope is that in my lifetime I can continue to support women who are seeking real nourishment, women being called to go deeper, until they reach the jeweled inner-door to their own self-center, their own truth, and can define for themselves what it means to live a nourish-ing life. This book is for those of us who are ready to create nutriment for our souls, far beyond the five food groups.

Isabel

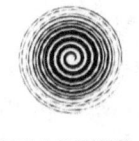

CHAPTER 1

Book Three: Why Me?

I believe I wanted to write this book all along, even before I started *Eat Your Words* (my first book) and then again, when I wrote *Bod Behavior* (my second). I wasn't ready, though. As shameful as it is to consider, I don't think I could figure out how a woman like me, who still couldn't slip into her "perfect" dress size (but could occasionally slip into a very "imperfect" eating day) would be entitled to write a book in the first person, from her own wisdom—sharing on the subject of how to truly nourish the self. Then I caught myself. One of the cruelest tricks the mind is prone to playing (which literally robs us of living a life that feels nourished) is the belief that we have to "arrive" somewhere in order to be good enough.

Even before *f-ing* Cinderella, women felt society's tight timeframes put upon them. They had X hours (or seasons, or years) to earn the revered role of princess chosen at the ball, and on all accounts, they should focus on prepping for that fantasy to come to life, rather than face the ghastly existence of living *sans* validating prince, undesirable—and thus impoverished. But you know, even Disney has re-written its scripts these days, performing an about-face in recognition that women have value even if they struggle, and—maybe even more so—have value for showing vulnerability in their struggle, and for their ability to triumph over oppression. By the time Mattel caught on, and even Barbie was going through her own personal identity rebranding, I'd also had enough of my self-limitations. If these fictitious plastic symbols had the brawn to bear the wisdom they'd gained from years of living in packaging or on paper, then I sure as heck could share what I know is true about how to live a life that is nourishing, because I know what it is to have committed deeply to that path. Like many other women, I've experienced the hellacious hardship of slipping from self-love and having to give all it takes to miraculously locate and then get on that horse of self-love again and again, riding off into my own sunset—on my own, fed by the sun and sand.

One beautiful gift of entering my sixties was that I finally got a good, true grip on the crippling mindset that plagues most women, and was able to really reverse it. That is, the belief that "only when you get to point X, will you finally be enough to have Y and Z." When I hit sixty, I recognized that I'd inevitably reached point X after decades of spinning around the sun, and accepted that I was enough; that in fact, I was beyond having Y and Z—I could hold the whole dang alphabet. I will say, it's not a totally empty adage that "youth is wasted on the young." It would have been great to give myself permission to know I was *more* than enough when I was twenty-one. But I do believe the freedom we find when we learn to truly nourish ourselves—at any point in our lives—is ageless and priceless. To nourish our own lives by our own standards and to find expansiveness and freedom in mind, body, soul, and spirit is eternally valuable, and it echoes generationally beyond ourselves.

So here I am, creating an offering for women struggling with body image, food, and diet, even though I'm not fully "over" my own issues in these areas. I still avoid the scale, struggle not to criticize myself in the mirror, and I still sometimes work out my anxieties with food. When it comes to transcending outworn behaviors around food, it's tricky, because food is not something we can quit cold turkey (and honestly, thank God, because in my opinion, there is so much pleasure to be had in all things food—including cold turkey). But because there is no "switch" to turn food off when we have any kind of addictive relationship to it, we have to make a life-changing about-face: we must learn to "eat" food rather than "use" food. And because we first learned how to relate to food in early childhood, our transformation in our food relationship must start with exploring and transforming our entire life narrative around sustenance, value, and presence. To live our way into being inside-out self-nourishing women, we must learn to reparent our inner-child—the one who, for whatever reason, missed the love-filled lesson on how to get the spoon in her mouth, at a pace and in a style that could really feed her mind, body, soul, and spirit.

Food has been central to my family's life and culture, the core of our vocabulary in many ways. Not to generalize (but, to generalize), this is largely because we come from a vibrant Italian agricultural heritage. The cuisine from that region, and our ancestors' relationship to it, is imprinted in our DNA. My family arrived in the United States by boat, empty-handed, carrying nothing but a dream and the farmland food-centered work focus that had been in their bloodline for generations. To be honest, I can hardly wrap my mind around what their voyage was like—what it would be like to travel for weeks without serious amounts of snacks in my bags, and floating in the ocean without knowing for sure where or when I'd get my next meal. My family made their way in the United States; in fact, they grew their new existence by creating restaurants—and when they had children, we worked as a family in the world of restaurants, together.

That's the space I grew up in. There was no "togetherness" without our faith in food. I often joke that our family's love language is "short-order cook"-style. That means our texts will read something like, "Did you get this done?" or, "Make it happen, fast!" The survival-mode intensity and work ethic my family exemplified was sometimes hard to swallow, to say the least. I figured out early, however, that I could swallow food to compensate for my discomfort, whether that discomfort came from absorbing my family's energy or just dealing with my own lack of boundaries, and, as a result, my dissociated sense of self. I believe that in our close-knit family, I wasn't really sure where I started and my relatives began. Metaphorically speaking, when things got hot in the kitchen (which was pretty much every day), I internalized all the heat as my own. Whatever critical words I'd hear my father yell out when agitated I took to heart as truth. Like many children, I internalized my parents' feedback (which was usually critical) as simply my self-image. I then responded with some version of safeguarding, which usually translated as consuming something with sugar in it. Sugar, let's say, became "my favorite auntie." Food sufficed to fill the spaces that really longed for my family's loving encouragement; for the reassurance that just being me would be enough. Despite my environment, my spirit's nature could not fully be repressed. It wanted the freedom to express itself, to know and voice my feelings, and, even more, to relieve an intensity that seemed generationally handed down. But without knowing how to safely be me, I lost myself in food.

I admit I have the same verve and the same fighter's mind as my father. I have his operational management abilities and tendency to be quick to defend (which, let's just say, has definitely provided me with more than enough material for my necessary growth and transformational work). Even though I see that I do "come from my family," from the get-go, I felt different—I can't say I'm the black sheep, but I may be the pink elephant in the room.

There was a language of energy within me that felt outside the capacity of my clan to speak, an undeniable sense inside my psyche and my soul. I felt connected to something vastly wide and cosmic, and that there was something way beyond our little town that mattered. In some ways, I may have been tapping into "energy" as a means of dissociating from my own body, as though some spirited part of me lived outside of myself. Regardless, I found a positive outlet; seeking spirituality allowed me to connect to something that felt full, affirming, and alive. And so I spent decades obtaining master's-level certifications in multiple energy modalities.

My discomfort led me along the path of learning, as it always has. I am a constant enrollee in Life Learning 101, which is largely why I write, as well—because I find learning fascinating. In this way, learning to access my spiritual "gifts" enabled me to see others' lives abundantly unlocked, and protect their highest calling. I could connect to a sacred, highly visual state—a kind of luminous pink bubble realm, and manifest abundance for you, me, and our community (and to be honest, I could even psychically access your grandmother, if you needed me to). However, I couldn't access my own body. I still had the perspective that spirituality, and faith, and all the places I could show up with reverence in integrity existed *outside* of my body, *beyond* the everyday routine. When it came to life-in-a-body, I continued to numb myself out on the regular, specifically using food. I don't think I was even aware of the fact I wasn't *in* my own body, or really feeling my sensations and emotions. Nor was I likely aware that many of my actions were responses to stimulation of my long-held patterns, which I interpreted as uncomfortable. When I look back now, though, I do see that I lived for years and years without feeling much of a range of sensation, or any emotion beyond what was deemed acceptable in my family (basically, hot-sauce varieties of extremely peppered anger).

I wish I could say there was one linear path that allowed me to find my faith not just in external, spiritual, or cosmic places, but equally within my own body, because I would then give it to you directly. For me, there wasn't just one light that showed up in the dark, but a million lights, many of which I couldn't see, even the ones that had been there all along. With my help and readiness, they turned on one by one, ultimately illuminating the realization that eating is a holy, spiritual act.

I came to see, little epiphany by little epiphany, that what and when and how I feed my body is the most powerful rite of reverence I can regularly make in this lifetime; a spiritual pilgrimage to my own inner-temple. Where once I had lost myself in food, I finally came to feel that when I open my mouth to eat, I am showing up for myself. I realized that when I'm eating food, I need to find myself. When I endeavor to take a bite, consume, and swallow food—I am acknowledging reality; I am cocreating with life. Relating to myself, and connecting with eating, is the same sacred rite and ceremony I'd sought in the far cosmos, light-years from my pelvic floor. I wrote *Nourish* because I want us to gain faith in ourselves—especially as women. We are all part of a vast, spiritual cosmos, and I wish for you to feel the light and glory within your being, not only in how you choose your food, but in how you choose your life. This was the missing piece for me all along.

Consider for a moment this symbolic scenario. Imagine you are playing a computer game, and you've created this virtual "you" character that you have to move around with your cursor, staying right on top of her virtual body. Now, imagine that all these other distractions come into your character's field of view while you play your game, and that your virtual you is stimulated by the things in her environment. She's pulled in various directions by people she knows, or tasks she needs to attend to, states of conflict, random glittery and gold possibilities that could help her mystically ascend to levels two, three, four, and beyond—the all-time gaming champion. But in all of these moments where your character has a million things flying into her realm, if you take your cursor off her—off of yourself—your virtual you loses her ability to be in her world. She is rendered inoperable. She dissolves with some gaming sound to mark her disappearance—she loses a life. With this analogy in mind, I can say I have fully realized the importance of staying with myself; with my body, my mind, and my breath—the spirit of life that feeds my soul.

I have seen how I have disappeared myself—whether in a bag of chips, an argument, a giant temptation, or the self-criticism that can loop in my mind, in a sort of internal extermination of my self-worth. I know my work here is to learn to stay with myself as the safe place to check in, to get the feedback that I am okay, to trust that I am enough. I want to share this "gospel" of *Nourish* that I know is inherently all of ours—to spread the nourishing news that as women, we can truly find respite, solace, and self-care in our own bodies. I believe that my commitment to stay on the path of cultivating presence in my own life is actually bettered by helping others to do the same. I believe that we're here, as women, to learn to truly nourish our lives together. That being said, *Nourish* is not about reaching a goal. Rather, it is about being in life. I will say, however, that once I really made the commitment to keep my cursor (so to speak) on my virtual me—or, work to find embodiment on my own trajectory, rather than losing my sense of self in the stimulation all around me all the time—I began to feel life from my body. I could better connect with the world, sensing my response, naming my needs, feeling my "being" alive within my environment. When I realized that I could have a felt sense of home inside of myself, I became more aware of the kinds of self-criticism I looped through my own head on the regular. Once I had tuned into the negative messaging I was giving myself, I couldn't tune it out. I had no other choice than to do everything I could to become less critical of myself—to activate a more loving internal dialogue. I had to develop a more consistent means of listening within and hearing my internal world, rather than only firing demanding self-directives at it. Ultimately, this entailed really embracing that I am an eternally changing collection of cells in process; thoughts and feelings in ever-evolving states and expressions. In learning to listen to my own physical body, I got more real with who I am and more tolerant of where I am, and in a lot of ways, I stopped hiding. I got to step up to living in a greater felt sense of love and pleasure—and do the things I care about not just because I "should" or because I might "win," but because I could feel that these things bring me to life. (Side note, however: there is nothing wrong with having a "winning" mindset. But when we aspire to win to lift up our own truth, our joy and others', and catalyze more truth and joy in the world, winning takes on a whole new meaning.)

Nourish may not take you to your perfect size, but I believe it can allow you to override the ideals of perfectionism, and to obliterate these ideals with a much more all-encompassing aliveness that is—actually—you. Your personalized equation for what a nourished life means is, actually, you, fully as you are, loving and accepting yourself in whole, and the energy this weaves through your character, your heart, your thoughts and actions; how you give and receive in the world. When you read *Nourish*, you'll learn that you already have the tools to embrace your life in full, and in these pages, you'll find the encouragement and guidance to remember that you are brave and capable and invited completely to be here in the universe now. To live self-nourished doesn't mean you'll never "slip" or "mess up," or find yourself face-planting into chocolate cake, for example. You may even take ten steps in the direction you call "backward" for every inch you move forward—and then you'll find that you can soar. *Nourish* is not linear. On this path, you will discover the illuminating steps specifically inside you, until you can walk with self-love and embrace your stride—whether forward or backward—with patience and self-compassion, defining for yourself what it means to take flight. This is how we grow the ability to truly feel our lives as our own from the inside out, learning to listen, to trust, and then to create our unique offering from our dreams, from a physically embodied space.

This book, like the *Nourish* app and my previously published books, is founded on the notion that when we can dismantle the self-deflating, self-criticizing mind, we stand a real chance of seizing the day, and of seizing our lifetimes in whole. This book isn't about getting you to stop eating so you can successfully run on empty. That never worked for me, and I don't believe it works for anyone. Rather, *Nourish* is an invitation for you to select the life ingredients that allow you to feel full—a fullness beyond food; the fullness of taking care of your whole being, mental, physical, and spiritual.

I want you to have the self-connection and vocabulary you need to wholly express yourself. I believe that as women, our female instinct is more essential than ever in this moment in time. I learned, through discovering a body-based means to find the words to know and express my feelings and sensations from the inside out, that instinct is most accessible when we can feel our own heartbeat, or feel ourselves breathing. When we can find deep peace by simply accessing the sense that we are alive, settling into ourselves, breathing, and listening—this is when we can begin to really know our power. I believe that the opportunity to drop in and hear ourselves, to have the safe space to cultivate self-love—that is a basic human right, though I also know that many people in the world do not have access to a peaceful environment. However, if you are a person who has a safe space in the outer world to develop her inner-world, this is all the more reason to grow your personal power, as a woman, and cultivate appreciation for the opportunity to do so. This is the way we can lift each other up, and increase the number of women in the world who feel truly encouraged to empower themselves.

So, yes—once upon a time, I did think I had to physically shrink into a tinier version of myself to be big enough to write this (or any) book. Then I embraced a deeper truth. My body thrives much more when I learn to listen and love

14

it, rather than force it to shrink or look differently. I don't believe I can share my vision only when I've reached some end goal, a place where I never struggle with my sense of self again. If that were the case, I'd probably have to write this book from my grave. My path is about committing to my whole-person health, and that's why a central component of my own transformational work requires me to step off the train of self-limitation—so here we go! I maintain a greater inspiration for knowing that the collective female consciousness beckons the heck out of us to step into our greatest selves, and to define what living a truly nourished life means by our own standards. We have been swallowing self-limiting constructs handed down either by our families or societies at large for lifetimes, but we will not do that here.

This is your book if you're seeking to live at large, within yourself, and move far beyond crumpling up the wide canvas of your life to fit into a very small lockbox. *Nourish* is your book if you know you have something in you that is profound—even if you don't know exactly what it is. *Nourish* is your book if you want to weigh your worth, beauty, glory, vitality, and joy by your own standards, rather than believe that someone else's exercise schedule, diet, or lifestyle plan will validate your worthiness. As you read through *Nourish*, you'll have the opportunity to engage in deeper explorations related to all the themes we will cover in these pages; a chance to tap into transformational practices that, I believe, are key to shifting our whole being toward the energy of nourishment.

These opportunities to dive into *Nourish*'s explorations are collected in a final chapter at the end of the book, but as you make your way through the pages, you'll find offerings in bold italicized letters related to given "explorations" (e.g., *see Exploration 17!*). You are then invited to flip to the back of the book and find the numbered exercise that correlates specifically to the section you're reading, and dive in then and there to personally explore your relationship to self-nourishment. Or, if you prefer, you can give yourself a moment at any time to engage with the explorations section on your own, at your leisure. I do fully recommend that if you want to get the deepest experience of this book as a true life-nourishing activation, the explorations are key. Whichever way you choose to engage with this book, remember, take whatever works for you here, and leave the rest. To live our own uniquely nourished life means we listen most keenly to the greatest source of wisdom we have—our inner-self.

Uncollapsible: The Art of Staying with Self

Most of us arrive here seeking out real, soulful nourishment, exhausted from a journey of being food and diet-focused. Maybe we've classically struggled with disordered eating, controlling our weight, and years of food confusion, or maybe we feel we live through a filter of managing when, how, and what we're eating. Then we come to a kind of "moment." It might be a subtle calling at first, though sometimes it's a full bullhorn requesting our spiritual surrender. The bullhorn is our soul, it turns out, crying out to access a deeper meaning in existence. Our days must be marked by something greater than calorie obsession or an enslaved relationship to a food product! We long to retire from "using food" and enter a life of relationships—including cultivating a real relationship with the way we feed ourselves and honor our whole physiology—in which we can truly nourish our own life, and the greater life in which we live.

16

From my own experience, I know that food issues can directly lead us to our own inner-doorway—a way to find embodied presence within ourselves. Heeding the call to iron out my rocky relationship with eating eventually (and I emphasize—not overnight, but eventually!) led me into a world I'd never imagined, where I could connect to energy both spiritual and grounding in the act of deep self-care. Finding residency within the body allows us direct access to a bubbling well of opportunity where we allow ourselves to rise. We learn to move with an energetic language, a valuable currency we've discovered within ourselves, without collapsing ourselves under external or internalized self-criticisms. Speaking of discovering language, it seems the term "uncollapsible" hasn't existed quite yet in the English language (until now, at least), but it's key to our story here, and high time to define it. As you'll see, our new word—uncollapsible—will be thoroughly demystified and actively used throughout these pages, and will serve as a great guide for us to glean what it means for each of us to uniquely claim our nourished life.

Of course, the foods we choose to put in our body deeply inform our state of mental and physical health (and not only what we choose to eat, but how much of it we eat; how fast we eat it; when, where, and why we're eating; and also, what we're telling ourselves as we eat!). Food is complex—in one way, it's *simply* food, but in another, it is the holiest rite we take every day. It is the literal and figurative expression of the sacred. It's a source we've worked with as humans since the beginning of our time, from seed to harvest. It has been central, defining us as individual people, while also globally bringing us together as one. We all have food in common. Where it has historically been challenging for us to embrace each other's so-called differences, our culturally unique cuisines have provided ground for us to share something we can universally agree upon: we all need food, and we appreciate culinary excellence!

Food is also a beautifully symbolic summary of how we choose to soothe, satiate, and support ourselves in all aspects of life, to cultivate our health. In this way, food gives us a lifelong opportunity to explore cause and effect, figuring out the correlation between what we eat and how we feel. For example, if, like me, you've specifically struggled with all things food- and diet-related, you may have experienced trying to eat something prescriptively "healthy" that left you somehow feeling not so great afterward—or even pretty crummy (no pun intended)—even though your food "should" have made you feel "good." Maybe you've found that an externally prescribed diet worked for a while but wasn't sustaining you through all the dynamic states of your beautifully ever-changing body. Or else, at some point, that prescribed carb-free, dairy-free, or whatever-else-free way of eating didn't feel so freeing. Or you might have eaten something "healthy," but in a state of anxiety, in a hurry, on the road, walking out the door (as I've tended to do much of my life) and ended up feeling unsatisfied, suboptimal, or even craving something more.

I've come to realize that everyone's "food and eating issue" plays out as uniquely as their fingerprint. Perhaps your situation is that you listen to what your body craves, but you consume food beyond a point of physical comfort, accustomed to a long-held pattern of eating-till-comatose. And then we have the "multiple-voices" food plan. For example, in the morning, our inner-dialogue surely says one thing about how we'll eat according to our highest intention, but in the flip of a switch at some point in the day, a war begins internally. By the evening, dinner becomes more a battle to survive than a relaxing event, with fork and knife as ammo. Before we know it, we've quickly piled some "forbidden" substance into our mouth, swallowing without fully chewing, in a state of rebellion and self-sabotage. And just like that, food has become full-on psychological warfare.

If you're like me, you may have gone through periods in your life where your habits regularly led you to an aisle of highly processed food. The corner store becomes some bizarre upside down vacation destination: part Disneyland, filled with color and light, and partly the place we go to escape the unceasing merry-go-rounds and rollercoasters of life. Perhaps you are in some kind of food-chemical dependency with raw sugar, or artificial sweetener, or even a so-called naturally flavored substitute. Maybe you've woken up for days, weeks, decades, committing again and again to becoming what you'd consider a graceful eater, someone capable of having one or two bites of something and then putting her fork down with agility and forgetting all about whatever is on her plate. Perhaps you've dreamed of being able to get through that "crave-o'clock" hour, but then the craving clock just strikes again, and no matter how virtuous your gallant efforts were to eat one "healthy" way or another, you succumb to something you've decided is sinister. Salty, crunchy, coated in sugar, gummy—whatever the craving-*du-jour* is, it will ensure-*du-jour* that you feel worthless or shameful afterward. Or it could be that none of these examples express your unique, complex connection to how you do food. Truth is, we could fill a book just by listing all of our unique food behaviors, so if you don't find yours in the above examples, please know I recognize our own "food thing" is not one-size-fits-all. In this way, when and if we go to free ourselves from our personal food prison, it can feel so hard to find someone, or a source, or a school, or any place where anyone understands our particular struggle. Even so, all of that considered, I truly believe that if you've come to this book seeking to unlock a deeper code to finally, truly figure out how to nourish your life, after exhaustingly outwearing the food-fixated, fix-myself-with-food form of life, then you are ready to understand how your relationship to food and eating reflects your relationships in all areas of your life. As you pass through these pages, hopefully in an engaged, self-connecting capacity, you will come to a new place, where you define for yourself what it means to live a fully nourished life.

When we begin to see, and I mean really see, as in "full-senses-on-board *get it*," that our food relationship is a reflection of our ability to stay in relationship with self, we get to focus on nourishing our sense of felt connection to life, and the food thing starts to fall away. Food becomes a place to practice sacred relationship and deep appreciation. And, even more, food is a great mirror—a place where we see the extent to which we can be present and stay with ourselves as we live through the experiences we create. For example, we might learn to see that in the same way we hurry with our food, we are hurrying through our life activities. Or we might see that as much as we've wanted all the things on the menu, once we get them or consume them, we're not even satisfied; instead, we've turned off. Or, in instances where we've overfilled our plate, we come to truly grasp the extent to which we've overfilled our mind, to the point we can't even be present. Or else, if we avoid eating to "get stuff done," we might discover we're avoiding listening to and feeling our inner-child's needs, because we don't know how to let her show up while trying to truly achieve something. We might see how we've overridden our inner-child with the demands of our inner-oligarch, our inner-director, or our inner–management team, who are often demanding we achieve one version or another of perfection.

When we come to the space of surrendering to the perfect imperfection of our nature, we gain the opportunity to cultivate self-listening. When we're led to that doorway of self, we find that food was never the crux of our problems, or the route to quelling our pain, or anything else—food was, all along, not our enemy, saboteur, glittery reward, or dangerous descent into self-loathing. We liberate food so that it can become what it is: a profound expression of vital, edible substance; a relationship to receiving energy that we'll cultivate for as long as we're alive. To reach the point of freeing ourselves from painful food fixation, we get to thank our food journey for providing us with the opportunity to gain amazing insights into our inner-psychology. We can become grateful to our past patterns we've had with food—they've been a kind of therapist! In healing our connection to food along our life journey, we get to observe how we care for ourselves through the fundamental act of eating—the most primary relationship we have. We get to determine what nourishment we need to support the whole garden of self we're growing.

When we learn to approach food believing we're enough before we take our first bite, we have established a true relationship with sustenance. We can now allow food to do its job of providing input to our cells and, ultimately, influencing how we feel in our body. When we arrive at the act of eating in a state of being able to listen to our needs, we can receive the intelligence of food, hear what it is telling us. Food gives our body hydration, fiber, key minerals, and vitamins for our whole self—and it can also light up our senses. When we develop an uncollapsible belief that we are worthy of nourishing our whole life, and that we are already enough, we become more adept at taking in food's life-affirming qualities. We choose food that helps our bodies feel affirmed by life, rather than beaten down by it.

For years, I conflated any uncomfortable sensation or challenges I experienced with the desire to eat. I didn't know hunger. I knew, instead, the feeling of anxiety or sensory overload and the need to quell it with something edible. Instead of knowing how to handle my own or others' reactions or the curveballs in life, I simply dealt with it all through food. At the same time, I'd fight food head-on. I made it my answer and my problem. I believed that if I could just do food differently, I would figure out how not to crumble in my life, how to stop checking out, numbing myself, or disappearing into a forbidden dessert. I lived toward the goal of my desired weight, inhabiting the story that I wasn't good enough as I was—as I am. I could blame feeling both "too much" (too big) and "not enough" (not thin enough) on, yes, food. Focusing my mental energy on food was, in some ways, convenient. I'd made food the place I played out my feelings—which was maybe easier than dealing with the complexity of where my feelings really came from, or what was causing my discomfort. Does this sound familiar? Can you relate? *Want to dive into how you are relating to food and why? See Exploration 1.*

In my relationship with food, I could see how I was collapsing my sense of presence, literally vacating from my felt experience and shutting off the overwhelm running through my body, by vanishing into a bag of chips or anything containing that five-letter word, s-u-g-a-r. I didn't have any other coping mechanism to handle the sensations and feelings moving through me, so I surrendered in full to food. My call of "hunger" was a deeper call to feel secure, to escape a sense of foreboding danger or threat—ultimately, a call for survival. I used food to feel I could make it through and retreat to someplace safe—even if the danger I felt was just in my head, and the respite I sought was simply a break from my own looping critical thoughts or sense of overwhelm.

It makes sense we'd go to food for psychological safety, because from our earliest days, as babies, we connected food with being safe. We'd cry for food because it ensured our survival. When a baby has a need, she triggers an alert to let her caregivers know. She cannot safely provide for herself—rather, she is dependent on (usually) her mother and her environment for her sustenance. Ideally, she learns, in time, through her relationships with her family and her community, to feed herself and grow her life on her own. She assimilates, participates in the intricately woven experience of living. Ideally, in this process of finding her own self-care autonomy, she believes she is 100 percent warranted to take part in life. She feels deeply invited into her whole experience—her sensations and feelings—to express who she is in full, demonstrating her affections, her needs, and her desires. At best, she learns to recognize and trust what she feels, and, even more so, how to soothe herself when she is uncomfortable, as well as distinguish her own discomfort from others'. Our transition from infancy through adolescence into adulthood is inevitably riddled with unique challenges, which (ideally) give character to our personhood. However, our early learning years are not always filled with the most effective coaching strategies to ensure we successfully become independent self-nourishers. Parents sometimes forget that school begins long before kindergarten, and we are being provided with the most fundamental lessons in how to nourish ourselves from the beginning of our growing lives.

In this book, we will explore what it means to develop an *uncollapsible* relationship with ourselves. So that, no matter what experiences we are undergoing in life, or which external events may trigger our ingrained behavioral responses, we have the means to stay with ourselves. Specifically, we will cultivate our ability to maintain an intact and unshaken sense of self as women, regardless of external or internalized pressures. We will secure our sense of being uncollapsible—a state where we know for sure that we are plenty, we are just enough, we are exactly right for ourselves. To be uncollapsible is to have access to our self at all times. We have the resources to drop in and listen to our needs, practice self-acceptance, and respectfully respond. Uncollapsibility is our most central domain, a basic state of self-connection that I believe is a universal human right. However, it can be a lifetime's work to acquire the tools of self-compassion, self-acceptance, and surrender that are key to truly living with ourselves instead of collapsing ourselves. When we collapse, we lose our sense of value, presence, embodied sensation, or self-connection. We may collapse to momentarily shut off our overwhelm, or give our power to something or someone else because we do not believe we can stand up in it. We may also habitually collapse because we believe it's the "right thing to do," or because it's more familiar to believe in our limitations and see life as a risk rather than an opportunity; because we haven't learned to believe our lives are filled with greatness. Collapsing can be hardwired into our physiological system, transcending our own life and extending back through generations of our ancestry. Even our neuronal pathways might be wired to collapse, thanks to humans' recognized negativity bias, keeping us on alert for danger. When we live with this negativity bias switched on full-time, you could say we are perpetually ready to spiral downward. By contrast, being uncollapsible is about learning to trust spiraling *up-ward*, to stretch into our sense of being and aliveness as a gift—and letting that be enough. *Want to understand what self-collapse means for you? See Exploration 2.*

Being uncollapsible is about recognizing that we're nourishing our lives not only through external substance (and, specifically, food), but through our internally felt sense that we are enough. And we start the query right here and now, by asking the self in the gentlest way, "Self, do you feel like you are enough right now?" We just ask . . . and then we listen. We listen to the wavering, quivering, intense, impatient, explosive, sullen, screaming, or wild voice within, and we practice allowing it to express itself so that we can hear what's really going on. Our internal dialogue, the inner-narrator that tells the story of the movie we are playing out, literally makes or breaks the quality of our life.

Here's what's amazing about an inner-voice, according to science. Evidently, not everyone has a full flow of words brewing within at all times, or even the occasional few phrases rolling around inside their head. Not all of us have a play-by-play announcer, an orating 1-800-future-danger predictor, a megaphone preacher, or an am station broadcasting inside us, available any old time we tune in. I wasn't aware of this, because I happen to be one of the 30 to 50 percent of humans on Earth (according to scientific research) who do have a richly verbal inside *speaker.* It seems the brain is equipped with an internal signal that is quite "voice-like," and which allows us to filter out our own experience from the auditory cacophony of the rest of the world. I've tuned in to enough Radio Inner-Isabel to know that mine typically speaks in declaratives, especially around food. "Order all of that." Or, "Make sure you eat this because you might not be able to get it ever again." For me, my self-worth declaratives activate my food-related internal-dialogue declaratives like dominoes. When my self-talk affirms some version of "you are not enough," the inner-voice soon decides, when eyeing a restaurant menu and preparing to order, that "it is not enough." It's as though an inner-monologue decides that if I want to feel free, have fun, relax, and liberate myself, then I should, say, liberate half the dishes from the restaurant kitchen—and bring them straight to the party at my table.

So much of my growth and development work has been about hearing what I tell myself and shifting negative self-talk. (For example, the name of my first book—*Eat Your Words*—focused on the potency of my own inner-dialogue and the way I show up in my life.) Even if you don't hear thoughts or words internally, scientific consensus confirms that you do have some sort of internal-state operator, a kind of "in-charge" assessor of reality that's giving orders or directions, or determining your reality filter. Yours may be solely visual, or led by enteroception (your felt internal state), or maybe your reality is guided by a blend of all of the above, plus your own secret sauce. What I do know for sure is that how we feel about ourselves, and how we affirm those feelings, is absolutely primary to living a nourished life. Our feelings inform our choices, and our choices affirm our feelings. It's an amazing circle of life, but that connection can feel, instead, like a vicious circle if we aren't tapped into self-love or self-respect as we make life choices.

Living an uncollapsible, self-nourished life is not a one-and-done prescriptive diet. There's no solution someone can model for us on TikTok and guarantee the same results if we adopt it identically. Living uncollapsibly is also not a practice of the kind we'd typically consider— some workout to commit to regularly and then *voilà*, we've transformed. The Nourish way of life is more of a seed; it's something we put into the mix of life that invites us to love ourselves, despite all of the outside influences we've taken in (especially as women)—influences that encourage us to believe that, for one reason or another, we're not worth loving. Nourish is a perception shift; it's a way to accept who we are while also actively choosing to go for the greatest version of ourselves. It's a way to check ourselves and say, "Am I *really* too old, too fat, too prone to failure, too unusual, too much, too XYZ to participate in life the way I want?" And then Nourish is a compass—so that we can say, "Oh, this direction is mine. This is how I can stay close to myself right now. This path brings more of me into the picture—ah-ha!" Yes—Nourish is the ah-ha path. It's how we proceed when we maintain quintessential curiosity about ourselves and move beyond limiting self-assessments. In the inner-dialogue of Nourish, we learn not to say "you look old" or "you look fat" or "you look tired" every time we look in the mirror. Instead, we might ask, "How can I see my reflection right now in a way that allows me to appreciate what I see? Is there some way I can value myself more in this moment, or at least accept myself where I am without creating a catastrophe in my head? Is there some way I can make a doable choice for myself today that gets me closer to 'thrive' than just 'survive?' Is there some type of joy I could bring into my body that I could access for free? Is it my breath, is it my bed, is it the sky, is it a book, is it a friend?" Nourish permits us to address ourselves like children when we need extra support tying our shoes. Nourish never stops acting with self-compassion, and—even more—when

Nourish can't, she stops. She surrenders, and either recognizes that she's having a moment that will likely pass, or accepts that she might need support.

In this light, I think you may agree that it's crucial we remember: when we decide we're ready to become uncollapsible, we're not trying to fix our state. Remember, we've already exhausted, fruitlessly, all those things outside of ourselves we thought might "fix" our reality. Instead, here we learn to shift our inner-language, or our internalized sense of self, and get educated about what really nourishes us. That is key. We must learn to find value in asking ourselves now and through all time, "What will nourish me now?" In this way, Nourish becomes a guide, and step-by-step we develop our ability to stay present and not lose ourselves to shutdown, whether in reaction to our food thoughts or to any other situation or substance. As a result, we get to really feed our whole life, and enter an era where we claim the liberty to define what nourishment is for ourselves—a truly major win for womankind. Hurrah!

While this book is not (and I stress *not*) focused on changing how you "do food," I believe that the following pages *will* allow you to see that your relationship with food offers an opportunity to practice cultivating uncollapsibility and strengthen your love for yourself. On the Nourish path, we get to cultivate resilience, self-reliance, and self-nourishing presence in our relationship with food, and take this into our whole lives, into the reality we're creating. We grow the ability to strengthen a more consistent, uncollapsible sense of self-value, which ultimately forms the backbone of a life richly lived with presence, self-acceptance, and self-love, amid all the myriad inevitable ebbs and flows.

I hope that sounds amazing to you, because a nourished life is here for you—and you are ready to live beyond any outworn patterns or behaviors, or externally imposed rules and prescriptions, that are keeping you from being all you truly are on this planet.

The Importance of Defining Nourishment for Yourself

Much of this book is going to be about you answering to yourself—because this is how we learn to hear the moment of truth inside ourselves. The only way I've created real shifts for myself is by finding my own takeaway from an experience, so that this new internal orientation inspires me, from within, to reach for something different. Also, I believe our truth changes—especially what feels true in our human mind at any given moment. This is both the beauty and the challenge of seeking transformation. It's most often the case that we don't really change until we have no other choice, when our life depends on it, or when the possible outcomes of change are definitely worth the difficulty of going through it. I believe that even though we're made of "monkey minds" that are apt to change on a whim and respond to stimuli without much self-control, and even subscribe to a particular perspective because, well, it's all we've known, that we are also capable of recalibrating at any time. We can create a new standard of self-love. Our lifestyle, choices, and style of self-respect can shift with the right support. To help us shift, we need to get into the Nourish mindset. We must feel together here, in a safe and loving space. I want you to feel, as you read these words, how much I know for sure—like 1,000 percent—how powerful and great you are, and how much capacity you have to live from a place of deep self-connection and loving focus. Change does not have to happen in a bootcamp only. It can be gentle—it can be nourishing. I'm a fan of not laying out a strict protocol for "what you have to do" from the outside in to achieve real internal shifts. In this space, I'm more prone to ask you questions. I want you to feel yourself alive inside these pages, because we're doing this together. Let this space invite you to enter the sacred temple of yourself, and to listen in with reverence for your truth, allowing yourself room to be whatever feels true to you in that moment. Here, I want you to describe what "nourish" means to you in the context of your whole life. You can include food, of course, but I want you to also list anything that you feel benefits your existence. Your answer will be uniquely yours (and will change depending on the moment, of course). For example, your answer might include any physical movement you enjoy, any media (music, books, podcasts, etc.) that stimulate your mind in ways that feel nourishing. Your list might include family, or friendships that are true-blue; physical locations (like places you love to travel to); or places of comfort, like your bed, the couch, the bathtub—wherever!

As you think through what nourishes you now, try to keep in mind that you are not in a competition with yourself. You don't even have to come up with more than one thing—or anything at all. Right now, you might be feeling that nothing at all nourishes you; you might feel bereft of anything namable that you find nourishing in your life. If that's the case, that might not mean you are lacking abundance; you just may not be in the state to appreciate or receive what you actually have. That's fine, too. On some days, you might feel that dozens of relationships nourish you, numerous places bring you comfort, and many activities nourish the heck out of your physical and spiritual being. On other days, you might really feel unsupported, that you don't have enough, or even that you can't stop wanting more, meaning you miss being present with all the nourishing things you actually have. Maybe you forget to look up and take notice of the simple nourishing things in our universe—like catching a toddler's first saunter around a park in spring, the joviality of a café on a Sunday, a stranger getting the door for you—and that's okay, too. The important thing here is to just observe yourself thinking about this question and come up with your own answer. "What nourishes me?"

You can speak your answers out loud, or write them down, or just take mental notes. The more actively you can participate, the better. Observe your thoughts and see if you can work on accepting them without self-judgment. When I say "without judgment" here, what I mean, more explicitly, is that when you consider what nourishment means to you, you might feel guilty because though you have so many things in your life, you still don't feel full. Or maybe you feel disconnected to a real, energized enthusiasm about your existence. You might feel something like an unending sense of pressure, or be convinced you're living a minimally expressed life when you could be "so much more." You might feel guilty because you feel you aren't choosing the healthy, nourished lifestyle you say you want, or grabbing a nourished life by the horns. What I mean by "without self-judgment" here is that we simply watch how we feel about ourselves as we wonder what nourishes us; we see what comes up and what value we place on ourselves about it. We ask ourselves who is making up the criteria, or the rule book, about how we're supposed to be living or feeling. Are our ideas coming from what we're longing for inside, or from some external demand we're placing on ourselves to live a glorious, special, out-of-the-ordinary "would you look at her!" kind of existence? Of course, while I believe that we are each profoundly important, what I am trying to highlight is that even the most benign-seeming, littlest self-judgments can negatively impact our ability to flourish as women. And to flourish, in fact, is the ultimate expression of Nourish. We'll start to see how these small self-judgments, even the smallest of them, escalate as self-deprecating patterns that we use to keep ourselves small. For example, self-judging thoughts like, "How is it that I am three pounds heavier today than yesterday? I am hopeless!" or, "Why did I eat that bread? I have no self-control!" become like heavy garments we cloak over our opportunity-rich lives. We pile judgments on ourselves until by the end of the day, there's no more room for the light of possibility to get in.

By dimming our light, we miss the path, the open and receptive road that will lead us to opportunities, whether that's a new friendship, a dream job, a heart-warming romance, or something as small as simply noticing a beautiful flower. Sure, exercise and nutritional science confirm that the human body can benefit at different times from specific ways of eating and even maintaining a range of weight for optimal physical health. However, if you are unable to see yourself, love yourself, and actively participate in your own life, all the dieting and healthy food in the world will not get you there. So it's time to put yourself first and make a vow that before you harshly tell yourself untrue statements—or emphasize feelings or beliefs that are limiting—that you will have your own back at all times. It's time we begin to listen within to hear what we need to build a nourishing, well-lived life. *Want to explore what you really need to feel nourished from the inside out? See Exploration 3.*

The etymological roots of "nourishment" come from Latin and Old French, meaning to nurse. Self-nourishment is truly an act of self-nursing. As adults, when we nurse ourselves, we parent our most fundamental needs; we tend to ourselves, and we grow our intentions into actualizations. In French, one derivation of *nourrir* (or nourish) is *nourrice*, which translates to nanny, as in someone who nannies a child. In adulthood, then, how we nourish ourselves is an expression of how we nurse and nanny our entire existence. It's inevitable that, as humans, we will all go through periods of self-doubt, whether they last days, weeks, or even elongated seasons! Heightened but finite periods of self-doubt, however, are different from consistently operating from a baseline pattern of self-limiting, self-dismissive, maladaptive behaviors. When we listen in, we activate our inner-nurse and engage our unique mode of self-care. We learn to recognize and acknowledge what we need, which might look totally different to anyone else's needs. We get to fall in love with our inner-child just as an inner-parent should—unconditionally! From here, self-nourishment becomes a wide field rich in possibilities; there are no limits to the ways we get to take care of ourselves and grow our whole life.

If you are like me, you may have excelled in life by managing your affairs from deep in survival mode, going-going-going and making great strides in many areas. Nourishment, however, is not about how well you can perform or how much of an ace you are at the doing; rather, it is about how profoundly you can participate in your being. The space of being: this is where all the healing happens. It's where we brave fully opening to life, and find not only that we truly believe we are worthy of taking up space in the world, but also that we already have the building blocks to grow something extraordinary in our lifetimes, from a place of real self-connection. From "being" we find our nourishing tools—the ones that not only nourish our body, mind, spirit, and soul, but also extend into all our relationships. Our community, our family, our friends—they too are nourished by our shifting into a place of deepened presence. As you grow your uncollapsible self, you'll see your cultivated sense of self-nourishment carried into every connection you foster in your life. You will be aware of how you nourish life when you speak to others, how you can empathize, celebrate your own and others' achievements, and endure moments of challenge. Nourishing energy is the spark of life, and so we take this light to find the doorway into our inner-world. With the light of nourishment, we can richly recognize our core connection to all of life. Embracing self means fundamentally believing we deserve to have roots; to be here, in reciprocity, giving and receiving energy—part of the ecosystem of the universe.

CHAPTER 2

The Nourished Brain: What Signals Are You Perpetuating, and Why?

I spent years waking up and setting an expectation for my-self to "eat perfectly" that day, only to end up hitting the self-destruct button every afternoon, right around happy hour—when many have their celebratory "day is done" cock-tail. This happened again and again. I had evidently traded in the opportunity to have a social drink for a moment with an illicit snack in the controlled environment of my parked car, alone. Go figure. In the morning, I was convinced that I didn't want to do this, but later in the day some part of me obviously did, and that's not only confusing—it's spiritually exhausting. I knew that my behaviors had to have a pretty strong grip on my brain, because in every other aspect of life, I was more than capable of being true to my word and doing or creating exactly what I set my mind upon. If I was saying one thing to myself but doing another, I figured there had to be some serious crossed wiring in my brain that was causing my own plan to misfire. I wanted the facts, the concrete science, and the biology around why we might repeat behaviors that keep us shut down.

I had to understand where in my brain I had incongruencies and what brought on this consistent self-collapsing. To cultivate nourishment, I needed to get what it cognitively meant. What does it take for the brain to obtain a state of feeling self-connected, to be satiated and able to practice enough self-regulation to make supportive choices so that we can feel safe, congruent, and trustworthy with our own self?

Just like any other facet of our existence, our brains are unique, with unique circuits and balances of chemicals. It's not possible to produce a general, one-size-fits-all description of how behavior, thinking, and eating cues work on the level of cognition. It's essential to realize that while scientific understanding can offer general principles around our brain states and neural patterns, our individual experience and behavior can vary widely, and addressing complex issues like stress management and behavioral change often requires personalized approaches. That's exactly why quick-fix, Band-Aid solutions to our issues don't usually help in the long term. Your brain, for example, might appreciate more sleep or quiet time, whereas a friend's might feel most replenished in a stimulating social space. You might zoom in to the sounds of your environment, while another person might feel more visually stimulated and unaware of the sound altogether. You might be able to handle a heavy load of stimulus to a region of your brain, while another person might be absolutely triggered and overstimulated by that same input. What's important is that we learn to get curious about ourselves and consider how our own brain is wired, because it's unlike any others.

Once I got on the brain train, I learned that nourishment isn't just a sweet theme, symbol, or theory; it's deeply rooted in a network of complex neurological processes.

Most of our brain functions, in fact, are wired around the process of when, how, why, and where we might get nourished, and what risks and rewards that might entail. For example, take the hypothalamus, nestled near the base of the brain in the limbic system—one of the oldest components of the brain, evolutionarily speaking. The hypothalamus plays a huge role in regulating our vital functions, such as hunger, thirst, sleep, and temperature, and also acts as a control center for emotions and hormones. Anatomically, the hypothalamus confirms the deep connection between our cues for being hungry or angry or tired; in fact, they can be hard to tease apart. It's small, but the hypothalamus is like a Grand Central Terminal responding to an influx of signals transmitting through the body—and specifically, it's dealing with all the hormones that regulate our appetite. For example, if you've been even a little bit interested in food and diet and have ever gone down a weight loss–infomercial rabbit hole, you probably heard of leptin, a hormone that lets the hypothalamus know the precise amount of energy stored in the body. When energy stores are sufficient, leptin effectively reduces appetite. Then, on the other hand, we have ghrelin (yes—very close to gremlin), which is coined the "hunger hormone" as it tells the hypothalamus to increase appetite when our body believes it needs more energy. If our stress levels are hitting the ceiling, our brain is given the signal that we need all the energy we can get to function, so that we can fight if needed, or survive our battles. This is why sometimes when we feel the pressure to get things done, we end up feeling the inevitable overwhelm of crave-o'clock, especially if we've spent all day in our programmed "go, go, go" mode, overriding all of our body signals. This is just when the ghrelin alert comes on strong, like Gizmo on fire. If you're in this place, it's no surprise you might find yourself (like I did for years) unable to practice self-control around colorful corner-store king-size packages of taste-enhancing additives made to keep you coming back, unable to eat just one.

When it comes to trying to break free from maladaptive behavioral patterns, we often put extreme pressure on ourselves to change. Unfortunately, this pressure ends up increasing the likelihood we'll turn to these self-collapsing behaviors—a phenomenon that can be described by neuroscience. While all the brain regions are connected, stress from self-imposed perfectionism and pressure majorly affects the prefrontal cortex in particular—that's the exact area responsible for our decision-making as well as how we express our personality, moderate our social behavior, and regulate our emotional responses. When we want to achieve something but we can't relax into the process, putting massive stress and pressure on ourselves, we wreak havoc on the prefrontal cortex, which then signals to the hypothalamus, impacting the body's regulation of hunger and satiety.

Simply put, when we allow our own "inner-tyrant" to lead the way, our well-intentioned goals can swiftly lead us to neural dysregulation, leaving the prefrontal cortex in a constant state of overactivation or dysfunction. And when this happens, we've set ourselves up for those uncontrollable behaviors of self-sabotage—the only way our poor brains can relieve their incredible tension or cope with a horrible fear of failure. The brain, after all, is an organ. Say your intestines were responding to stress in one specific way every day. Would you personally insult your intestines, saying something like, "I've been telling my large intestine to digest fiber better every day, but it's not listening to me! Why?!" No. Instead, you'd likely realize that your intestines need a different kind of energy to operate more efficiently. Similarly, as an organ, the brain is just responding to stress as an organ would—naturally. It needs a nourishing environment in order to feel safe to operate at its best.

Among other endocrine responses, stress triggers changes in the way our adrenal glands secrete cortisol, which then impacts hypothalamus regulation and leads to a confusing mash-up of hormones going all over the place in our brains. Suddenly, lines get very blurry between how we think about ourselves, what actions we need to take, and what sensation we're feeling. With leptin and ghrelin hormones misfiring, our overwhelmed brains will zoom in on one thing, something that can placate the mayhem—a prime opportunity for us to obsess over food, craving, calories, crunching, and consuming something that will translate to comfort. When we lose our way internally, when we cannot find our sense of mental self-composure, there's no time to feel—we have to survive! Then, no matter how much we've worked to change the script, we'll find our way to that old go-to friend, some self-sabotaging eating behavior. We let our plans for the day, our greater inklings of what we want to create, and our vision of vibrance and confidence crumple into a crumbling warm cookie, dunked in milk. And we find comfort there and think, maybe, for a moment (before self-judgment sets in) that we are being nourished.

Now, I don't want to knock our coping mechanisms. I truly want to thank every cookie I've ever consumed during secret hours in parked cars, like some villain hiding out from the FBI behind a gas station. Those cookies allowed me to keep some sort of handle on my life, to get through a surfacing memory I'd not processed, or deal with the workload I'd put on myself, or quiet some looping self-criticism going through my head. Those cookies were there for me when I couldn't be bothered to come up with another palliative option. Plus, those cookies didn't talk, they didn't require me to make future plans with them, they had zero expectations of me, and they were a better choice than some of the harder substances I could have consumed. I believe that the way to graduate from our patterns is not to put undue pressure on ourselves, which will inevitably only lead us to feel more like failures. Instead, I've learned that the only way to let go of some of the old behaviors I'd held onto like baby blankets, convinced I needed them to get through the night, was to literally write a love note to them. I recognized them as the old forlorn teddy bears in the closet that they were, and I learned to trust in a more adult version of myself, who could honor how I coped without making myself wrong. I recognized my patterns as the way I'd been best able to find comfort in moments when I'd needed it and had no alternative options. In this way, I found true appreciation for these old, engrained modes I was still clinging to, which provided me with some familiar self-soothing. I was then more able to recognize that these long-held behaviors were like my oldest companions, and that I did not need to make myself wrong for returning to them for so many years. Instead, I reinforced within myself how ready I was to find a new way to care for my needs. *Do you want to learn to recognize and give thanks for your past "coping" patterns as a way to create new room for a deeply self-nourished life? See Exploration 4.*

Changing our brain might be easier if our whole self-collapsible pattern was just about the neuronal-firing waltz between our prefrontal cortex and the hypothalamus. If this were the case, we could take one simple herb, a magic pill, or a trip to the doctor to get our brains completely sorted out. But the story of how you think about yourself and how that triggers your mental patterns, and specifically your relationship with food and eating, goes way beyond just two sections of the brain. Remember, when it comes to understanding how our cognition plays into our patterns, though the brain is "just an organ," it's also one of the most complexly interconnected technologies on Earth! Wrap your mind around this: At any given moment, the regions of the brain are firing billions of neurons, most of which are habitually wired into their specific firework pattern. Most of the day it's like an exaggerated Fourth of July firework bonanza in your head. Most of these signals moving through your brain, communicating between and through lobes, are attempting to consistently confirm that you're safe, to assess the risk of all potential safety failures, and to keep you alert to any moment your security and safety are possibly threatened. Let's just say that after 150,000 years of our humanoid brain evolution, we're quite stacked with alert notifications. At pretty much any point, even if we've just been flooded by an excess of dopamine or bathed in oxytocin, neurologically, we can still rally up and ready for potential warfare. And what neurological role does "numbing out" play in relation to this state of rapid fire in the brain? When we reach for food, alcohol, drugs, Netflix, shopping, etc., these downregulating substances give our brains the temporary message to deactivate our stress responses, because perhaps (and just perhaps) the threat of war has ceased. Not always, but sometimes, when we find ourselves in this situation, it seems like the soul is given just a small window, a tiny taste (sometimes literally a taste) of what it might feel like to live without the eternal pressure of internal or external conflict. We are granted a temporary reprieve.

Obliterating our stress permanently isn't necessarily a biological ideal. Humans are hardwired to detect threat and feel fear, and have spent a significant amount of energy evolving our ability to do so. We need potential threat—to some degree. It makes life compelling and gives us purpose, allowing us to pursue and secure access to things that are vital or scarce. Developing the flexibility to transition in and out of stress states and self-regulate between these moments of "fight, flight, freeze, rest, or digest" nervous-system signaling is key to our physiological health. It's called "homeostasis," or, we might say, one's ability to flow, let go, receive, and respond to life in a way that is not extensively self-harming nor harmful to others, and ideally helps us to cultivate effective conflict-resolution skills. However, some of us seem to automatically operate at higher states of stress, where we may feel perpetually under threat, even if we're not aware of feeling this way. Our stress-response patterns are influenced by many factors, including inherited conditions, early childhood experiences, and the collective sociocultural environment. Specifically, the experiences that we are not able to process physiologically—whether from a one-time event or compound experiences—can linger as micro- or macro-traumas. It is often unprocessed trauma that negatively impacts our neurological functioning. Whether trauma is consciously recollected or remains subconscious, it can influence and perpetuate repetitive or related maladaptive behaviors—our "trigger responses."

It would be irresponsible, in writing a book about nourishing our whole physiology, not to properly highlight and attempt to define at least a broad concept of trauma—or, as some may call it, "the T word." In fact, I have written articles on the complex subject of understanding trauma, such as "On Trauma, Identity, and Disembodied Eating Behavior," (*Medium*, December 2023). In that piece, I outlined the significant increase in popularity of the term "trauma" over the last decade in schools of psychology and therapeutic healing, and noted that it is sometimes misused or easily tossed around. The term has even been touted as the "word of the decade," with *New York Magazine* describing it as "America's favorite diagnosis." So what do we mean when we say "trauma," after all? Pioneering psychological and somatic experts have worked to respectfully define trauma in a formal capacity, as well as to develop modalities toward healing it, bringing trauma to the collective attention in an accessible way so we can speak about it more universally. These experts include Dr. Peter Levine, creator of Somatic Experiencing, and Dr. Daniel Siegel, professor of psychiatry and cofounder of University of California, Los Angeles's Mindful Awareness Research Center. Other significant contributors to the field include Trauma Research Foundation president and author of *The Body Keeps the Score*, Dr. Bessel van der Kolk; Dr. Gabor Maté, who introduced the phrasing of "little-t" and "big-T" trauma; and Dr. Thomas Hübl of the Academy of Inner Science.

To summarize these experts' collective offerings, we can consider trauma (whether ancestral, from early development, or from recent experiences; whether repetitious or occurring in one single event) as an overwhelming experience that disrupts the mind-brain-body balance. Here, it's important to differentiate between two types of experience: moments when your body's systems respond to a stimulus by dysregulating temporarily before returning to homeostasis, and moments when the nervous system dysregulates and *does not fully regulate itself afterward.* To illustrate the first scenario, let's imagine you're looking down at your phone and also trying to cross the street. Suddenly, you hear a car honk at you because you're in their way. You notice your whole body having a physiological response—for a fleeting moment, you're revving for an accident. Then, when you realize you're not in immediate danger, your system eventually normalizes. That is a systemic response of your nervous system getting dysregulated and then returning to some type of regulation. In the other scenario, let's imagine you're perpetually looking at your phone while crossing the street, and you're constantly checked out with a device dependency that's manifested from chronic stress, and this is impacting your ability to safely participate in the world—this behavior may, in fact, be a kind of trauma response.

Trauma, specifically, impacts the nervous system. It then goes on to disrupt our emotional and physiological regulation, in either the short or the long term, depending on how we deal with it. Trauma is psychosomatic, which means that our unresolved psychological pain is linked to chronic illnesses, chronic maladaptive body-wide manifestations, health-threatening patterns, disconnected states of being, and addictive behaviors. Experts on trauma emphasize its impact on the brain's functioning, particularly in areas related to safety and threat detection. (This is why it's impossible to speak about nourishing safety and transforming our behaviors without acknowledging what we carry, consciously or subconsciously, as trauma.) Trauma filters through to our ingrained responses and states of being. When we are traumatized, the actions we take are informed by experiences we have not processed, whether these experiences are individual, generational, or societal, since trauma can impact us collectively as well as individually. The work of learning to recognize traumatic experience and be present with and process our trauma is deeply linked to the work of learning to nourish ourselves. The above-mentioned teachers provide countless resources to help us dive deeper into being informed about trauma, to support both our own experiences as well as how we relate with others. *Do you want to take a moment to understand what the word "trauma" means to you? See Exploration 5.*

What's so powerful is that in the wake of trauma, we might end up building our entire behavioral landscape—which informs our choices, our life expression, and even our identity—out of a response to what happened; a coping mechanism designed to make us feel safe. We may not have been given any model of healthy boundaries, of knowing where we start and another person's input or energy begins. We may grapple with feeling our identity is "wobbly," that we don't really know who we are. We might dissociate—feel numb, dislocate from our own physical form, or ceaselessly fall into a single safe emotional response, no matter what we are really feeling or what anyone else is feeling. In truth, trauma may *rightfully* be the word of the decade or the true source of every malady, because for many years our culture encouraged us to airbrush over everything we really are. We failed to recognize where we'd been hurt or hurt others, collectively and individually. Until recently, in fact, the notion that leaders are strengthened by vulnerability was unheard of. (Thanks to Brené Brown for bringing "vulnerability" into our vocabularies as a close second to "trauma.") There's now a bit more room in the collective consciousness to consider our early patterns, to stand in our vulnerability and see how those first formative influences are like the innermost rings of a tree, influencing the way we expand into the world and into ourselves throughout our lifetime. We now have more tools to consider how our sensory experiences, from our prenatal moments right up to our current adulthood, shape our inner-landscape. And we have more tools to see how imbalances in our mind-brain-body, left unhealed, can lead us to normalize living in nervous-system states of high alert or "hyper-arousal," where stress becomes synonymous with simply operating in the world. On the other hand, we might also learn that a mind-brain-body imbalance has led us to stay in a consistent state of downregulation. Here, we remain disconnected from a felt sense of life's energy; without this resource, we may feel lethargic or dissociated from emotion. We might slip into subconsciously reciting a mantra of, "It doesn't matter, I don't care," or even, "I don't matter, no one cares."

When it comes to the brain and the state of being on alert, feeling hypervigilant or energetically drained in response to real or perceived stress—here, we discover the role of the amygdala. Like the hypothalamus, the amygdala is part of the limbic system—the network of the brain that performs the primary processing of our emotional stimuli and assesses potential threats. The amygdala collaborates with the prefrontal cortex, enabling it to assess threat levels, inform our decision-making, and regulate our emotional processes. Let's take the "fight-or-flight" response, in this context. Though the brain, as noted, is a complex and multifaceted system, in the simplest terms we can break this response down to a series of interactions between various brain regions. If the amygdala detects a potential threat, it sends signals to the hypothalamus, which then rallies the sympathetic nervous system and the prefrontal cortex—resulting in a release of stress hormones like adrenaline and cortisol.

In the framework of Nourish, we can look at the cognitive patterns of our stress response in terms of what happens when we don't feel safe. This emphasizes how essential it is to consistently anchor our whole physiology in a deep sense that we are, in fact, safe to be in our own lives, in our bodies, in our brains, and in our collective environment. I believe that more than establishing a "healthy diet" prescribed by an external protocol, we should start by figuring out how best to support connecting to a felt sense of safety in our bodies. If we are caught in a wheel of self-harm or dissociation, constantly sabotaging our own efforts through food or the way we think about food or the action of eating, then we are likely living with a trigger pattern rooted in not feeling safe.

Many of the women reading this book are high-functioning, extremely successful women (even if we're too humble to self-describe as such). We've achieved significant accomplishments, whether by creating wealth, attaining a strong professional position, or raising families—or all of the above. To add to this, we've likely supported others, helped to greatly shift their own life circumstances, or even miraculously healed their pain. We've traveled solo, we've stood up for the underdog, we even know—deep down—that there's no mountain too steep for us to climb when we're willing. We know we're strong enough to stand in the eye of the storm when stuff hits the fan. Therefore, when it comes to *why* we're doing what we're doing with food and eating, the idea that we're feeling unsafe might not immediately click. We might be operating with the notion that we largely *do* feel safe in our bodies, in our minds, in our lives, in our independence, and in the greater world. We may feel, on a conscious level, physically secure in most situations—unintimidated. (In fact, we might actually intimidate others with our so-called confidence.) However, even if we show up to our life's challenges like we're on center stage, ready to stand up for ourselves and give the world what we've got, we may still lack the deeply self-compassionate, self-connected, dialed-in sense of safety that would allow our brains to really know that we're okay. We're enough. We can be brave and even take great risks, but still have a message somewhere inside of us that keeps our mind-brain-body from really drinking in the nourishing sense of being safe with ourselves, with our own company. We still might not deeply feel that we belong to our lives; or that we can stay with our bodies, uncollapsible; or that we have what it takes to "make it."

For me, it wasn't so easy to learn to look under my "I have it together," "I can get it done," and "call me to put out your fires" and acknowledge the tender parts of myself, or understand how feeling unsafe came hand in hand with my negative self-messaging. Step by step, I learned to hear when, beneath my judgments of myself or others, there lurked a sense of not feeling safe, or that I was enough in the world by just being me. Without self-worth as a core energy fueling my actions, I was keeping my system in a stress-response state. For so long, my sense of success correlated to how much I was able to cross off my to-do list, while going one thousand miles an hour. Once I prioritized growing awareness and presence, I was able to see that I carried an underlying belief that I wasn't safe enough already, just as I am.

For example, I often felt extremely sensitive about what other people thought of me. I didn't want to care, but I often felt thrown off by this feeling nonetheless—even if I had no real evidence to back up my reactions and suspicions. If I heard a compliment, I couldn't absorb it—really, physically feel it, or stop to receive it. I couldn't let myself be nourished by others' loving reflections, because somewhere inside, I didn't trust their words. That, in turn, came down to not trusting my *own* internal dialogue about myself. When we operate from this state, how can communication ever feel safe? I started to see that despite how much I'd learned, all the certifications I'd received, the courses I'd taken, and the investments I'd made to acquire my many skills, I was still being influenced by the deeply-rooted negative self-concepts I'd seeded in my early developmental years. I still had these response mechanisms—or, we might say, trauma responses—built from the critical messaging I'd received in this lifetime, as well as intergenerational messaging; ideas of self I'd personalized from my family's limited sense of their own greatness. This is how I realized that creating a deeply comprehensive, internally well-communicated sense of safety in my own body would be a kind of golden ticket, granting profound growth in exchange for the simple act of listening in and embracing where I needed to feel nourished in the seat of my being. In this way, I saw that there is a vast difference between working to arrive at a point of finally "having enough" (i.e., "being enough") and, on the other hand, living from a foundational belief of already being enough. The sense of self-connection, and ultimately self-love, that comes from living this way—create the rich, fertile soil from which grows our unique, generative expression.

So how do we get on board with feeling safe? It's hard to simply tell the mind, "Okay, now and forevermore, all of your thoughts need to reflect self-compassion." Even the best spiritual and scientific writing will confirm that our process of thinking is messy. The mind may not always be working for the body, and the body holds that evidence.

The body tells us if something is "good" or "bad" for us—and what works one day might not work the next. But our minds don't always want to listen to our bodies' shifts and rhythms. Mostly, we're dealing with minds that are wired to seek whatever requires the least energy expenditure for the greatest immediate reward. (Which is to say, most times, the mind will likely choose a Snickers bar over a four-mile uphill climb, whether we want to admit it or not.) Usually, the mind would like to find relief as soon as possible—would love to give up immediately and retire if something requires physical strain. The mind would like to "get there," or have permission to clock out, and even check out—take a load off. But despite all of this, I do believe our minds, brains, and bodies can truly align with our higher choices to nourish ourselves. Our brains need to safely believe that choosing nourishment in the long run is actually rewarding! It isn't exhausting or overly taxing to take care of ourselves. Even if we do take the four-mile ascent, the Path of Nourish shows us, step-by-step, how to connect to our choices, our bodies, our environments. Nourish helps us to keep our eyes open to the possibilities, to the beauty, to the opportunities we have. The way we learn to grow a sense of safety in a nourishing life is to stay connected to our resistance. To listen to it and parent it, informing ourselves regularly (and somatically, with the breath and with our spirit on board) that we are valuable and worthy and even graceful when we take care of our bodies, both while eating and in all things. What's essential is that, even as strong and capable women, we learn to tenderly self-parent our own vulnerability.

If feeling more joy is our goal, then guess what? To feel joy, we fundamentally need to feel safe. True nourishment requires physical, psychological, and spiritual safety, cultivating relationships with safe spaces that we can trust, including the relationship we have with our own inner-world. When it comes to food, I believe that our root issue is that we don't trust ourselves enough. We don't trust ourselves to know what nourishment we really crave. Or we might not trust ourselves to even be around certain so-called tempting foods—we can become scared of ice cream. Whatever your safety story is, in order to create safety within, you have to learn to listen to the wisdom of the scared places within yourself. You have to get curious about the phenomenon, the feeling, and the deep function of safety in your life. *Are you ready to uncover what safety really means for you? See Exploration 6.*

Many of us were strongly encouraged by our families or our communities, who did their best to make sure that we grew up to be strong, independent, and unstoppable women; women who wouldn't give too much credence to the fact that the world is not universally safe for us. While we may have wonderful externally strong traits as a result of their encouragement—or else what they modeled to us through their own behaviors—we may also have learned to override any part of ourselves that felt unsafe. We were shown that in order to be all-powerful, we shouldn't give any attention to any part of ourselves that doesn't feel 100 percent secure—or, if we feel insecure, we should use that feeling as fuel to go even harder toward our intimidating dreams. As a result, many of us have never gotten to know and embrace our vulnerable genius. The parts of us that don't feel safe are suspended in a time or place where they experienced tumult, shame, threat, humiliation, or even felt at risk for their lives. These parts were dismissed (or, as the Internal Family Systems therapy model may put it, "exiled"), meaning that we lost the opportunity to get to know, to encourage, and to grow significant aspects of ourselves—aspects we might need in order to live out the fullest flavor of our life's expression.

These less secure parts of the self, however, possess valuable information—information we need if we want to step into our whole, unlimited, liberated true nature. These parts can help us to know ourselves as truly full, not from food or overeating, but from feeling our lives are enough. We might not yet know this part of ourselves that doesn't feel safe, because maybe we overrode it. Maybe our personal version of "unsafe" doesn't look like it would in the movies. No one is attacking us from behind in a dark, scary alley, so we might not be able to track the ways we don't feel completely comfortable simply being ourselves socially, or how we lose our sense of self around some people. Because there's no one physically shooting us down, we might not be aware that while we're speaking to our team at work, we are carrying an internalized feeling of discomfort. We may not notice that on some level, we feel that our lives are at risk; that if we say the wrong thing, we might not get shot, so to speak, but we might very well get shot down. If there's nobody obviously booing us off a stage, we might not realize that we are secretly running a program through our bodies that says we have failed, or that we are neither lovable nor good enough, or that we have no talent and are certainly loathed by those around us. We may not note that we're chronically exhausted from giving too much away without healthy boundaries, or else upset because we gave something to others expecting something in return, but received nothing. We might not realize that we don't feel totally safe to express ourselves, or might fail to recognize how often we feel on edge, even with family or close friends—perhaps fearing that someone might verbally attack us. And then, we may not notice that even when we're alone, we are holding on to this slight sense of being perpetually unsafe. Maybe we feel threatened by the prospect of always being alone, or that we're not lovable, or that there's no one to love. These feelings of unsafety can be so subtle, but they can keep us numb, in low-grade states of chronic stress, or in physical pain. Often, this subtle sense of lacking safety is built of past experiences or stored and replayed patterns. From times when we did not feel safe. In response to those experiences, the brain does its job, keeping us suited up in the boxing ring with our amygdala on high alert, or else chronically exhausted from having fought for so long. While the amygdala doesn't tire in the same way as, for example, our legs might tire after a hike, living in a state of prolonged amygdala activation can contribute to the development of anxiety disorders and other mental health conditions—like disordered eating. Living in a trauma-induced state of chronic stress or anxiety creates a negative cycle, since it tangibly affects brain function, impacting our neural circuitry and neurotransmitter levels. If we're dealing with a low-grade conscious or subconscious sense of feeling unsafe for long periods of time, our brain's ability to emotionally regulate, cognitively function, and make decisions will be impacted. When we're operating on a less cognitive capacity than we need to make nourishing decisions for ourselves, this lack and the decisions we make because of it perpetuate stress and fear cycles, as well as the physiological symptoms related to these stress states. In your own life, can you think of any experiences—recent or distant—of feeling unsafe? And did those experiences have lingering effects that still influence your behavior or live in your psyche now? *Are you ready to recognize where you've not felt safe and why? See Exploration 7.*

The great news for those of us who want to create a truly nourished brain (and life!) is that changing our brains is actually possible. The whole body naturally leans toward wanting to heal, especially if the elements needed to improve its state are already there. In this way, we can leverage our brain's inherent ability to rewire itself, also known as neuroplasticity. Yes, positive thinking is, in part, informed by the food we feed ourselves, the trillions of microbes brewing in our guts, and the fertile ground they make for our clearest thinking. But just as much as the foods we consume, our regular actions and mental constructs profoundly inform our mental states. Our brain's greatest neuroplastic potential is activated when we nourish ourselves with conditions that allow us to become more mindful, less contemptuous, less irritated by ourselves or others, more compassionate, and less likely to fly off the handle or get dragged under the bus. You can be the world's greatest longevity expert, but if you are creating high-stakes, painful patterns in your own mind, or limiting your joy and freedom in some capacity, I don't believe that any amount of supplementation or diet is going to help you live a long and happy life. Our brains can change when we more frequently create new avenues and adventures for our physiology; when we seek out invitations to find new ways of being, and step outside of our habit of perceiving life as a threat. We change our brains when we grow the practices that allow us to feel life as safe and welcoming—and a magical place where we can truly belong. *Want to make new neural pathways toward self-empowering behaviors? See Exploration 8.*

In this light, a key commitment we make to ourselves when we step self-lovingly onto the Path of Nourish is to regularly ask ourselves the question, "How am I choosing to experience reality right now?" When we ask this question and listen to the response, we get to see our stark truth and key into our own inner-state. Are we working for or against our true well-being and joy? By taking regular inventory (whether throughout the day, in a dedicated practice, or in whatever way works for you), you allow yourself to begin to consider which shifts you might need to make in order to really step in the direction of nourishing your life. For example, how often do you think, "I GET to do this," when you do something you literally signed up for, something you're choosing to commit to—whether that's getting ready for a work meeting, taking care of your physical health, or even jumping on a plane to take a vacation? Do you realize that you "get" to do your activities, or are you somehow creating stress and a sense of burden at every step?

How fully do you feel that you are the creator of your own destiny as you go through the movements of your life? If you can't allow yourself the glory of being fully where you are, knowing you deserve to be there, and allowing some facet of your experience to fulfill you, then guess what—you're much more likely to turn to food as the way to safely fill up. If you aren't allowing yourself to receive and appreciate your life as *enough*, as being a fertile ground for you as a creator cultivating your destiny, then you're likely to miss the beauty that is available for you to experience in the here and now. It makes no sense to wait around for that "thing" to happen for you, for that person who really gets you or loves you to come along, if, for example, you're unable to receive what is already showing up for you in your life. All of this might sound like a basic account of setting yourself up for success, but it's the most elementary, fundamental tools we must really put to work if we want to make a nourishing shift. Gaining the ability to hear what we're telling ourselves about our lives is essential. If you're spending your time making sure you do all the "right" and "positive" things for everyone else while internally feeding yourself negative input, it's time to recognize that no one but you can do the inner-work to change what's happening inside you. Our lofty aspirations don't matter at all if we are poisoning our inner-worlds with self-diminishing energy. All the happily-ever-after billion-dollar Hollywood stories mean nothing in comparison to the love story you really have in this lifetime—with yourself.

The complexity of life—both our internal biology and all the stimulation around us—makes it no simple feat to drop in and listen to ourselves patiently, so that we can gauge what we might need in order to feel both enough and deeply connected to the life we're creating. Stepping onto the Nourish path isn't about becoming passive, bypassing what we actually feel, or force-feeding ourselves messages like "I'm enough" or "I've got this" before simply going on with our days. All positive messaging to ourselves is welcomed, of course, but it's essential to note that Nourish isn't about sugarcoating life, or making out that it's filled with nothing but amazing opportunities while entirely dismissing our inner-critics, with their strong negativity biases. There are definitely situations in our lives where we need our critics! For example, a moment of complete meltdown from the critic can help us to recognize our upper limits and, in response, brave tough actions, like finally taking that leap, creating a challenging external change, be it moving house, leaving a relationship, changing careers, or letting go of a limiting belief system that just doesn't suit who we are anymore. As we know, life is filled with peaks and troughs, ups and downs—there's no way out of that! At times, we will certainly face soul-crushing grief and labor through deep pain. The art of nourishing our inner-world so that we are aligned with ourselves and deeply engaged with reality includes honoring our discernment and our skill in scrutiny—the capacities that allow us to, for example, size up what is and is not working for us. When we truly nourish our lives from an inside-out state of staunchly believing in our value and not collapsing, we're not glamorizing reality, nor our role within it. No. We are committing to being eternal students who learn by going within, who prioritize creating the profound shifts life calls for on our personal evolutionary journey, and who unconditionally respect ourselves. When we nourish, we learn to catch even the slightest moments where we might need something—perhaps to affirm a core boundary in order not to disregard our real truth. Self-honoring in itself provides us with the tools to help us stay uncollapsible. And as hard as it can feel to shift long-held behavioral patterns that our brains have played out and replayed, it's valuable to consider that even the smallest actions can catalyze neuroplastic changes that might lead, someday, to major change!

According to neuroscience, about 40 percent of our behaviors are completely habitual, and up to 90 percent of our actions are carried out subconsciously. These statistics make it seem really hard to find ways to change our ingrained thinking and actions. That is where something magical comes into play—namely, our human ability to cultivate self-awareness and presence. When we get present to our patterns and behaviors, we start to see that even more than the actions we take, it is the way we feel about ourselves and the stories we make up about our lives that really impact us. It's one thing, for example, to make a specific blend of tea on most days because you really believe the tea is, generally, something your body likes. Maybe it helps wake up your digestion or makes you feel mentally focused.

But if we're making this tea in a rush, or focusing on some negative, pleasure-limiting story when we're consuming it, with our minds elsewhere, then really, what are we enforcing in this ritual? Not pleasure!

Think of something you do each day that is part of your habitual protocol. Maybe it's brushing your teeth or getting undressed at night. Now relive that experience in slow motion in your mind and consider: What are you thinking and how are you feeling about yourself while you're going through the motions? How do you feel about the task? Are you tired, bored, do you feel comfortable in your body? Do you criticize yourself or avoid some part of yourself while you get it done? Do you let yourself settle into the moment and feel present with whatever you're doing? Or is everything a means to an end? Are you multitasking? Say, is one eye scrolling on your phone searching for something, or taking a call, or starting something else while you're still in the middle of this task? Can you let yourself settle into one thing and let that be enough—or, in today's go-go-go digital world, does it feel like an archaic concept to take time and be present with a basic task when you could fit in two or three others at the same time? What are your actions and thoughts showing you about the way you're experiencing the world? Is your mind aligned with really appreciating the sensation of being alive and settling into life? Or do your actions mostly reflect your urgency to move forward? Moving forward, of course, is a wonderful thing; it's how we focus, find purpose, and get feedback about ourselves. If, however, we are moving forward because we feel like we can't breathe until we "get the job done," or that we're simply "not enough" until we get there, or that "everything is in great danger" until we safely make it, then how are we feeding our lives with anything other than frustration and pressure?

Consider now, are there any daily activities in which you would like to land more deeply in order to feel really present where you are? Are there daily rituals—whether they're choices that reflect what you think is healthy and supportive for you, or else things you do to relax—that you could cultivate experiencing more fully? Can you see how simply shifting your habitual thinking in your daily actions is an invitation to create a more delicious, nourished life? Can you see this cost-free opportunity to become aware of negative self-concepts or energetically draining thinking, and that doing so can help you to transform your whole orientation to your daily tasks? Imagine how much room you might make for the lush energy of life to get in. Now, how might you commit to making this shift? *Would you like to bring more light into your everyday life? See Exploration 9.*

Here's the key: We can't really outsource this work to anyone else. We are the only ones who are full-time employees tending to the true needs of our internal being, in charge of creating our real behavioral shifts. While others can provide us with supportive materials, encourage us toward opportune situations, or serve as profound mentors, ultimately, we have to commit to ourselves on our own. We have to do the work from the inside out to learn to hear, tolerate, accept, love, and respect ourselves. We can spend thousands on the best transformational coaches and proactively work to create behavioral change in some areas of our lives, but still secretly sneak off when no one's looking and find a genius way to play out our stories of self-sabotage. Don't get me wrong; having external support and community is truly essential for our brains and beings—but *we* are the only ones who can put our best intentions into practice. We're the only ones who can tell if we're actually meditating or, in fact, sleeping, or creating our grocery lists. How do we become truly self-accountable? We need to think one step at a time and build consistency—and from there, we can grow real momentum. If we want to work with our brains, we need to give them the kind of material they need to send and receive signals of feeling sated, safe, and successful. I believe we can start by cultivating some appreciation for some of the simplest but greatest gifts of life—and regularly. This way, we can access all the free resources built right into our body systems, which can help us to make supportive choices for ourselves that strengthen our optimal behaviors.

I've called myself my own most difficult student numerous times, as I've often resisted the most effective, simple practices that would support real transformation and well-being, seduced by my own inner-saboteur. So I understand if you're someone who can listen to all the self-improvement podcasts, or read about breathing practices and the power of sleep, or whatever it may be, but still somehow choose to binge on a Netflix series into the small hours. I understand if you still breathe through your mouth most of the day, no matter how many studies now tell us that nose breathing can help effectually oxygenate the brain, or if you fall short of your various self-care ambitions on the regular for seemingly no good reason. The aftermath of choosing a behavior or action that doesn't lead us to optimal health might not feel good, but when we haven't put our faith in the power of living a nourished life and feeling worthy of amazing experiences, our suppressed emotional needs speak out. They might say, "My heart's deep needs are unmet. I need some sense of connection, so I'm going to placate my painful longing through this pattern of zoning out in my safe little bed at night. I'll sate my longing for fulfillment by eating these delicious snacks under the covers, staying up past my bedtime, and watching this simple love story with a happy ending. This way, I can numb out the part of me that can't deal with what she's feeling. And even though I want to get up feeling like a badass tomorrow, instead I'll let myself feel less than valuable—and get taken down tomorrow by my own sleep-deprivation hangover! It's better than tolerating this emotional discomfort and coming up with some other alternative—I'm way too exhausted for that." Somehow, setting ourselves up to operate in a subpar state can feel more comfortable than doing the work to feel safe in our bodies, to trust our actions, and to engage fully in our lives. Sometimes, making the choice to have, say, a nighttime mindfulness practice, to focus on something as simple as breathing in and out of your nose and connecting to the energy of life, feels like too much to do. Our unprocessed trauma continues to conduct our lives, and so we forgo the opportunity to let ourselves rest. We don't even give ourselves the level playing ground of waking up deeply rested and ready to love ourselves.

Setting Your Nourishing Tone

Remember, when we want to support improvements in our system state, or our felt sense of physiological being, we can begin with small steps. One small step that can help take care of our system state is regularly setting what I call a "Nourishing Tone." A Nourishing Tone is an energy we connect to that tends to our whole physiology from the inside out, and allows us to feed our life at its core with the nutrients of joy. Setting a Nourishing Tone allows us to cultivate awareness of what our inner-state is telling us, so that we can observe how that state impacts our entire reality, and then gently shift our whole physiology toward the energy of self-love, and, ultimately, toward feeling open to our potential. According to neuroscience, we have trillions of opportunities to form new neural pathways that, over time, can become stronger than the old patterns that lead to self-collapsing into a downward spiral. We can learn to, as I call it, spiral upward by regularly setting a Nourishing Tone for ourselves. While there's space for each of us to "hone" the right practice for ourselves, creating a Nourishing Tone really breaks down to about six steps. Note that you can do these steps for any amount of time. If you want to dive in deeply, you can spend a whole day exploring them. Alternatively, you could create a morning practice where you set yourself up to prioritize your inner-state of well-being throughout the day. You can also learn to do these six steps as a quick calibration, a kind of instant energy transfer that reminds you to stay connected to your own value and listen to what you really need in the moment. Also note that these six steps can take a lifetime to cultivate! For this reason, we must give ourselves the grace to patiently grow our garden of self-love.

Six Steps for Setting Your Nourishing Tone

STEP ONE: Create the space to connect with yourself and drop in to hear what you are experiencing. Feel your sensations and listen to your thoughts. The more slowly you move through this "inventory" process, the more likely it is that you'll get to feel into your true internal state of being. The primary focus of this step is to practice being absolutely tolerant and welcoming toward whatever you're feeling—even your negative thoughts or uncomfortable sensations. The key is to not make yourself wrong or try to change what you're feeling. That's no easy feat, but you can achieve it by simply noticing what arises. If it helps to respond to what you notice, you can simply say to yourself, aloud or internally, "I hear you. You feel—." Even better, you can write your feelings down! This is where journal-based writing practices can be so helpful (as you'll find in the explorations section at the back of this book).

STEP TWO: Implement whichever body-based practice for connecting to yourself works best for you. (This might be a breathing technique, or movement, or simply putting your hands on your heart or belly, or any physical and energy-centered method that helps you to turn your attention inward.)

STEP THREE: Gently begin to assess the story you're telling yourself in response to the feelings and sensations you're holding, by lovingly investigating what lies beneath each sensation, until you get to the root cause. For example, if you feel physical tension in your stomach, your accompanying narrative might be "I need to eat." If you feel anxious about an upcoming meeting, your storyline might be "I'm trapped." If you feel pressure to get something finished, you might be telling yourself "I'm losing time!" Once you hear that statement, and, even more, feel it in your body—listen further yet. What does "losing time" mean to you? That you'll never get to where you want to be? That you won't make it in life, thrive to the degree to which you think you "should" thrive? Listen deeper still, asking yourself a question like, "Underneath the feeling I'm having, what is my belief system?" Keep going, listening for the root energy. Listen inwardly to your body's story, the "reality" you're creating for yourself internally, but also notice the stories you're making up about the environment around you because of these internal narratives.

STEP FOUR: Engage the power of your imagination—something you may recall doing effortlessly as a child. Using your ability to visualize, connect to a calming, loving, soothing energy. If you can't find it at first, use your body-based practice to keep inviting the energy in. You can even say aloud, "I don't know how I bring it in, but the energy of safe, connected, loving care now floods my body." You can say, "I'm not sure how to do it, but I am deeply opening to the energy of nourishing, loving, caring light." Repeat until you allow yourself to soften, find connection, and receive a Nourishing Tone. Let the nourishing energy move through your whole body and beyond you, into the ground and then deep into the Earth's core. As if you're painting your inner-landscape, feel the energy color you with whichever feeling you long to bring into your life now, and know that it's in your power to spread this Nourishing Tone throughout your physiology, as a deeply sustaining resource. Notice the quality of the tone, its colors, and how it invites your body— your heart, your nervous system, your breath—to relax into your own life and trust yourself.

STEP FIVE: Keep opening to the Nourishing Tone as it spreads through your body, until you know you are filled up. Once you sense that you are full of your own inherent power—your Nourishing Tone—allow the tone to spread all around you, so you can connect with your environment. Breath by breath, moment by moment, notice how your body feels in space and strengthen your sense of feeling safe and connected to your life—self-aware, self-connected, and connected to your reality. You might want to say aloud, "I am now connected to myself, and I feel the nourished connection between myself and my life."

STEP SIX: Repeat this simple practice of filling yourself up with your Nourishing Tone whenever it is helpful and however often you like. Think of the experience of setting a Nourishing Tone as like soaking in a tub, getting a massage, or having an exquisite moment of self-care. Your Nourishing Tone also attunes you to the gentle, expansive, creative potential of life, and allows you to welcome it in. The more you do this exercise, the more quickly you'll notice when you start to tell yourself a negative story or disconnect from your own power, and the more patience you will learn to have with yourself. You will learn to notice rather than judge, and to ask yourself questions like, "How am I loving myself now?"; "Am I feeling enough as I am?"; "Do I believe in my ability right now?"; and, "Am I telling myself something true, or is it informed by my fear?" And it all starts by getting curious. Cultivating curiosity automatically opens us to the energy of receiving joy!

Ultimately, setting a Nourishing Tone helps us to learn new pathways and let go of our outworn behaviors, effectually but entirely without force.

When we shift our internal state from a place predominantly informed by critical, self-deflating patterns to a realm of nourishing possibility, we begin to allow ourselves to feel already enough, just as we are. We finally drop those voices that shake our foundational sense of self by repeating expressions like, "I won't succeed," or, "My time is over," or, "I'll never find my focus," or, "This always overpowers me," or, "I'll never change." Which repetitive, deflating thoughts do you have? Do you know? Even if you can't hear the inner-dialogue, do you know which feelings you have about yourself that make you feel less than? Are you able to recognize these modes or patterns of thought? Can you see how negative thinking or holding chronic stress is like a program that sets you on an inevitable path to self-collapse, a path that will loop back time and again to this same shut-down place and space, where there is nothing else to do except reach out to something else, outside of yourself, just to make it through the moment? When we don't practice self-care, we'll always reach to other substances to attempt to find a reprieve. Setting a Nourishing Tone puts us in our own driver's seat. *Want to explore self-empowerment vs. self-collapse? See Exploration 10.*

When it comes to supporting ourselves to really connect to our bodies when we're setting a Nourishing Tone (STEP TWO), it is often the most basic practices, gestures of self-connection, or active intentions expressed through ritual that help us to create an intimate space with ourselves. If you've learned to live with a low level of self-connection for most of your life, imagine that you are entering a new relationship with yourself, and that as with any new relationship, it will take time to get familiar. The best way to grow self-connection is to show up consistently, becoming a good friend to yourself. We may notice that when we begin our self-connection practices, we don't seem to experience much. Over time, however, the more you practice setting a Nourishing Tone, the further you will be able to deepen into your energy and feel a connection between your body, mind, spirit, and soul. In turn, you will naturally shift away from the internal patterning that no longer serves you. The Nourishing Tone becomes not only the energy that generates through us, but the energy that generates *from* us, ultimately activating our intrinsic magnetic charisma. Isn't it amazing? Carving out a few moments for yourself in the day to charge yourself up with *you* fuels your power as a creative being and amplifies the natural energy of your soul and spirit.

One of the most profound and basic means to grow self-connection is through getting to know the power of your breath. Specifically, when we make a regular date with ourselves to simply focus on the sensations in the body when we breathe, we start to appreciate that our breath is, in fact, a powerful technology. We see that we can drink in the energy of life when we inhale, expanding our sense of self-connection and growing our feelings of internal safety. And we find that when we exhale, we can let go of what we don't need and come to a really quiet space inside of ourselves. Starting with just five or ten minutes of regular practice will support significant shifts toward nourishment; shifts that will not only change your eating behaviors, but make you feel fundamentally stronger in the world.

It's fascinating to unpack the science of the breath. If you are a more or less physically healthy individual, that means you have about twenty thousand opportunities to breathe every single day. That is an abundant, lottery-winning number of breaths, which you get to take without even having to consciously dote on the effort. Breathing is so essential to us that we've made it "autonomic" (or automatic). Otherwise, we'd likely be complaining about it! Basic breathing is a natural talent that comes easy to most of us—but being more mindful of how we breathe can be a major game-changer for our neural patterns. It's wild to think that in such a consumer-oriented world, one of the most powerful brain-transforming drugs we have—mindful breathing—is completely, entirely free!

For us humans, oxygen is our primary fuel source, absorbed through our lungs, our bloodstream, and the cells of our bodies. Our breathing patterns influence the balance of oxygen and carbon dioxide in our bodies. These levels affect our metabolic rate and our blood pressure, which—get this!—impact our perceptions of hunger. In other words, a simple alternation in your breath can shift your physiological state, including your energy use and your sense of hunger. For me, as someone who had been so focused on diet, the functioning of my body, and the root cause of my struggles with food, this was a giant eye-opener to learn how profoundly my own breath impacts my sense of satiety. I was someone who'd lived quite disconnected from her own respiratory processes, at least on the level of consciously practicing health-invigorating, energizing breathing. My longtime go-to was to judge my body as malfunctional, seeking one specialist or another who could confirm that some part of my system was failing to absorb nutrients or work properly—and then needed to be "fixed." Yet I'd not considered how my breathing patterns, informed by long-held mechanical and psychological behaviors, were the first frontier in providing essential fuel for my entire neurological and biological health. I'd sought the best-trained experts to help me heal my emotional hunger issues, all the while overlooking the humble teacher always available to me—my own breath, and its innate power to help me overcome my emotional hunger, while also supporting my cells to hydrate themselves and retain the nutrients from the food I did eat.

Ancient cultures around the globe recognized the breath's importance to both health and sacred connection. Breath awareness practices sat at the heart of embodied learning modalities, and were respected as key to energy cultivation, foundational to creating our entire destiny. Long before health-tracking smartwatches and Fitbits, breathing practices were a known way to intrinsically connect with our vital signs. In truth, Western science is just catching up, confirming that yes, breath-focused practices (whether breath retention, breath elongation, breath-based relaxation, or other diaphragmatically engaging breathwork) significantly and positively impact our neural functioning. Breath practices have been proven to lower cortisol rates; enhance emotional regulation; and support the amygdala, hypothalamus, and prefrontal cortex to regulate our stress hormones. If we want to massively beautify and optimize our brains—guess what we can do. You got it! We hold a great key to our life empowerment in the creative source of the breath.

Modern researchers have specifically highlighted the advantages of nostril-based breathing (which pressurizes our oxygenation process, helping to filter out toxins and nourish our organs, and is also antidotal to conditions like sleep apnea). Additionally, it turns out there is a "breathing sweet spot" where we are breathing neither too little nor too much, but our system's unique Goldi-locks, just-right amount. There's research on the positive impact of retaining the breath (which you may be familiar with in techniques like "box breathing," where we inhale for a count, hold for a count, exhale for a count, hold for another count, and repeat). In a world where our digital interfaces seem to scream out to us even from our first wak-ing morning moments, it can take some concerted effort to put breathwork into gear. When we do, however, we start to notice significant differences in things like our impulse control throughout the day, the clarity of our cognizance, our ability to function without crashing (energetically or physically), and how much we criticize ourselves. Breathing practices, especially slow and deep breathing, can activate the parasympathetic nervous system, which enhances re-laxation and promotes brain activity in regions responsible for sleep regulation. This means that breathing practices can increase the quality and duration of our REM and deep-sleep stages—truly nourishing stuff! Improved sleep quality, as most of us know firsthand, can greatly enhance our cognitive functioning and emotional regulation. This is because in our best sleep states, the brain gets to detox deeply, and we refine our neural processing power and consolidate our memories—a total nightly reboot! You can sleep for significant hours in the night, but if your breath is disturbed or you are mouth breathing (or snoring), it's possible you're not really getting the nourishing sleep you need—and then it's all too easy for the behaviors that will take you down to take hold.

Consider this: Do you often choose to stick with an old habit of not regularly connecting to your breath? Maybe it's more familiar and feels safer to keep yourself small or even "deflated" (i.e., collapsed). Beginning a breath practice can be truly triggering, and if this is the case, we have to be extremely gentle with ourselves. If you notice that you want to check out anytime you turn your attention to tracking felt sensations like breathing, I encourage you to seek out a safe space—whether with a teacher or in a self-guided ritual setting—to explore staying with your sensations. Make a date with yourself to relax, to get into your body in a way that allows you to unwind. If that feels unrealistic, ask yourself what you need to make that goal achievable. Sometimes, we might feel we aren't attaining our self-set goals in an "accountable" way, but perhaps the problem is that we haven't broken those goals down into doable-enough steps. Things that seem simple (for example, making time for a breath practice) can actually be more challenging than some of our bigger wins (such as managing major work projects, dealing with significant professional responsibilities, and achieving goals at work). We think, "Oh, no-brainer, I'm going to make time for self-care, of course." But then it's a week, two weeks, a month—and we've still not started toward our goal. Maybe this is showing us we need more support around the goal; we need more simple steps toward it. For example, you could start just by remembering to take a few deep breaths while you shower. For most of us, the shower should feel more or less safe—hot, steamy, comfortable, cleansing. This is one reason people sing in the shower. So take a moment, exhale, sigh. Breathe and feel how breath physically expands your body, stretches you open. This is a simple, achievable start. Once this starts to feel comfortable, your breath awareness might start to extend outside of the shower, for instance, to the moments after waking up. Perhaps, in those moments, you could bring your hand onto your heart and feel the rhythm of your chest moving up and down. If we start with even three breaths, taken mindfully in the places we feel most inclined to relax (like in bed or in the shower), we can slowly cultivate the capability to commit to sustaining, say, two minutes of breath-aware presence. In this process, we begin to feel inside ourselves and investigate ways to foster loving kindness there, taking small, nourishing steps toward a fulfilled life. *Do you want to take a moment to oxygenate? See Exploration 11.*

There are innumerable ways we can integrate subtle but significant shifts in our brain patterns and activity. In fact, I believe that most of our lives can be filled with moving in and out of one self-loving, life-connecting practice to another. For example, something as simple but precious as exposing our faces to sunlight can help decrease the sensitivity of the amygdala (which you might remember is the part of the brain involved in fear responses) and strengthen the prefrontal cortex (the part associated with reasoning and our ability to manage our emotions). Being around animals or people we love enhances the functioning of both the prefrontal cortex and the amygdala, promoting the release of beneficial brain chemicals that reduce stress. Through small acts of self-nourishment, we can make the big shift toward reducing the impact of fear and stress responses in our brain—which then helps us to avoid acting out our cognitive overwhelm through maladaptive food and eating behaviors.

The benefit of putting nourishing acts into practice may sound *so* obvious, but even so, it can be challenging to anchor a consistent habit. And yet every time we choose not to give up on ourselves, not to collapse, but instead to care for our being, we are writing a new script; actively creating the potential for a new neural pattern. We shift from living in the stories and patterns that no longer serve us—stories of fear, of being unwelcome on this journey of existence—into the realization that we can write new stories, completely and profoundly. We come to see that being human is all about our capacity to make significant psychological and neurobiological shifts.

The truth is, no incredible creator has ever worked from a place of belittling and beating down her tools. She creates by taking the utmost care of her resources—loving her colors, her brush, the canvas she has. Creation comes from being moved—from the feeling that we possess the energy to express something true. When we dial into the innate art of nourishing ourselves, we step into our true role as the artisans of our own lives. We lead our lives through self-questioning, asking ourselves, "What do I need in this moment to tend to my life experience?" or "What will truly support me to move in the direction of loving myself in full?" When we embrace self-nourishment, we realize we have chosen ourselves as our truest companions. *Interested in step-by-step, doable giant shifts? See Exploration 12.*

When it comes to creating nourishing practices, many of us don't consider how essential it is to cultivate joy. We've learned for so long that in order to find "focus," we should keep our brain regions in a state of tension, existing in a semi-triggered mode of emergency. Here, we're ready to fight, ready to defend our agendas—fueled by stress hormones that keep our defensive responses ready to fire. In this mode, we are likely to live in a way that's well armored with our heart energy guarded and less open. When we're protected like this, it's difficult to let joy seep through and impact us, difficult to fully surrender to being moved by others' affections, or even simply be vulnerable. Just like when we set our Nourishing Tone, if we can't receive the joy of connection, we can't give off an energy that allows

73

others to connect to us. For some of us, even the idea of letting joy penetrate our hearts and fill up our whole bodies may seem simply theoretical. That's because, as powerful women, many of us have learned that if we want to achieve things and be successful in this world, we can't allow ourselves to soften. We can't afford to risk deeply receiving pleasure, mentally or physically, because then we might be susceptible to another's actions or behaviors. We might think we need to stay tough and not involve our actual emotions, which could allow someone to knock us off our feet. And so instead of feeling joy, we might feel something like a sliver of satisfaction when we believe we are heading successfully toward our goals. When we feel we are inching closer to some internally imposed benchmark of perfection, we may take a moment to recognize our strengths, and interpret that as joy. Joy, however, is like the breath itself—it is a kind of gratitude we get to feel, mixed with awareness and presence, and it really accelerates our progress on the Path of Nourish. The more joy we feel, the more we learn to choose self-nourishment as a lifestyle. Can you remember the last time you felt joy that had nothing to do with getting somewhere or looking a certain way? If yes, when was it, and what were the circumstances? If you can't remember right now, how do you feel about trying to cultivate a kind of joy that is truly unconditional? *If you'd like to proactively welcome joy into your life, see Exploration 13.*

No matter who we are, where we've been, or what we've gone through—who failed us, or who we failed (even if we've failed ourselves)—we can always remember and reconnect with our Nourishing Tone, because this tone is inherently part of us. We can commit and recommit, again and again, to filling ourselves up with the life energy we seek to feel whole and self-connected. The more we do so, I've found, the more our hearts start to lead our life journey, showing us the way. Joy allows us to relate more profoundly to both ourselves and the world. When we prioritize joy, we allow ourselves to open more often and even emit our radiance, shining our glory to others. When we connect to ourselves—a capacity that's built into our human nature—we access a moment-by-moment guide to tending to ourselves, with humility, acceptance, grace, and true commitment. We learn how to feed ourselves with the energy of life itself, so we reach to food differently. Look at the way you relate to food. Do you feel overwhelmed by it? Stressed? Upset? Or are you constantly returning to the sensation that you never have enough? Maybe you feel bullied, or that you, in fact, bully through your eating experience. Say you're in a long, entangled, dysfunctional, love–hate relationship with food. Doesn't it make sense, then, to consider that at the core of this relationship, you are actually crying out for relief; for some internal, essential foundation or internal clarity that allows you to successfully, intelligently, and organically take care of your whole being? How can we reach out for anything to feed us, to satisfy our bodies—how can we expect to register nourishment at all, if our internal states are operating on programs that do not allow us to ground into our self-worth, settle into the moment, relax, receive life energy, and feel that we are safe and we are enough?

CHAPTER 3

Corpus: Your Body of Knowledge

S etting a Nourishing Tone does not, of course, involve only the brain, or even only our neural circuitry. It's true that we cannot function without our brains, but whenever we make a choice, we onboard much more than this organ. Our brains are, in truth, fully informed by our bodies. In fact, some neuroscientists consider the "thinking mind" to be a body-wide system. Not only do our neurons extend through the whole spine, flowering a full nervous system through every network of communication in the body, but we are also more influenced by the trillions of bacteria in our bodies than by any other facet of our biological composition. To believe that thinking (not to mention all the hormones that inform neuronal activity) is a cranium-centric operation is to disregard the truth that up to 90 percent of our neurotransmitters are made in the digestive biome. No part of the body stands alone; in this, our physiology is a beautiful microcosm of the elemental interconnectedness of all life.

Many of us have consciously or subconsciously found our environments, cultures, or our family atmospheres challenging—or, we could say, "unnerving." When we chronically feel uncomfortable, unwelcome, or unable to settle into ourselves and our interactions with the world, we might become cut off from our body-wide navigational systems—literally unnerved. In these conditions, our thinking is not informed by an embodied state—by our "interoception" and "proprioception," or, respectively, an internal body-wide sense of perception and an ability to assess how the environment feels in our body. Body-wide thinking helps us to come into our full selves and discover our gifts, our sense of presence, and our unique offerings in the world, drawing from the emotions, sensations, and experiences of our physical sense of being. What has been your relationship with feeling your own body? Do you easily feel overwhelmed, unable to interpret what's happening from the inside? Do you feel that your body is constantly giving you the message that there's something "wrong" with it? Do you sometimes fail to notice how your body state changes in relationship to any stress you might feel? Is there some way you regularly access, tend to, or even soothe the sensations inside you? On a scale of 1 to 10, how able have you been in this lifetime to feel your body? Do you notice how foods impact aspects of existence like your sleep, your heart rate, and your mood? How do you respond to what your body feels? Do you override it while trying to "get stuff done"? When you experience conflict, do you react before dropping in to note what's present in your body? Are you taking more of an initiative these days to step fully into "thinking with your whole body," and if so, how has that been? Does your body work for you, or do you work together, as one? *Want a simple way to drop into the body? See Exploration 14.*

Aside from dancing and being physically on my feet most of the day in chronic go-mode, I didn't really cultivate any concerted sense of my whole body as a "thinking vessel" until quite recently. As I shared earlier, I didn't heed the call to listen to my body as a source of wisdom for about six decades. My first book-writing mission was really an answer to a call from my subconscious, which was requesting that I start to learn to take inventory of myself, including feeling my physical body. I went through quite the emotional process, reviewing my younger life and feeling the ways my body had paid the toll for whatever I wasn't willing to face or encouraged to process. As a survival mechanism, I had convinced myself that some things "didn't matter"—that I should just "get over them" and "not care"—but my body, it turns out, couldn't fully play along. Rather than feeling or respecting what my body told me (for example, the physical sensations of being confused, irritated, triggered, exhausted, or physically unwilling), I decided something was wrong with my body. I needed to ignore it so I could get up and go, get on with life. I learned that the only way to connect with my body was to label it as wrong. I looked wrong, I moved wrong, I weighed wrong. And either at the same time or soon after, I decided that something was also wrong with my brain. Even into adulthood, when I believed I had arrived on the path of self-love, I still spent so much time seeking out proof of my wrongness—for instance, often looking for medical or holistic specialists who, in exchange for my payment, would confirm that, yes, something was wrong with me.

Of course, learning about our physical conditions often means seeking out medical and therapeutic professionals to help us discover what we're holding onto and how to better bring balance into our lives. This is absolutely part of nourishment. What I mean here, though, is that for years, I hadn't done the basic work of befriending my own body. I continued to consult one expert or another with the deep-held sense that I wasn't okay, because underneath every feeling and sensation I could physically connect to was the idea that it wasn't enough just to be me. Eventually, I was fortunate enough to find somatic-centric experts trained to support processing some of these outdated but deeply rooted beliefs, perpetuating stories of wrongness clouding my perception. And rather than confirming that X, Y, or Z was happening in my body and I needed to fix it, they helped me to see that I was already unbroken, and to brave feeling and connecting to my own body and cultivating awareness of my felt sensations. I had a lot of resistance to sitting with my sensations, but working to become more tolerant of my own feelings led me to the epiphany that listening to the body is a path to creating a more coherent physiological state of internal operations; a semblance of self-organization. Healing the disconnection from our inner-state is the first step toward feeling enough—toward feeling fundamentally satisfied with our exact lot in life, as well as fully believing we are worthy of the energy to grow. I had to really experience the sensation of better befriending my body—and, as I've stressed, I am an eternal student in this school!—because unless I know what "enoughness" feels like, no forced protocol will land. Nothing will stick.

I am aware that few of us are given the opportunity or education to learn to value the act of checking in with our bodies. We learn to locate how we feel by thinking things through rationally. We learn that an emotion doesn't really "exist" unless we can name it, even though a lot of mysterious, beautiful, multidimensional, intuitive feelings are difficult to name or describe. Consider also that each language has its own words and ways to express body-based feelings, and some have more than others. Japanese, for example, ties emotion to physical sensation with the common use of words, including *hara* (or gut-related intuition or courage). Finnish has a concept called *sisu*, which describes a blend of inner-strength and stoic determination arising from within the body. Mandarin Chinese links the physical and the emotional through words that directly translate to sensations, like the phrase *xīn tòng*, which means "heart pain"—specifically the kind that arises from deep sorrow. Hindi expresses the physical–emotional connection through phrases like *dil khush* or "happy heart." But though there may be hundreds of words we could use to describe our felt sensations and stored feelings, we often fall into using only a handful to locate or comprehend what's happening for us—and generally even fewer when we go to express those feelings.

For instance, typical responses to "how are you?" are limited to "good," "fine," or "okay," regardless of how one might truly feel. Specifically, if we're having an unsavory emotion—something like what the Germans call *schadenfreude*, or "feeling pleasure in another's misfortune"—we might find it easier to simply deny what we're feeling. Or maybe we're a little mystically befuddled by *sehnsucht*, another German term that translates to an intense yearning for something far-off and indefinable. If we're feeling something unclear, ambiguous, or even impractical, it makes sense that we might deny our feelings, and definitely not talk about them in passing conversation. How, after all, can we yearn for something we cannot name, or some far-off place or person that we may not even know, as *sehnsucht* suggests? When you consider that our neurons can fire trillions of possible pathways, it's kind of a miracle we've organized any emotion into something we can understand at all! Because it can seem so complicated to recognize a sensation, to know why and when it started, and then how to actually soothe these sensations, it's often easier to try to extinguish our feelings with an external fix. This is why emotional eating has been so darn handy. You could try to sit with whatever intense, hot discomfort you're feeling—or you could sit in a comfortable, air-conditioned movie theater, stocked with popcorn and your beverage of choice, and, instead of sorting out your own feelings, watch a love story that has conflict but also resolution. Through the safe divide of a screen, we can handle reenactments of war, historic pain points, and other massive failures in human history that lack empathy, justice, or morality. We can clearly follow the folly, frenzy, and fret woven into stories told through lights, camera, and action, because they're outside of ourselves and they're visually and narratively comprehensive. This is why we love film. The truth is, we don't get a clear, directly comprehensive movie of what's happening on our insides—a means to illustrate the complexity of our inference, our emotional reception, how we're precisely digesting, processing, and handling our feelings, nor even what's precisely informing them. In fact, working to connect to what's happening inside of ourselves can seem like going to a movie and sitting for two hours in front of a screen with no clear plot, just a blur of moving colors and random impressions, with little bits of fragmented, nonlinear information and phrases here and there.

Neuroscience shows us that we can have bigger reactions to our own life events or experiences than might seem reasonable, particularly when our minds and bodies are still being informed by early, unprocessed experiences. Many of us enter our days already filled with pressable buttons—microtraumas just ready to go off if someone does or says anything that rubs us the wrong way, regardless of their intention. We might spend most of our lives walking around just trying not to get rubbed the wrong way!

And with so much external information to process, along with the "hidden" activity of our inner-worlds, it can seem nearly impossible and even threatening to make time to feel into what's going on inside ourselves—to listen within, without judgment. Perhaps, then, rather than trying to "figure out" what we're feeling with our logical rationale, it's more pragmatic to develop a practice of simply listening to, feeling into, and accepting what we feel. Specifically, while certain discoveries may help us unpack aspects of ourselves, we may never fully "know," in any logical sense, why we are experiencing the sensations or emotions we're carrying. However, learning to shift gears and first listen to what we are sensing, rather than rush toward logically solving (or relieving) whatever is creating our discomfort, helps us to grow more self-informed. How can we know if a lifestyle choice we regularly make or a relationship we're cultivating is truly nourishing for us, if we don't stop and listen to our actual needs and desires, and the ways our bodies are speaking to us? *How do we practice nonjudgmental body-based listening? See Exploration 15.*

If you're anything like me, you may sometimes find it difficult to empathize with your own feelings and "grasp" your inner-experience, without reacting with self-criticism or judgment. You may find that you can listen to a friend *sans* judgment better than you can to yourself; you may even tolerate a stranger's physical, intellectual, or emotional challenges better than you do your own. If a friend shares that she feels insecure, stressed out, or overwhelmed by the tasks she faces, we might be able to simply fire away with gracious advice, clear—from our outsider's perspective— about the steps she needs to take to transform her strife into success. Yet when it comes to the challenges in our own lives, we might feel too stuck, limited, or overwhelmed to take the time to feel our way into the heart of the matter, to trust our gut instinct, and to truly believe in our ability to achieve our goals. When it comes to making shifts for ourselves, finding our way from challenge to success might feel unclear, less obvious, or simply too hard. With others, we might be keen to name the feelings they're probably experiencing—but in our own lives, we often opt to disconnect altogether rather than brave the depths of what we're holding inside of ourselves. Instead of parsing our more complicated sensations, we settle for assessments like "I'm hungry," in order to bring those sensations to a quick end.

We might fall into patterns such as feeling interested in an idea, a project, or an activity—or even believing we "finally" have the gusto to transform an aspect of ourselves that isn't working for us anymore—but then, when it comes to knowing how to love ourselves enough to make the change, to commit to the steps, one at a time, we meet feelings we can't "sort out" immediately, and opt to shut down our previously determined efforts. We may deploy familiar quitting phrases—"I wasn't good enough" or "I didn't have what it takes"—rather than brave the slow, deep work of setting on the path, and ultimately, generating momentum to take flight.

Patiently expanding our emotional, sensation-based, body-centric sense of self-connection helps us realize that when we may think "we can't," we're actually just having a nervous system response, and it doesn't mean that we need to collapse our dreams or quit on ourselves. We can expand beyond the few emotions we are comfortable with naming (for example, "I'm so angry!" and "I am too tired") to recognize a fuller picture of what's happening for us, which allows us to better tailor how we comfort ourselves. What feelings or emotions might you skip over recognizing inside of yourself? How might learning to be with your feelings and sensations help you grow self-compassion? *Are you ready to broaden your emotional vocabulary? See Exploration 16.*

The Patterns of the Body and Locating Energy

In my late fifties, walking around my family's hometown in Italy, I saw a woman who was in a better state of physical fitness than I was even though she seemed significantly older than me. I watched her effortlessly ascend a hillside while I struggled to catch the breath it took to make it to the top. At that moment, something clicked. I realized that my body wasn't keeping up with my brain's agenda of "go, go, go," and for the first time, rather than look to the universe to somehow transform my energy through spirit, I decided to look to my body—and start a running practice. Even though I'd identified with being a dancer for some years, running was a new challenge for my body, and I ended up having to listen to it patiently every day in order to reach my goal, step by step. That goal was to get through a multimile race back home in the States. I did end up participating in that race (and getting through the finish line, too!), but that wasn't the real source of the achievement I felt. It was something more. I'd connected with my physical body and moved at its pace for the first time, rather than trying to force it to move at my mind's speed. I'd opened a door to a new way of being, a new understanding that there was another intelligence to heed, one that wasn't outside me on an etheric plane, or simply logical either, but was based, instead, in my body. More than that, I finally saw that I could—and should!—include my body in my equation for spiritual growth. *Do you feel you might be ready to shift some long-held patterns around moving your body? See Exploration 17.*

Until I started working with my body to train for a race, I'd never really shared aloud about my relationship with my body, my weight, or my relationship to food. I would discuss almost any challenging detail about my life with friends or family, but never admit to struggling with my weight or even being an "emotional eater." Meanwhile, I conveniently sought out healers who worked within my comfort zone; in particular, any healer whose modality centered around past lives or a mystical sense of self was a green light for me. Like many people, I didn't feel called to check in with my body, likely because I knew it would entail confronting some pain or discomfort inside me. Even when I did begin to check in, I'd immediately get so mentally exhausted that I'd fall asleep. Once I recognized that my body was part of the mystical self-actualization I had been seeking in the cosmos, I began to prioritize ways to connect to and ultimately care for it as a source of energy. For me personally, that meant investing in regular exercise and body-based therapeutic modalities, namely acupuncture and somatic exploration sessions. I understand it can be hard to find the time or resources to invest in ourselves. But whatever our budget is, I believe that when we find the will, we can access the opportunity to care for our whole selves, ultimately arriving at the wisdom of the body as the path to self-love. More than any other place we might look, it is the body that holds our truth, expressing the way we're digesting the realities of our lives.

To note, we don't need to majorly raise our resting heart rate or go to physical extremes in order to tune in and listen to the body. However, if we make some concerted effort to enter a state of either physical, rhythmic motion, or even supportive relaxation, we often have a better chance of dropping in and hearing what our whole physiology has to say. The essential thing, obviously, is that we discover whichever unique activity or ceremonious rite allows us to connect to our own inner-process—that is, discover the way we can best nourish our internal experience. As we cultivate that experience of self-connection, we slowly learn to apply this feeling in other areas of our lives, including eating.

In this way, we can begin to appreciate that eating is actually a complete opportunity for body connection. It is literally a moment of nursing ourselves, because remember, *nourir* means "to nurse"—or nourish! When we open our mouths to eat, we bring the Earth's bounty to our lips, we meet the elements that have evolved through all time, and we reap the sustenance of nature, assimilating the genius of the living world into our living bodies. What could be more sacred than this? Eating is our holy temple, a temple we enter through the genius nature of our own physiology. The sacred hymns in this rite are the feedback we get from our body, which sings a holy song as it relaxes into, receives, and accepts sustenance, bringing us into presence with the fact that we are alive, here and now. We are so darn alive. When we eat, we can feel that we are both fragile and strong; we have strong jaws and delicate tissues; we enter a flow of motion that requires proper mastication, breathing, and swallowing. We feel our bodies' inherent ability to create, and also that in order to create, we must receive. When it comes to our food and water needs, we are absolutely vulnerable. This makes eating an amazing opportunity to humbly fall to our knees, as though at the feet of the creator herself. And when we eat, we also get to rise to the occasion that we are worthy, simply by being part of the world's energy exchange. We get to be eternal beginners, allowing our taste buds to open, noticing the flavors and textures of what we take in, and allowing ourselves to experience pleasure. And with each meal, we are given fresh permission to try again; to do our best to care for ourselves. Eating is a merciful teacher.

So what happens to us when we lose control around food—or, at the other end of the scale, when we try to over-control food? When we lose our sense of self—*collapse*—around food, who do we become? Which part of self shows up? Is it the part that feels there's nothing for us in this life other than whichever food we're grabbing? Are we longing for ground; for something warm, something comforting? Are we trying to slow ourselves down and so using food like a car crash—a way to hit a wall that shuts the engine off? Do we just not believe we are good enough or beautiful enough to get to relax, receive, enjoy, and delight in our senses—so we must wolf our food down like the worthless creatures we are? Do we keep ourselves from eating things we find delicious, or are we fighting the fact that our bodies truly want food that's opposite to our family's cultural cuisine? When we recognize food as a route to true reverence for our own bodies, we see that our hunger is part of the expansive nature of all life. The body is made to want to heal and find harmony. It is naturally geared toward all things Nourish. It has the power to produce milk, to shed and replicate cells, to bring in new fertile opportunities. Our bodies have done everything for us—including giving our spirits a place to dwell! And it is possible to learn to find the sacred in our own bodies just as they are, and allow our eating experiences to reaffirm our oneness with sacred energy. *Would you like to make eating sacred for yourself? See Exploration 18.*

As someone who feels most able to consciously transform herself in the right type of shared space, one-on-one experiences with healers and group work have been the best way for me to unpack my relationship with self and retrain my nervous system to feel safe in an environment with others. The nourishing connection we can cultivate in the company of truly supportive healers, friends, or colleagues allows us to practice being compassionate to ourselves. When I took on the mission of writing this book, I knew its contents would be fortified by the wisdom of one of the most nourishing body-based healers I've met in this lifetime.

Thus, the following pages are devoted to sharing a conversation between myself and an expert practitioner of Chinese medicine, qigong, energy, and health, Mark J. Romano. In my sessions with Mark, I've received the incredible benefits of both his skills as an acupuncturist and, over and above that gift, his support in cultivating a greater sense of my own embodiment. Mark shines so much light on what it means to nourish the mind-body-spirit, drawing his illumination from multiple influences, including insights from his seemingly intrinsic connection to classical Chinese medicine and his heart-centered practice of qigong. Mark has been a great guide for me, ushering me toward recognizing the power of life and spirit in my own physical body. I share his words here in the hope that his perspective will fortify you and key you into the powerful life energy and spirit inside (and around) your body, helping you to grow an ever-greater capacity to nourish your whole life.

On a snowy New England morning, Mark patiently allowed me to ask him dozens of questions on all themes Nourish and more! What emerged is the following interview with Mark J. Romano.

Isabel: Mark, I'm hoping to gain some insight about what body-centered, whole-self, psycho-spiritual nourishment means from the perspective of Chinese medicine—and your perspective as a practitioner focused on "qi," or vital energy.

Mark: In Chinese medicine, nourishment is connected to the Earth element. It encompasses something broader and deeper than food itself, or even the energy we get from food. Nourishment is more than what we're putting in our mouths, and it's not just related to what happens inside our bodies. Nourishment also includes our sense of connection, our ability to feel safe on the planet and around others, and how we receive energy from the whole environment—including light, sound, smell, texture, and receiving others.

It's important to remember that in Chinese medicine there is a lot of complexity and nuance. We can't really limit our experiences to one organ, for example, but we can look at aspects of nourishment in relation to the "spleen–stomach meridian" in Chinese medicine, which is considered an Earth element. Meridians, to clarify, are the mapped, located, and named pathways or channels through which our vital energy flows, which connect various organs and systems in the body and help to facilitate balance and health. And nourishment is connected to the nervous system perhaps more than anything else. In other words, in order to really receive nourishment, we need to be in a safe or allowing state where our nervous-system regulation allows us to absorb energy efficiently or in a healthy way.

Isabel: How do our organs get associated with certain energies?

Mark: The oldest form of Chinese medicine, Classical Chinese Medicine (CCM) was initially a more abstract sense of "energy orbs" interrelating within the body; a philosophy that described the inherent connection between life and nature. It was nearly lost in the communist regime, but came back as what is known as Traditional Chinese Medicine (TCM). In TCM, the focus was placed on mapping, locating, and naming these orbs of energy in relation to the organs and meridians of the body. The root of Chinese medicine, however, is in the foundation of feeling energy, or prioritizing feeling the energetics of an individual's body.

Isabel: It's quite interesting that an intuitive modality of medicine focused on feeling energy was not "safe" to practice during political strife. There have been so many instances where it seems the predominant socioculturally enforced message has been, "Whatever you do—don't feel!" Historically, we humans have often had to fight for cultural permission to feel comfortable and to acknowledge and nourish our vital potential energy, rather than operating from a closed-down place. When I consider this, I realize that the struggles so many of us have with our own relationships to self-nourishment are about so much more than our own personal stories.

Mark: This makes me think of Thomas Hübl's work, specifically on what he calls the "collective nervous system."

[Author's note: I later researched Hübl's work on collective trauma, and thought to add a note about it here, since it both helps to elaborate on what Mark shares and provides insights into what makes up our collective nervous system.

As mentioned in an earlier section of this book, Thomas Hübl is one of the world's preeminent educators on the subject of trauma. In a December 2018 conversation with Gabor Maté titled "Healing Collective Trauma" (Science and Nonduality), he describes how the human nervous system is complexly composed of parts that respond to our own individual experiences and those that respond to intergenerational and collective experiences. Our collective trauma is a community- or society-wide—or even global—network, composed of what Hübl calls our "shared disembodiment," creating a kind of "mass anesthesia, where we don't feel certain things together."

This collective net of trauma becomes a societal structure we're born into, which we learn to call "normal." Even if we don't call a traumatic event "normal" at the time of occurrence, Hübl notes that our shared traumatic life events become normalized, or ingested, as our collective behaviors and then handed down as a kind of operation manual for living in our shared system state. Even when it isn't triggered, our group nervous system still exists, like a "dormant force." In some ways, it expresses the strongest features of our culture or society. Hübl emphasizes the parallelisms of trauma, meaning that, just as our own trauma keeps us from listening in and really hearing ourselves, it also keeps us disconnected from responsibly listening to global struggles or caring for the health of our planet. In this way, our trauma effectually cuts off the flow of our energy in the greater world—which has significant implications on our health.

Hübl argues that the true problem is not that we are lacking the capability to be sensitive as people, but that we don't have the clarity to understand ourselves, to connect with the foundational emotions or beliefs that inform our behaviors. So how can we take responsibility for knowing what we feel? One clue Hübl shares is the observation that if we are still charged, feeling stuck, or struggling once we believe we've identified the root emotion of a given perception, then we likely haven't actually touched the depth of its roots. We must go deeper.

Hübl believes that to create clarity for ourselves, we must do the work to discern between our traumas: Which traumas do I hold that are mine; which have I inherited, and which belong to our shared experience? He argues strongly for the necessity of learning to feel—a skill that can seem so rudimentary. Yet when we live numbed out, plagued by bouts of anxiety, or in persistent psycho-emotional-physical discomfort, without the clarity to locate the emotional charge we're carrying, it is very difficult to have a true understanding of our whole selves. Hübl sheds light on the essential process of learning to listen to and feel into the body as a means of unlocking trauma.

And now, back to Mark's insights!]

Mark: To give an example of the "collective" nervous system, I think of *The Bear*, a show about a chef and his life experiences. Specifically, there is an episode in the second season called "Fishes." It's a perfect example of how we are not only nourished by food, but by our whole collective environment. There's a shared dinner with an angry mother who is cooking this classic Italian meal (. . . a meal known as the Feast of the Seven Fishes). Out of her whole family, she's evidently the only one who knows how to prepare it correctly. She asks her family for help, but no one can meet her standards—and so, as a result, she's just yelling the whole time. Here she is, making an amazing meal with this incredible setup—everything's perfect. But everybody is so uncomfortable. They're all just waiting for the top to blow off on the meal. They sit down—with this beautiful meal in front of them. They're with all their loved ones, but there's this energy of explosion in their shared space, and so no one enjoys the food. This is the perfect illustration of the collective nervous system. It's impossible to really nourish oneself, to really receive, if the whole container does not hold the energy for nervous-system regulation and peace. When it's not safe, and we feel nervous, we simply can't be nourished.

Isabel: When we bring in the discombobulated experience of most family meals, it makes sense that as adults we might exhibit long-held eating behaviors like secret snacking or never sitting down for a meal. Sitting down for a meal might literally feel like sitting down on a landmine! Strained eating environments impact our ability to rest, digest, and give energy to the organs. Mark, can you speak more about the connection between our energy and specific body organs?

Mark: As I mentioned, each organ has a spirit connected to it, which helps us to name or give a location to energy. If I say a condition is in "your liver," on an energetic level this might be related to your sense of boundaries and how you're responding to others. You could be feeling frustrated in a specific situation, or impacted by a confluence of things. Here, we may not be talking exactly about your physical liver, but about the "spirit" of it. For example, in Chinese medicine, the spirit of your liver is called *hun*, which could be described as a soup of the collective unconscious; a type of watery, dreamlike energy. Say in this soup of the collective unconscious, I'm one kind of vegetable and you're another, and we form the soup broth, or a collective unconscious, together. When we have healthy liver energy, we can differentiate feelings in the shared environment from what we're feeling individually, and we can discern how we're feeling from how another person feels. We are then able to access the energy of compassion and understand that we are in relation to others, because we can retain healthy boundaries in real time in our shared physical space. That's the *hun*.

Isabel: So, for example, let's say you have a business meeting, and you feel like your boss doesn't like what you're sharing, and you start to feel really uncomfortable. Say your boss is just not feeling well, but you interpret it as some failure on your part. Then, after the meeting, you can't shake the feeling. You feel sort of raw or even worthless. Would you say that's a liver agitation—where we haven't created healthy boundaries between how we feel about ourselves and how another might feel, and, as a result, we lose our sense of personal comfort?

Mark: In relation to the "soup" idea—that we're sharing a collective unconscious and we need to discern self from other in the shared space, or delineate our boundaries in a healthy way—yes, that's the liver. But also, oftentimes, one emotion is influenced by other emotions. We're not just "one thing" in some static state; we are composed of different parts that influence our totality. A person's total energy is informed by their outer state, their biology, their psychology, their microbiome, and their neurons—and all of these are complexly layered and interrelated.

Isabel: For so long I assumed that if I had an emotional problem, or felt overwhelmed by a situation, it was something I was thinking, a cognitive pattern I had to change or relieve. My work with you has helped me to understand that we're not just storing ideas, patterns, or states of being in our heads; that there is a dimensional, physical, manifested component of our body patterns. Let's look at more emotions and how they're expressed in the body. For example, let's take fear—can you describe how fear might impact the spirit of our organs?

Mark: If you're feeling anxious or worried, like you're looking into the future, somewhere outside of yourself, and unsettled, these emotions are likely connected to the spleen, the stomach, and the Earth element. Lungs are about feelings of impermanence in life, and also death—which is part of the life cycle, like when the trees lose their leaves. In Western culture, we don't really like to focus on the impermanence of life, so fear is also connected to the lungs and kidneys.

Isabel: It's amazing to consider that, for most of us, the body and the emotions are conceptually kept separate—but here is a whole mode of medicine that has had such a healing impact on so many people, even in the West, and it completely connects our felt experiences and our bodies. Now, one more organ-function question... say something is going on in your personal life, but you can't share it. It's like you have to hide your felt sense or your truth around your partner or someone close to you, and it makes you feel like in some way you can't be present. Or say that you feel like you can't be present in general. Which organ would that be?

Mark: The kidneys—which are associated with water—are the organ that usually indicates the most rooted sense, which allows you to feel safe and not gripped in fear. In your body, the sensation is that you're able to drop down. The liver will also respond in this type of situation, where you might feel agitation because you can't relax around your partner.

Isabel: Oh! Now say you experience something, like an event or an intense, unexpected interaction, and it shocks you?

Mark: Shock would be something like what we call a *shen* disturbance—a disturbance to your spirit. This will affect your kidneys, which respond to the energy of feeling dissociated or stuck in a fight-or-flight response.

Isabel: It seems that, when it comes to eating behaviors, many of us are operating from an energy I'd call "aftershock," where our lives seem to be informed by old traumas or long-held patterns. When we're living in "aftershock" and we get triggered, it can seem like our only option is to go to food. We might be feeling anxiety or other uncomfortable emotions, but even if we don't know exactly what's provoking us to eat, we might just have this intense need to turn to food. Why do we reach for food in situations where we're uncomfortable?

Mark: In the case of emotional eating, there can be patterns where food becomes a symbol of feeling safe or creating connection, whether we're quelling our individual upset or, in the case of a family, where collective distress is soothed, even if temporarily, with food. For example, I have a client who lives in a pretty overwhelming home environment. There are various stresses in her family and a lot of arguing. After they've had a fight and everything starts to finally calm down, they return to connection by baking cookies—and eating many of them, together. We could say that when the nervous system is raw, the "boundary energy" has been used up. That felt rawness, having no internal sense of boundary and protection, needs some way to be soothed, nourished, and appeased. So, sugar, which (at least initially) releases serotonin, kind of "helps" the body cope.

Isabel: Boundaries and sugar. Honestly—that sounds like the name of a great book—which I should read! Can we talk about the connection between the energetic body and our behavior when it comes to sugar, and specifically what I'd call sugar addiction? What is sugar actually doing physiologically—what am I using it for? I want to understand how this fits into the equation of self-nourishment.

Mark: Let's say you experience a stressful interaction, and as a result, your blood sugar spikes. This happens because in response to stress, your adrenals increase cortisol production, and elevated cortisol keeps insulin from effectively doing its job. From this stress response, the hormone insulin can't help your cells uptake glucose. So glucose remains in the bloodstream, and this elevates your blood sugar levels.

When your heightened stress begins to subside, your cortisol levels decrease. This reduction allows insulin to resume its primary function, and so it rapidly clears glucose from the blood into your cells, which leads to a sudden drop in blood sugar. This blood sugar "crash" is what triggers your sugar cravings. Basically, your body craves a quick source of energy like sweets and carbohydrates to quickly restore your blood sugar levels. You're craving to counteract the sudden low you're feeling, to regain the energy you had grown accustomed to during the period of high stress and elevated cortisol.

Consuming sugar actually is part of the stress cycle, however—it perpetuates the pattern, you could say. That's because the sugar initiates a feedback loop in your body, a subsequent rapid increase and decrease in blood glucose levels, and a physiological stress response that exacerbates the cycle of cravings and stress.

Isabel: And that's how sugar dependency and stress dependency become entangled as a whole-body pattern! Creating stress, then crashing and craving the sugar—going from high to low—becomes a normal state. Living in a consistent shock-and-stress-response cycle keeps us in that high-adrenaline state where we can "do do do," and get all of our work done—overstimulated; it's how we remain "productive." Psychologically, the sugar becomes a kind of temporary buffer to deal with stressful events, but then also a way to keep us pumping adrenaline and repeating the cycle.

Mark: We can also look at the pattern this way: When you have a stress response and you release blood sugar, but you don't actually use that sugar to, say, physically fight a lion, it stays in the blood. When things cool down a bit, insulin will actually turn that extra sugar into fat. So we could say that when we don't feel safe, our body will respond to that threat with cortisol. Then we need to sedate ourselves, so we'll reach for sugar, for serotonin, which will help sedate us. The extra energy becomes stored away as white (inactive) fat. Weight is a form of protection, we could say, because we're storing energy—as though we're preparing for the future, to ensure our survival. We get into a cycle of not feeling safe in our lives, and storing up extra energy so that we have enough for the future. Underneath this sugar pattern is really the question, "Why don't I feel safe?"

Isabel: So, if we're storing fat, say, that might be because of fear about our survival. Even if that concern isn't conscious in our minds, we could be holding these thoughts unconsciously; we might have inherited them from the generations before us. So to clear these patterns, we need to shift our looping patterns of living in stress and placating ourselves with sugar. We need to figure out how to find a true sense of safety and feel that we are enough; that we have what we need. We need a way, a means—other than this physiologically harmful pattern of numbing ourselves with food, since it really just perpetuates the cycle of believing and feeling that we are unsafe and we don't have enough. And when we have a "not-enough" mentality, we're always searching for "more," which is exhausting in itself. We grow exhausted from the constant comparison, judgment, overwhelm, overstimulation, and confusion that come from fundamentally believing we're not enough and we might not make it in the world.

It's important to create shifts for ourselves that are soothing, soft, and really healing to our systems, rather than traumatizing. This will allow us to feel safe to start walking a path of step-by-step changes to build different, evolving patterns or rhythms that shift us away from a cycle of sugar highs and lows, of up and down, elevating and crashing. We can learn to look at this condition as a call to grow self-trust—to become sacred guardians of our whole sacred selves. This way, we can figure out which thoughts, actions, activities, and adventures help strengthen and support our bodies and brains, daily, regularly, and at intervals. Maybe we start to take a midday walk, or enroll in a deep breathing class, or connect with others—something that lets us relate to ourselves and to our environments, and helps us to grow that sense of safety deep inside of ourselves. From that place, we become more familiar with regularly listening inward, and checking in with what's really happening. Then, when we think we feel hunger, we can ask ourselves, "Do I have an appetite for some food, or do I need to care for myself on other levels? What am I feeling? Does my body feel safe, and if so—how do I know?" We make it our agenda, and then gently, step-by-step, we learn to really believe, really know from the inside out, that we are already enough, and that we have what we need.

Mark: I believe that the most effective way to shift our behaviors is to create practices that help us to build a real, grounded sense of safety, and support us in creating new patterns that nourish us and foster our relationships to ourselves and to others. A practice can be any activity where the emphasis is on connecting with our internal state, with how we're feeling. Even horseback riding or Pilates—as long as we are in a soothing, safe environment where we are able to drop into our bodies—can help us to cultivate greater interoception, self-connection, and rich relational ability.

Practice helps us cultivate respect for the diverse "soil" from which our lives grow, so we can grow a sense of familiarity, a trust in feeling nourished and safe. In the same way that we thrive when there's diversity in our plants' soil, we want to cultivate the ability to relate to diverse parts of ourselves, and a diverse, rich ability to relate with others, to our spirits, and to our physical bodies.

The more we foster a sense of being self-regulated, safe, and secure, the more often we'll find that our emotions and our body-physiology can strike a healthy balance. If we don't have boundaries, then we're not really in a sustainable or safe environment—wherever we are. We won't have the appropriate way to say "stop" or "no," or feel what's right for us and conduct our own lives—whether we're dealing with eating, food, relating with others, making any choice, or creating any behavior.

On the subject of the relationship between eating and feeling safe and well-bounded, I would add that, in Chinese medicine, the tongue is connected to the heart. If we don't feel safe in the spirit of the heart—which is a seat of the mind, and which brings us a sense of feeling warm and present and relaxed—then we might reach for foods that taste rich, like perhaps a high-additive snack that's engineered to have a highly addictive flavor. We create a behavior that cements in our minds a correlation between taste or crunch or saltiness or sweetness, and feeling safe and okay. On some level, we think we're going to be nourished when we go to these foods. Metaphorically, however, these highly addictive foods are almost like the parent who says they're "here" for us, but isn't actually emotionally present. It's the same thing. These foods are empty vessels of love.

100

We can get programmed pretty early on to reach for these ultimately empty foods as a substitute for the empty presence of our parents.

Isabel: Presence is so essential, especially when we are younger. This is how we learn what safety and security mean—from how these are modeled to us. Some of us don't realize, if our parents were physically in the picture, that in a way we still grew up alone. Or even if they were present, they may not have been present to the fine, sensitive needs of our unique selves, and so we might have felt abandoned in ways they weren't even aware of. And the primary way we learn to "fend for ourselves" is in the food we choose and the way we feed ourselves. If we're operating from a sense of being unsafe and insecure, and if our parents haven't modeled presence and self-care to us, whether in how they care for us or how they care for themselves, then we might play that out by checking out ourselves, and using food to start doing so at a young age.

We might be especially likely to play out our trapped feelings with food if we're raised in an atmosphere that, like Hübl says, shares a collective net of trauma, where the underlying rule is that we just "don't talk about stuff," where we operate by navigating around our past hurts and ignoring things. In that situation, we learn early on that this is how we should behave, too. We normalize numbing out, ignoring our sensations, not expressing ourselves, and getting our psycho-emotional-physical needs met elsewhere—for instance, a box of cookies or a bag of chips. And we can do all of this subconsciously, not even realizing the complex pattern until, as adults, we find that it has become chronic.

Mark: Yes, and that's why we practice being present. It's not like we have to be present 100 percent of the time;

that would mean achieving some high state of enlightenment. Instead, we practice. We learn to value the felt sense of connection and to recognize key moments when something is calling us to be fully present, to fully connect with ourselves or be present with another. In those moments, and when we're transitioning into and out of them, we give our full presence. In general, people don't get educated culturally, in school, on how to do this, so we have to train ourselves sometime later. Learning to cultivate presence is like training your soul to be in your body, to be present with yourself, with the people around you, and with your environment.

By the way, it might be useful to add that this kind of presence we want to cultivate, it's not the same as being in a high-alert, battlefield state. It's not just about being aware; it's about being aware *with presence.* You could say that awareness is in the head, but presence is the heart, and feeling grounded, safe, and secure is related to your belly. So being aware *with presence* means grounding into your physical body.

Isabel: So if I'm aware in my head, but not present in my heart, my stomach might interpret everything I feel as "hunger," even if what I'm really craving or needing is to become present, engaged in my heart—and bringing that energy into my stomach to feel grounded, safe, and secure? Gosh. This is a giant takeaway for me. Let's just say, I hope to become even more present to this dynamic.

Thank you so much, Mark. You've given so much here. Is there anything more you'd like to share on the subject of nourishment?

Mark: I'd like to mention something author Charles Eisenstein shared—that if we want to learn to take care of the Earth, we have to love the Earth and not just try to "fix it."

102

I think it's the same here with the body. For us to take care of our bodies, we have to love our bodies, and not see them as a problem to solve.

Isabel: I love that. More than any diet or protocol, it's learning to cultivate the awareness and presence to be with ourselves that allows us to fundamentally nourish ourselves. We work to gain clarity as we feel into our boundaries and our senses of personal, generational, and collective energy—and through practices, we build the feeling of safety from within, grounded in our bodies and connected to a natural flow of life that moves through us.

Mark: Yes. In Chinese medicine, there is a central channel—the *Chong Mai*—that is described as a house. Within this house channel, we can access another core channel that runs through it, called the *Zhong Mai*. More than just a house, *Zhong Mai* translates to the *felt sense* of home. In other words, when we make our house our home, another channel shows up; the head and heart and stomach find alignment and center. In adult life, this is our work—to make our house our home.

What do the words "presence," "awareness," and "grounded" mean to you? When you contemplate, for example, the word "presence," how does your body respond? Take a moment to chant it internally, or even aloud. Can you feel the word "presence" in your body, and if so, where does it live? Is it in your head—or in your heart? Visualize the word actively in your imagination, and then internalize it so that you can feel it energizing you, nourishing you. Imagine presence being an energy that comes into the garden of your being and waters your internal senses while connecting you to your environment, and to the moment.

When you picture this, what do you notice? What do you become present to? How comfortable do you feel in your posture right now? What is your body saying to you?

Consider also that you can run different *forms* of nourishing presence through your whole physiology. What *quality* of presence would you like to carry in your being? Whatever you need right now is available to you: gentle presence, generous presence, stabilizing presence, compassionate presence, energizing presence, loving presence, self-committed presence, focused presence. We may notice that we are longing for, craving, desiring a sense of being comforted—truly a version of safety—while not generating a presence that carries the energy of comfort. Are we comforting the energy of our lives right now with our presence, or are we creating discord with our minds and stress in our bodies? How are we operating? What if the presence we long for is actually the presence we can grow within ourselves? How would you show up for food, how would you eat, if you were holding the energy of the presence you crave? Maybe you crave something to come cool you down, or embrace all that you are, or provide you with physical comfort or appreciative, attentive care. Can you imagine what it would feel like to be those things for yourself—to give your mealtime or eating experience, for example, the very presence you crave, the grace of appreciation and attentive care?

If cultivating presence feels a little elusive, we can, at the least, likely name the symptoms of not being present. Can you think of a specific example in your own life when you've perhaps lost your awareness and connection to your grounded sense of presence in the moment? When we lose awareness, we might, in the most obvious sense, forget where we placed something like our keys, or forget something important on our errand list. When we lose presence, however, we disconnect from our feelings, from our grounded sense of vitality, or even from our environment. We may lose touch with the feeling of having a place in the world, or being able to be in reciprocity with life.

Like Mark said, our physical presence connects the spirits of our organs—the energy of the heart, the stomach and its felt sense of safety, and the liver's soup of collective energy and personal boundaries—in an interrelated flow. As we grow presence, we may notice that we are able to settle more deeply into our felt experience—to let go of impatience and pressure. We may become less fidgety. Our eyes might find a soft focus. We may reach outside ourselves less for "stuff," since when we allow ourselves to take up space, we feel less need for things to fill our space. When we're present, we may be able to single-task more fully, shake out the restless energy of *doing-doing-doing* in favor of just being, because we recognize that we belong right where we are. Presence allows us to rest more in our felt sense of the moment, even if we're physically exerting ourselves. (For example, think about how present top athletes must be to champion a game with physical and mental cunning—and how do they get there? Practice! Practice fueled by passion and dedication engages the mind, body, and spirit.) And the body isn't the only possible doorway to presence—consider, for example, a master chess champion, or an incredible poker player—yet when we tap into the flow of presence, we become more fully connected to our bodies and engaged with our whole experience of living. When we are present, we might be aware of what's next, especially if it's pertinent to our task, in the way an archer is present when pulling back her bow, but is also thinking about hitting the mark at which her arrow is aimed. But we aren't focused on another time or place as a way to escape our experience in the moment. When our senses are all on board, we may recall various visions, feelings, or even textural memories in our bodies, but presence allows us to integrate this information into our felt experience and land more fully in the moment.

We have to follow Hübl's suggestions and develop the clarity to know what is "my stuff," "your stuff," "our stuff," "societal stuff," "generational stuff," and even "miscellaneous other stuff." It is my opinion that if we want to learn to make these distinctions, we must be prepared to approach our internal world with curiosity and a beginner's mind, rather than a "know-it-all" attitude. It can be easy, for example, to interpret someone's hurtful expression as "their problem," or something that has nothing to do with us. We might tell ourselves we need to put up a firm boundary to avoid being impacted by other people's energies. It's certainly possible to erect firm boundaries. But we can also build them from the soft energy of self-inquiry; from curiosity rather than rigidity. We can create a healthy boundary, or commit fully to our needs, by asking ourselves, "What do I need in this situation to take care of myself, to care for my own energy and respect my environment?" When it comes to discerning or clarifying our feelings, curiosity is often a more supportive tool than defense, which can keep us locked in familiar patterns of feeling edgy and irritated in our responses to life. Rather than creating structures that affirm our separation from others, curiosity allows us to build boundaries that support our connection to the world and expand our capacity to be present. As we know, it's not always easy to be present; life isn't all flowers and love. We must often be present to painful, challenging, tender moments—but these moments help us cultivate sympathy and greater capacity for heartfelt connections.

Even with tons of practice, we might not "do presence" perfectly each time. We might fail to be kind to ourselves, blur our boundaries, or find ourselves, once again, in the middle of a self-collapsing behavior. It is essential to practice compassion on our journey. Remember to be gentle with yourself; 90 percent of our actions are ingrained in our subconscious, and our neural pathways can seem more stubborn than a mule in mud. Also, while someone surely showed you how to tie your shoes (which I'm guessing you've mastered), it's highly unlikely that anyone directly coached you to be present as a toddler. It's possible, too, that no one sat with you when you had an emotion as a child, helping you to process the feeling and stay connected to yourself, or modeled healthy behavioral responses with their own. In many ways, we have to grow up aspects of ourselves now—parts that are still suspended in adolescence. Be prepared: these parts of ourselves can be challenging to deal with. That's one reason we've often chosen to ignore them! But we can look ourselves in the eye, in our mirrors, and remember we can do this. Seek out people who are also cultivating presence. Get curious; ask them how they work on becoming more present—and what's been difficult for them along the way. As we grow presence, we do our best to learn from the outcomes of our experiences. Keep in mind that we can be experts in many arenas, and also be beginners struggling with fundamental aspects of our functioning. And that's more than okay! We allow ourselves to learn, and we expand; our soil becomes more diverse, as Mark described. We make up our own rituals and rites, listening within. We become more creative as we get in touch with the vitality and beauty inside ourselves. *Are you ready to cultivate grounded and aware presence in your life? See Exploration 19!*

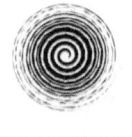

CHAPTER 4

Surfacing the Subject of Nourishment and Womanhood

Historically, it's safe to say that men have been given certain advantages and societal permissions to feel comfortable in their own bodies, just as they are. While we can't speak for individual men, it is definitely the case that the male population in general has felt less pressure to look beautiful, fit, youthful, and fashionable in order to secure their societal value. For a man, age is not typically a factor in his romantic eligibility; in fact, it may not be until the ripe age of his late fifties that he starts to consider the notion of parenting a child. Time is not slipping through his fingers; in some ways, he is granted a different timeframe in life altogether. In fact, in the eyes of those around him, his matured looks might even make him more handsome, more commanding, and more deserving of respect. While the tables are slowly turning when it comes to gendered beauty expectations, those tables are still made from masculine standards. From days of old, men have been granted greater authority to move through the world confidently regardless of their external appearance—in other words, they have been invited to accept themselves just as they are. Additionally, in many cases, boys are raised with an automatic license to pursue whatever ambition they choose, with no sense that there's anything holding them back. At first glance, this type of "believing in one's self" can seem to have similar apparent qualities to the kind of nourished essence that has been emphasized in these pages: unbreakable self-trust, self-confidence, and the ability to navigate life uncollapsibly. But our individual nourished path is not a generic, expected privilege provided by our society alone. In most cases, for us women on self-forged paths, we must find our own profound and delicious path of self-nourishment, and doing so is crucial to the work of exploring and transforming our individual trauma and the collective nervous system.

I am always keen to avoid incessantly focusing on limitations, especially if they are in the long distant past. However, I am also a proponent of doing the necessary work to collect parts of ourselves that we may have left behind—parts essential to embodying our whole-person energy, our self-worth, and our ability to feel safe and secure, just as we are. While each woman is on her own journey, we are part of a collective womenkind, and it is valuable to look at the strengths and beauty inherent in our gender, as well as not to be blind to some of the serious disparities we've historically endured.

For thousands of years, women have been aesthetically objectified; their physical appearances have been the currency that has determined their societal value. It is only in more contemporary times that we are beginning to see a larger quantity of women playing diverse roles on television or in movies—roles in which their internal worlds are integral to the script, rather than lost behind a winning appearance that is pleasing to the male gaze. These more diverse roles broaden our cultural sense of the kinds of realities women experience; they reflect the truth that we are characters who exist beyond male-centric storylines and peripheral roles supporting men. We have concerns beyond romantic sagas; we have challenges to overcome, relationships that mean much to us, dramatic processes besides men-focused woes, and ambitions beyond motherhood. Even though the world of cinema still has many miles to go, these more modern storylines might be an attempt to make up for history, which left out most stories about women. To say that women have been "underrepresented" would be a gross understatement. Even *The New York Times* recognizes that we are "missing stories" of women from the last 3,500 years; citing historian Bettany Hughes, the newspaper of record notes that less than 1 percent of all of written history has been devoted to sharing the feats and powerful contributions made by women. A Wikimedia initiative named "Project Rewrite" runs "edit-a-thons," where editors and contributors devote periods of time to filling in the gaps in history where women should appear. Their goal is to create some semblance of balance in the gender gap, as up until now, our historic contributions have largely been unaccounted for. What *has* been accounted for, and exhaustively, is our physical forms—meaning that when history does tell us about women, it's often to let us know how their physical appearances were regarded by men. (Nefertiti, for example, was the most beautiful woman in Africa, while Medusa was so repellent that she ruined men for all eternity with a single glance.)

We've objectified women's bodies—because we've been trained to. Whether it's the industries that run on the currency of female beautification, or the laws that historically gave (and in some cases still give) women no rights over their property or even their bodies, our culture has been built around disempowering women for hundreds or even thousands of years. However, just as we can each shift our behavior on the individual level, we can also make cultural shifts over time—and that's precisely what our society has been doing. With women coming together more profoundly in recent years, we are now more capable than ever of overcoming the limiting and superficial aesthetic requirements that have so long been placed on women.

In many ways, social media can uphold unachievable utopian lifestyles, idealized body images, and other peoples' perfect-seeming realities—which can make nearly anyone run for the airbrushed hills of Photoshop just to feel presentable. While this is a social media pain point we must confront, it's also important to recognize that social media has given women the opportunity to come together in numbers far greater than we ever have historically, helping us to see examples of deep female camaraderie and friendship. As we move forward, filling in our missing history, we will see that the effect of joining forces as women is different from the kind of male bonding we see in history. To speak in broad strokes, men have traditionally teamed up to play sports, compare brawn or brain, champion, earn, get the trophy, or adorn the medal. When women come together, meanwhile, it's true that we have often thrived in the kinds of games and competitions devised by men—but typically, we bond over something greater than simply trying to "win at all costs." The value of gathering together as women lies less in the energy of rallying to dominate, than in the empowerment we gain from the personal sharing of our stories. See, where one woman may long-believe she suffers something unspeakable all alone, another woman's bravery to share a similar struggle gives us the eye-opening awareness that, in fact, we are not alone. Because our stories have been stifled for centuries, we've often struggled privately, not knowing we were part of a shared challenge. When we hear other women divulge their truth, we get to widen the scope of what we believe we are allowed to feel and experience, and acknowledge ourselves in all parts of our cyclical nature. Most importantly, we dispel the outdated myth that we are "less than" or "not enough." When we come together, we can destroy any restrictive rules around what we can or can't be in this world. We can heal the shame we've internalized for too long for inevitably "failing" to meet some imposed standard that as women it's our job to be perpetually poster-perfect, glossy, and presentable. In the last decade alone, we've seen a significant rise in women being valued for our personhood rather than our appearances. Increasingly, women are sharing real-deal content—whether they're female comedians, entertainers, podcast hosts, or reporters. Women are showering our world with outside-the-box conversations and insights that cast light on discrepancies and inequitable standards—and more importantly, let the world know what it's like to be female.

When we come together, we gain more power to see the subconscious beliefs that have stunted our sense of what's possible, and which definitely no longer serve us as women today who want to live free and empowered. We each get to have our own little "aha moment" around the ideals and standards we've ingested and internalized, perhaps without even realizing it. Some of these can be giant, and some more subtle. For example, just recently, social scientists relayed that the optimal room temperature of office spaces was determined in the 1960s, based on the thermal comfort and average metabolic resting state of forty-year-old men—which is on average five degrees warmer than that of most women. To avoid being "difficult," for years, most of us politely put up with feeling freezing in many publicly air-conditioned spaces. Perhaps on some level we worry that if we share that we're too cold, we'll be seen as complaining, or being weak or too sensitive or—the worst of the worst—high-maintenance. In her book *Invisible Women*, which highlights the innumerable discrepancies we've often overlooked, writer Caroline Criado Perez calls the condition of catering to males in our social and industrial architecture "one-size-fits-men." Most of us have lived unaware of the masculine bias in our foundational structures, which support the fabric of our created reality. And even if we don't wish to devote our own personal lives to replenishing history books with the lost stories of powerful women, when we become aware of the outdated limitations we may have ingested around what it means to be female, we can become more present and conscious in choosing which reality to feed inside ourselves. We can find a greater sense of self-trust to bravely, even fearlessly, create our own destiny and unleash our full potential—knowing that though we forge paths that may not have been mapped in history, we are not alone. We do not have to walk the road ahead in blindness; instead, we can see each step illuminated by all the women who have come before us, whose spirits now chant for us to live our best lives, believing in all of who we are!

This is why when we set our Nourishing Tone, and whenever we check in with ourselves, it's supportive to consider the essential cultural changes that have come before us. We don't have to preach about our position as women, sermonizing far and wide, if that's not our life work. What is valuable, however, is to recognize that healing trauma and working with our nervous-system responses is intrinsically related to these cultural constructs handed down to women. As we become more aware of our internalized dialogues and our sensorial processing—not to mention the stories we make up about ourselves—we will find more patience and forgiveness for ourselves if we recognize that not all of our thinking belongs to us. There is an outworn diatribe in our culture, and just like our outworn behaviors, it's hard to shift. It is holding onto a dying idea, vying to survive because for so long this idea has been what our culture has known and how it has operated. This diatribe attempts to make us feel, deep down inside, that it's not safe or practical for us as women to explore or express our full range of self, and fearlessly draw on our talents. It enforces the idea that what ultimately matters is that we appeal to others physically; that we can only dare to be something or someone if we hold the "beauty card" or fit well enough into a physical shape that's acceptable in the eyes of others—and if not, we are offensive, intolerable, or have little value. We may or may not identify as feminists or feel comfortable using words like "patriarchy," but whichever terms work for us individually, awareness and presence are key to our embodied sense of nourishment, as Mark described. Becoming more aware of the cultural constructs that have played a role in the way we, as women, operate our lives, feel about ourselves, and interface with the world, helps us to better understand how to become uncollapsible. Nourishment, for women, includes exploring the ways our sense of self, our ideals, and our fixations are fed by culturally perpetuated information—information that has been enforced for thousands of years. When we decide for ourselves what's important to us—what makes us feel good rather than hating ourselves into a smaller dress size—we start to choose well-being from a place of inspiration, energy, and, above all, self-love. And it's not an overnight decision, by the way, to suddenly choose to love yourself after years of devoting far too much time to, for example, disliking your nose, or wishing your lips were fuller or your hair were straighter or curlier or whatever. We have to recommit, over and over again. And when we do, over time, we learn to spend more time celebrating our value than sitting in self-disdain.

A little more "herstory" for thought, on the topic of transcending the internalized self-objectification we so often get stuck in as women. Consider this: As far back as 25,000-plus years ago, when our stone-age ancestors crafted the Venus of Willendorf figurine, human societies have been focusing on women's bodies. (You've likely seen this curvaceous four-inch carving of the "ideal" woman's body crafted during the Paleolithic era.) The stories of women's intellectual achievements may have been left out of history, but our hip-to-waist ratios and bustlines have left an indelible mark. For example, searching "Marilyn Monroe's dimensions" yields four million results on Google. By contrast, if you google "Arnold Schwarzenegger's pant size," you get just 12 percent of that number. In similar disproportion, googling "actresses who have aged" brings up a whopping three billion-plus results, whereas searching "male actors who have aged" yields only 23 percent of that number. And there's more: "female actors who have gained weight" brings up ten times more search results than "male actors who have gained weight." The picture these statistics paint is that we are five to ten times more interested in women's sizes, weights, and physical features than men's. The numbers confirm the social message—emitted silently as well as bugle-blared over our own individual, internalized beauty battlefields—that if we want to have any relevance at all, we need to look a certain way. It makes sense, then, that when life feels overwhelming or we aren't sure how to choose what's best for our long-term path—or even what our long-term path is—that we displace our anxiety onto trying to control our weight. At least, we think, if we can control what we look like, we might have a chance at success, or love, or money, or value, or importance. And if we do have passion, or skill, or interest, or vigor and fortitude? Well, we'd better focus on our weight and our appearance so that society can bear to look at us. For we might believe that if we dare show up looking unattractive or unsightly no one will take us seriously. How could anyone accept what we have to share?

When we do the work of letting go of what no longer serves us—including self-limiting concepts that have been influencing women for centuries—we might find that we feel much lighter. We get to consciously choose a different way. Instead of thinking, "Will this diet help me look good?" we naturally start to ask ourselves, "Will this food make me feel good?" We begin to define what lasting beauty means for us, from the inside out. As we find the power to live by our own internal standards and values, we also become lighter. *Are you ready to explore and transform how social constructs of beauty have influenced your sense of self? Then see Exploration 20. And—Do you want to feel valuable as defined by your own standards? See Exploration 21.*

Redefining Power, Organization, Purpose, and Identity on Your Own Terms

If every woman has an inherent brilliance, why is it that so many of us struggle to actualize our best lives; to commit to ourselves and deeply believe in our own power? Why would we wobble in our felt sense of identity, suddenly uncertain about our purpose, or lack the momentum to self-organize sufficiently to generate our dream projects? It's useful to consider the histories and etymological roots of words like power, organization, purpose, and identity, so that we can understand how we want to define them as women.

The Latin origin of "power" is *potis*, related to meaning "lordship," "control," "right to command," and "military force." In this way, the roots of the concept of power suggest an energy that is inherently masculine. But what if for you, as a woman, power didn't look like dominating or controlling others, but rather like empowering your expansive truth and supporting others to do the same? How would it feel to rebrand the notion of power, filling it with the energy of the heart—feeding it with the source of love, so that it is expressed by softly flowering open?

"Identity," meanwhile, comes from the Latin *idem*, or "the same," indicating this word that has come to signify our very selfhood, in fact, describes sameness and consistency; a shunning of irregularity. And yet for female-bodied people, our bodies are, by nature, an expression of change. Our hormone levels shift dramatically throughout the menstrual cycle, with our estrogen and progesterone levels varying by as much as 500 percent at different stages of the cycle. Men, on the other hand, experience relatively minor daily testosterone fluctuations of about 10 to 15 percent. In this sense, the concept of identity is also male-coded. What if rather than feeling we need to be consistent in order to have identity, or express ourselves as though we are just one single color crayon in a crayon box, day in and day out, we can consider that our identity is an ever-changing palate of colors? Which hues do you feel you are today? From head to toe, heart to soul, what is your spectrum?

Does it feel truer to your free, female spirit to give yourself permission to be a flowing, shifting spectrum of energy, instead of something fixed and consistently the same?

"Purpose" comes from old French, *porposer* and Latin's *ponere*, related to "putting" or "placing," or "putting one in place." The roots of purpose, like those of power and identity, closely relate to linear, masculine ideas, such as taking direct aim, creating function, having a clear goal, or keeping a distinct object in view. And it's little wonder that the idea of purpose is so tied up with masculinity, since for centuries, it was male leaders and male-dominated industries that set civilization's targets. Men determined humanity's goals and aims, and the structures we would put in place (*ponere*) for generations to come. Even the words we speak were chiefly first recorded in the writings of men, for women were not historically encouraged to write—and if they did produce works of art, they often published under male pen names. The Brontë sisters, for example, originally released *Jane Eyre* and *Wuthering Heights* as Currer and Ellis Bell. What if the word "purpose" invited us, as women, not to fix a target in place and aim for it, but rather to let go? What if having purpose meant drawing our energy from a place of playfulness and ease—a place where our imaginations are stimulated and possibility feels unlimited? A place where we are simply dialed into the energy of allowance, feeling ultimately invited and allowed to write whichever story we wish as our own?

Then we have the word "organization." Originally, this word relates to the Latin term *organizare*, connected to *organum*—meaning "instrument" or "organ"—which became the medieval English *organisacioun*, "the arranging of parts in an organic whole." Later, however, the word gained popularity when it was applied to the notion of the organized military and institutions of authority. To this day, we often go to organize our lives with a kind of militant energy, getting our "ducks in a row" and "squaring things away" in an attempt to get our lives in gear. We can even see this organizational zeal in the layout of our very land, with its rural areas divided into agricultural squares, its cities built on grids, and its urban architecture of sky-scraping squares.

I believe that as women, most of us are naturally oriented toward a different kind of organizational geometry. In my healing work with women, I often use the energy of shapes like spirals, pyramids, and diamonds. I have found that using these sacred shapes in collective visualizations and our shared felt senses helps us toward transformative healing and deep catalyzation; it helps us blossom fully into who we are. What if your innate female wisdom does not work in a linear order, or organize itself just in squares? Take a moment to visualize the internal energy that helps you ground into your creativity; the energy that helps draw together the pieces of you that can manifest your vision. What shape is it? And does it feel forceful and intense, or is it more expansive and inviting?

What if power, identity, purpose, and organization didn't always have to have such linear meanings as history and etymology would have us believe? What if, rather than tracing the origins of these words back to a kind of outside-in forced control, marked by the ability to aggressively exert influence on others, you gave them a new, embodied meaning, set by you, on your own terms? When we decide how we want to define these words (and—ultimately—all words) for ourselves, we empower ourselves to enter a new relationship with these ideas. The words then become our allies—ways we are calling in and creating our profoundly nourishing lives. If you want to make this important linguistic shift, the table below is designed to help. Under the words "power," "identity," "purpose," and "organization," you'll find three columns. One column lists the words typically associated with each term in its original, etymological sense. It's important to note that there is nothing wrong with these original associations—in fact, there might be many times in our lives when we'll want to connect with the more "masculine" forms of power, organization, purpose, and identity.

Even so, in the next column, you will see some new words for you to consider and integrate. These new words are offerings—expansive and supportive descriptors that provide more context for our original terms, and are more related, specifically, to the energy of inside out self-nourishment. As you read through this second column, consider whether you align with these new words—whether they feel supportive to your mind, body, soul, and spirit.

You'll find that the third and final column has been left blank. This is where you can begin to list any and all words or phrases that you personally connect with, in defining your own highest sense of power, identity, purpose and self-organization. Feel free to draw this table out in your own journal if you need more room. Better yet, make it an art project! Draw out the table in whichever shape feels most geometrically soothing to your own spirit. The more deeply you connect to this activity, the more deeply you will imbue these words with your own self-empowering sense, dictated by your own reality.

POWER

Prior Terms	Expanding Terms	In Your Own Terms
Outwardly dominant	Inwardly listening	
Outwardly commanding	Internally refining	
Making a conquest	Taking inquiry	
Exerting force	Strengthening your own core and your practices of engaging with your core principles	
Taking over and taking control	Trusting you can navigate the unknown	
Supremacy	Self-possession	
Reigning	Honing self-love and being what you seek in the world	
Charging forward	Allowing pause	

IDENTITY

Prior Terms	Expanding Terms	In Your Own Terms
Rank	Range Expression Balancing your own needs with the needs of others	
Status	Already established as worthy just as you are	

Title	Possessing many gifts	
	Flexible	
	Multifaceted	
	Free to be whoever you choose	
	Free to change	
Authority	Interconnected	
	Communicative	
	Open	
	Participating in the world while setting others free from expectations	
Fixed position	Deeply committed	
	Able to let go when it's time	
	Listening and responding to your needs	
Influence (on others)	Authentic to your heart's wants and expression	
	Able to share, give, and receive	
Leadership (of others)	Able to listen to and (ultimately) accept your whole self	
Role	Trusting you have what you need to create the change you seek	
	Rising to the occasion for the best evolution of self	

PURPOSE

Prior Terms	Expanding Terms	In Your Own Terms
Mission	Embodiment	
Goal	Greatest expression	
Quest	Connected to desire and sense of being alive	
Cause	Subtle and nuanced truth	
Focus	Inner-vision	
Pursuit	Fiercely committed to self-connection, self-respect, and respecting our external realities as a reflection of how we treat ourselves	
Duty	What's true for your soul?	
Aspiration	Regularly remembering "I am enough"	

ORGANIZATION

Prior Terms	Expanding Terms	In Your Own Terms
Regiment	Intention	
Discipline	Passion and refilling your passion cup	
Administration	Self-accountability	
Institutions	Inner and outer fortresses	
Structure	Form for your free flow	
Delegation	Self-evaluation Willingness to look at the shadows and lights with discerning but loving eyes	
Systemization	Seasonality Willingness to shift with the tides and seasons Learning by listening	
Always on, 24-7	Resetting Tuning in to what you need in the moment—according to what's true for you	

Now for the fun part: Consider all of the terms you connected with in the second column, and the ones you listed in your third column as your personal definitions of power, identity, organization, and purpose. Write these words down and put them somewhere you see regularly—for example, on the door you open every time you step outside of your home and into the world. When you read these words, take them in as core values that give you a direct route to nourishment and self-connection. If you ever find yourself thinking, "Who am I do to this?" or, "I'm not enough to do that," remember that "power" is a word you've defined for yourself, which you already relate to and which is tangible for you. Or if you feel confused, you can come to this list to remember your own definition of self-organization, then return to your inner-sense of self to listen to what you need. When you question whether something or someone is distracting you from what's important in your life, look at how you've defined purpose for yourself, as a way to return home to who you are and bring your attention there. And if you ever find yourself wondering who you're becoming, or where to find the courage to truly express yourself in the world, evaluate what the term "identity" means to you, in your own words! Finally, remember that it isn't only the words "power," "purpose," "organization," and "identity" that have been solidified through time by what we might call the more "man-made" way of structuring and conceiving our realities. There are many words we may want to look at carefully and define for ourselves, as women learning how to really nourish ourselves and our relationships.

For now, let's explore self-nourishment just a bit further with these particular terms in mind. First, we'll take a moment to access what you might call your "higher self"—a version of you that can serve as a kind of role model; an energetic embodiment of a powerful, purposeful, self-connected woman who respects herself and loves her relationship to life. Consider you are sitting with her, your higher self, or that she is here, within you. Now answer the following questions from her perspective:

1. How do you feel about yourself when you look in the mirror? When you see your reflection, what do you tell yourself? What is the purpose of looking in a mirror? Do you judge your appearance by externally imposed standards? How do you find peace with having an ever-changing body?

2. How do you prioritize self-care? How do you know, for example, when it's time to rest? How do you know when it's time to be with others and when you really need to spend time on your own? How do you feel when you're all alone? How do you take care of your own needs when you're around others?

3. How have your personal challenges helped you move forward? What advice do you have about overcoming obstacles? How do you confirm your self-value? How do you organize your life to make the most of your experiences? Is there a practice that helps you to be present? What do you think is the most important key to finding self-love? Is it possible that connecting to self-love is as simple as saying, or affirming to yourself, "I already, inherently, have self-love and now I'm bringing it forward"?

4. When you feel upset, how do you soothe yourself? What do you do when you feel self-critical? How do you shift out of a mindset that feels negative? How do you take care of yourself when you're going through a difficult time?

5. What kinds of self-care do you prioritize and why? What makes you feel powerful? Where do you go when you need to remember who you are?

6. What do you do that makes you feel alive? What brings you the greatest sense of fulfillment? What do you want to make sure you get to experience in this lifetime? Do

you need anyone else to help you make your dreams happen, and if so, why or who? What lights you up?

Remember, you can check in with your "higher self" as a role model, mentor, and guide anytime you like. You already have the power to access the highest knowledge available to you—because it lives inside you. As the great author Alice Walker wrote, "We are the ones we've been waiting for."

Creating Choice: Trigger to Tragedy or Trigger to Transformation?

The thing about life is that sooner or later, we'll always be offered yet another invitation to show up as a beginner. As enlightened as we might become, and as keyed into our own inner-wisdom, we will inevitably encounter opportunity after opportunity to practice patience, to refine the ways we deal with discomfort, and to better understand what we're feeling. When we seek to nourish ourselves from the inside out, like dedicated mother birds, we work on building our nests every day, creating a rooted sense of well-being inside ourselves so we have a safe place to call home. With practice, and little by little, we learn to stay with ourselves, even in those inevitable moments when we feel thrown off balance.

For example, have you ever been at an event—maybe an intimate dinner with friends, or even meeting strangers for the first time—when someone asks you a question, or brings up one subject or another—and something inside you just *shifts*? Suddenly, you start to feel uncomfortable. Perhaps you arrived feeling open, communicative, and excited to connect with company. Then there was one look, or someone questioned something you said, or shared an opinion very contrary to your own, and suddenly you found yourself in a nervous system response. You might experience such a systemic response in innumerable ways—there are more than a trillion neural pathways waiting to fire inside you, following all sorts of ingrained reactive possibilities. You might, for example, feel a massive energetic drop, and find yourself suddenly able to focus only on finding an excuse to leave as soon as possible. You simply have to take flight. You mumble one excuse or another, then zip out as fast as you can, until you find someplace that feels safe and far away; a hideout where you can protect the rawness you now feel from head to toe. Or maybe you stay at the event and engage for a while longer, but your nervous system is wired; you're in fight mode. You might end up getting into a debate that escalates, your system telling you you'll be unsafe unless you "win," or prove the other person was out of line. Maybe instead you leave your body altogether; you can't really feel your limbs, your face, your stomach, or your thighs; it's all numb and frozen. You find yourself hovering somewhere above yourself, watching the event like an outsider, ripping yourself to shreds for never fitting in. To get through the evening, you turn to overeating, indulging in something sweet—and nobody seems to notice. It's like being absent from school, even while you're sitting right there in the class.

Fight, flight, freeze—most of us are familiar with these terms and even a few of our own personal trigger-response scripts. And if we're not already self-regulating with practices of self-care, we might find those scripts getting triggered all too often. Beginning to prioritize staying present with ourselves brings an invitation to become curious; to take inventory when we feel triggered rather than simply reacting in our habitual patterns. Specifically, we can use our experiences of feeling "triggered" as opportunities to create new pathways and better ways to care for ourselves, rather than collapsing our sense of self-worth and vitality. I call this opportunity the *T-to-T turnaround*. See, for most of us a trigger can bring us quite immediately (and to be honest, often quite unconsciously) to a place of total tragedy. And this can seem to happen in less than seconds—quicker than the speed of light.

Imagine you're driving down the highway in a pretty good mood. For some reason, you get off at the wrong exit—and it's going to add twenty minutes to your drive. Now you're going to be late to wherever you're going, but you're still trying to stay calm. Then someone honks at you from another lane. The next thing you know, your good mood is trashed. You're ready to get angry, to roll down your window and give the honker a piece of your mind. In seconds, you've lost your cool, your sense of safe self-connection and your grounded energy. You are now fully agitated, and it's not you behind the wheel—it's fury itself. Your body is no longer telling you that "everything is fine"; instead, you're on high alert, things are escalating, and you've successfully gone from trigger to the energetic embodiment of tragedy. Even if you think you still have it together, your body has entered a different energy field, where it's ready for everything to fall apart. You're in survival mode, and pumping out stress chemicals to deal with it.

This state of trigger-to-tragedy easily becomes our status quo when we aren't practicing self-compassion on the regular; when we aren't making the space inside ourselves to breathe and recalibrate. But what if we have the mindfulness to access a sense of self-awareness—and expand our perception just enough to consider what we're doing to our brain and body by going into tragedy mode? When we enter a rage pattern, which neural pathways do we activate?

How does our blood pressure and our whole-body system respond? What happens to our posture, our soul, and our spirit? Why are we choosing to put ourselves under so much pressure, to ruin our whole day in this moment? How available are we, in this state, to let the energy of love into our heart? Is this how we want to experience life? Do we have a choice? What if we can ride some self-compassion through our system, soothing our state and cooling ourselves off a bit? *Okay,* that voice might say, *I'm going to be late. I'll be okay. I need to take a deep breath and go one step at a time—then take another deep breath. Feel my emotions. It's okay. Whatever I feel is okay. Remember, I don't have to collapse my whole sense of well-being into this situation.*

Of course, there might be moments when we're truly in life-and-death danger; at those times, it makes sense for our bodies to feel charged, fiercely self-protective, or emotionally spiked. But in everyday situations when we're simply meeting the inevitable follies of life—like getting off at the wrong exit—it's safe to say that generating the energy of tragedy in our bodies does not support self-nourishment.

When we are triggered, we don't have to collapse into tragedy. There is another option we can work on cultivating, and it's what I call moving from trigger to transformation. This shift takes time to nurture. But when we have a practice that helps us cultivate a sense of safety, security, and nourishment, we have a stronger chance of responding to stress as an opportunity for transformation. Take the same small drama: We're on our way to a meeting, and we get off at the wrong exit. Suddenly, we're twenty minutes out of our way, in traffic, and being honked at by some person who seems a little upset, to say the least. As soon as we start to feel our body respond, we notice we have a tiny window. It's just a flash of a moment, but in it, we remember:

We can take just one or two deep breaths. We opt for the breathing rather than for revving up our system. We take a few more. These few breaths help our brain regulate the way it processes the experience. This is when we notice that we've been triggered—but rather than trying to bypass our body's response and telling ourselves to just "get over it," we check in and feel what's happening for us. We take a small inventory. We listen, and once we hear what's happening in our system, we can support ourselves; we can self-soothe in a healthy way. Maybe we tell ourselves, "It's okay. You're human, and you're doing great." Or maybe it's, "Everything is going to work out," or some variation on that. We bring our awareness and our unconditional positive self-regard to the situation, because it helps us stay present instead of reacting in an outworn pattern of collapsing on ourselves. We begin to recognize that "catching our trigger" is an opportunity to train our mind and body to live freshly in the present moment; to not close down but instead, ultimately, respect the life we have. In fact, we can begin to look at every triggering occurrence, chapter, and event as an essential step in catalyzing our personal and spiritual growth. *How are your triggers providing you with the opportunity to expand and transform? See Exploration 22.*

I know we can shift even our most significant trigger patterns, because I shifted one of mine, and in the most unexpected way. For decades, as my mother got older and her health declined, I lived in a pretty constant state of fear, resisting even really considering that I'd most likely outlive her and have to face the death of one of the most stable people in my life. In fact, it wasn't just that my personal life was deeply interwoven with my parents'; the whole foundation of my professional world and much of my sense of identity were built on the world they'd made from scratch as immigrants coming to America after World War II. When my mom was in her eighties, she grew increasingly frail. I dedicated most of my time to trying to keep her healthy and being present with her. I couldn't bear to think about how I'd get through her death, and my emotions were consistently amped up, reflecting my deep fear about losing such a precious part of my life. I tried everything to restore her vitality. We brought in nurses, holistic healers, all kinds of natural energy medicines—any and every modality to help her recover. In my mind, I was living in a state of tragedy. It was tragic my mom wasn't well—and, as a result, my nervous system remained in a constant fight response, fighting to beat the tragic odds and keep my mom alive. Then, at some point, there was a shift. I saw my mom let go of her own fight. I could tell that her body—that all of her— was ready to go. I had to recognize that the greatest thing I could do for my mom—the best way to love her fully—was to let her do it. I had to surrender my fight and turn my focus to being present with her, to just holding her hand. In my mother's last days, the heightened emotional experience of being with her gave me (and my family) no choice other than to be in our hearts. My heart's intelligence supported me to overcome some of the fear-based stories of tragedy I'd mentally perpetuated and to surrender, to accept—to let love lead the way.

As my mother began to pass, I felt connected to the gift of her life in a way I'd never felt before. I felt filled with her love and her wisdom in a way I'd never imagined. When my mother had left her Earthly form and I spoke at her funeral—to the large crowd of friends, family, and community members that came to recognize her life—I was amazed that instead of drowning in despair, I felt a powerful sense of transformation. I realized that I wasn't losing my mother, exactly; rather, I was gaining extraordinary connection to her light and essence because I could feel her transitioning to a different realm. In this sense of expansiveness and connection, I didn't collapse into a sense that I'd never overcome this endless tragedy; instead, I found access to a truly nurturing energy that filled my heart on the day of her passing and for many days and weeks afterward. In a gentle, even nourishing way, the more I healed from my mother's passing, the more I attuned to her ethereal light. She seemed to have found her place in a kind of timeless spiritual realm—and in that place, she's still there for me when I need her. (In fact, she'll show up even when I'm not expecting her, for instance, in a dream state, a surfacing memory, or the flavors of her many recipes that live on in my Italian family's fare.) The amazing thing is that what I feared even more than my mother's passing was that I'd be lost; that I'd disappear without her. I feared that everything she is and was in this world to me would be gone—but I haven't found this to be true at all. Every day, in fact, I feel my mother helping me become more and more of the full, nourished woman I actually am. I feel her encouraging me to form and express my own identity in the world; to share my own gifts. I find that her essence isn't only fortifying me, but has made the world a more beautiful place.

I share this story because I imagine other women may fear the passing of their parents or their loved ones. We don't speak enough, as women, about what it's like to lose our mothers or our closest and most beloved companions. We don't share enough about our fear of losing our deepest anchors of safety and security—and the way we can live in anticipation of tragedy, expecting everything to shatter, leaving us unable to function, take care of ourselves, or thrive. These fears are not who we are, however. When we remember that life is holding us, we tap into the true mothership of nourishment. If we ever feel triggered, we can draw on this source, through whichever practice, ceremony, or rite serves us best, and experience the trigger as, instead, an opportunity for transformation. We can learn to parent ourselves. And this brings us to a core foundation of self-nourishment; one that is key to any attempt to explore and transform the behaviors we're ready to shift: our early family arcana.

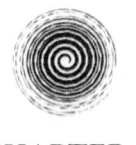

CHAPTER 5

Inherited Nourishment

W hen it comes to recalling our earliest years or describing our childhoods in detail, each person's memory ranges in capacity. Some of us may see just a few blurry images wafting past our minds' eyes, or feel a vague nostalgia when trying to recollect our first years, while for others, early events may feel ingrained in us, crystallized, as though they happened yesterday. Some years may seem significant, while during other periods, dates, names, and events blur together. Memory is biased, and the brain can be powerfully self-protective—which makes sense, really, on the anatomical level. Each of our brains is like a secret fortress, containing multitudes of folds, places to tuck away ideas and memories that make each brain as unique as a fingerprint. This many-folded fortress needs a complex architecture to make space for our estimated eighty-six billion neurons to fire. In a way, the folds of our brains are a kind of genius origami—if you unfolded the tissue and stretched it out onto a flat surface, it would take up about six square feet! Now consider that a single neuron transmitting information is microscopic—but with eighty-six billion of them, it still takes some significant surface area to squeeze them. You could say that each of our brains is like a little Manhattan, maximizing its space to accommodate so much bustling activity. With all this complex folding in our brains, suffice to say, there's a lot of real estate where content can get lost, and especially our earliest memories. And yet, it's in those earliest years that our brains are most susceptible. They are being shaped and molded—literally—and creating a framework for how safe we feel in the world.

Our first seven years are typically considered the most important in our development as individuals, and of those, the first three years are the most profound. However, neuroscientists have discovered that our cognitive function remains malleable well into our late teens and even beyond; in fact, there's evidence that the brain—particularly the parts dictating our executive function—is still undergoing tweaks and adjustments even until our late twenties. This might explain why so many of us are still "finding ourselves" as we near thirty years old, or performing massive 180-degree turns in our lifestyle choices well into adulthood. Still, it's in those earliest, "implicit" years of our development that our psychological state is most adaptable. Here, our sense of boundaries is completely blurred; there is little sense of "me" vs. "you." (This is clear if you've ever seen a child discovering herself in the mirror for the first time, and witnessed her total awe or delight in being able to control the movements she sees reflected, as though she's being parroted.) During these first years of implicit development, our sense of self and other is being formulated, which means that whatever we experience environmentally, including the behavior of those around us, deeply impacts the way our nervous system learns to respond. Studies show that, especially during our first three years, if someone is upset, we aren't just "empathizing"—we are literally absorbing their upset

136

as our own (which is particularly interesting in light of the concept of the collective nervous system Mark described in Chapter Three). If our environments often offer a sense of peace and calm, we internalize a felt sense of peace and calm. If transitions flow smoothly in our early lives, for example—if our caregivers create a regularity of rhythm that supports our essence—then our nervous systems stand a chance of smoothly calibrating to the transitions and relationships in our environments. In a way, the world is still much like a womb for us in those early years—we are really one with it. Because our boundaries are so undefined, it makes sense that, in these early years, we're easily upset by aggressive noises; that we react with tears or tantrums if we encounter something that agitates our systems, or if we're taken out of a natural rhythm abruptly. We express deep disturbance because we're at one with life; we feel it all— we've not yet learned any techniques to numb out, to turn ourselves off. Additionally, though we're packed with millions of years of evolutionary information in our little nervous systems and budding brains, we are, of course, unable to fend for ourselves out of the gate. We must learn from our caregivers how to do, well, basically everything—even down to taking care of our personal hygiene. We are left to simply trust that when we cry, our caregivers will discern whether we need to be changed, need to nap, need to be held or given physical attention, need food, need milk, or need something more subtle.

As we become more independent and start crawling of our own accord, reaching for objects, and playing with toys, we learn by mirroring the behavior modeled to us. And even when we don't directly mirror our caregivers, we likely internalize aspects of their behavior or emotions, which influence our interactions with the world. Consider, for instance, the impact of the patience (or impatience) our caregivers showed at having another mouth to feed (ours); the joy or irritation with which they taught us about basic survival. These responses were encoded in our still-forming minds as a kind of baseline. And it goes way beyond food: As a child, your entire sense of self, and all your agency, rested in the hands of your parents or guardians. The way your caregivers handled their interactions in the world, the way they literally cared for, engaged with, and reacted to their own physical and emotional lives, likely mirrors their energetic and physical handling of you in your earliest years. For example, if you had a caregiver with a tendency to be heavy-handed, to forget about things or be easily agitated, or one who, say, had a short attention span, it's likely that their care for you in your early, implicit years carried the same tone. As you learned how to engage with the world, you were filtering reality through the feel of your parents' touch, their perspective, their moods, and their movement. Today, you might feel similar to your parents or caregivers in some ways, and perhaps very different to them in others. Now imagine having to run the most fundamental parts of your current self-care practices through their skill sets, their behaviors, their sensory motor skills, and even their bodies—and voilà, you have a decent picture of what you likely felt in your most formative years. For better or worse, our parents hand down all of the obstacles and (ultimately) gifts we need to find out who we are as individuals—and more than that, how to operate in a world where we will always in the end be part of a collective. It's a brilliant design for spiritual growth, really, being born into these years of total dependency on others' parenting styles—a college-level course in acceptance and interdependence that we're enrolled in right out of the gate.

Reflecting on the emotional and behavioral impact of our earliest life experiences can give us great insight into why we might find caring for ourselves challenging as adults; specifically, it can reveal much about how we nourish ourselves. For many of us, those early years were not easy, to say the least, and they might even have been downright damaging. It's important that we empathize with ourselves, and sensitively recognize the full history of our lives. It can also be helpful to consider that no matter what anyone's earliest experiences were like, just getting through those formative years leaves *all* of us with ingrained behaviors and patterns that can seem impossible to understand or shift as adults. Some of these neurological–biological–physical imprints become lifelong scars; parts of us we'll carry forever. Even in such cases, we must remember that none of us are broken, and that we all have neuroplasticity; we can all continually form new pathways, thoughts, and behaviors— forming those life-giving habits and patterns *around* the scars of our childhood, when necessary. In fact, we can use our distinct personal challenges to ultimately energize our paths. You'll see many heroes in the world doing just this, achieving remarkable feats despite what others would see as difficulties. Think, for instance, of the competitive athletes with prosthetics, or the successful public speakers who speak of rising to success despite being born with significant genetic brain conditions. For some of us, our lifetime scars are obvious—we never have to guess what they are or where they came from. For others, it's more subtle, and requires waking up our feeling again, so that we can really explore ourselves. Sometimes we don't have just one root cause for what we're carrying; it was inflicted by a perfect storm of factors that might have lasted for some time, influencing whatever chronic and often complex physiological state or behavior we now experience. The more intimately we know our unique lifelong scars, the more effectively we can transform our triggers, and begin to approach them from a curiosity mindset rather than a tragedy mindset. We work with what we have, we find the road to lovingly accepting and listening to ourselves, and in return we get the greatest gift: we become open to opportunities more abundant than we'd ever have fixed our little-girl minds on, which allow us deeper joy than we'd imagined.

In all of our implicit and developmental years, the most fundamental and significant way we are taught to fend for ourselves as human animals is to learn how to feed ourselves. From our earliest years, we must figure out how to hunt (which might mean search the cupboards, beg for a sugary cereal, or request a snack). We learn—or try to learn—to engage in harvest, eating with siblings, making sure everyone has enough, sharing provisions. And, ideally, we learn to listen to our bodies: Are we full? Are we hungry? Has our hunger been acknowledged? Are we allowed to be sated? Do we get time to digest? Do we appreciate our meals or are we rushed? We learn to relate to the key thing that makes our lives possible: nutriment. Though some of us grow up learning to rotate crops and tend to the soil, with just 27 percent of the world directly employed in agricultural pursuits, it's safe to say that most of us grow up quite divorced from the physical labor it takes to grow food. In fact, in our earliest years, we might even think that food comes from the grocery store, or the restaurant, or from Uber Eats. However we orient to food, the places we find sustenance become an integral part of our lives. In these implicit years of being cared for, our food, and the energy and atmosphere around food and eating, make a significant impression on our thinking and the way we'll nourish ourselves long into life. Even in our first years, we're already creating our deep, complex physiological associations with hunger. On the symbolic level, we're determining what food represents for us, and to what extent we'll allow ourselves to settle in and feel sated, feel nourished—beyond food alone, and into all areas and energies in our lives.

We can start to find the roots of our current relationship to self-nourishment by investigating the archetypal concept of the "shared family meal." Can you recall what mealtime was like in your earliest years? Who was there? Was there an actual table you sat at, or something else, like a counter? Did dinner take place at a set time each day, and if so, were you anxiously awaiting it—was it when you got hungry—or was it when everyone else was hungry, or when someone got home from work? Did you have to adjust your biological hunger to a parent or caregiver's work schedule? Did you feel that mealtime, as a result, was all about a parent, or was it also for you—or for your whole family? Or perhaps you didn't have a set time for dinner. If so, how did that feel? Did you snack before dinner, eating what you really wanted in some solo safe space? After school, for example, would you fill yourself up as a way to transition from the intensity of the day, maybe with the TV on, too? Did it make you feel good, or did it just numb you out? Did you often snack so much that you didn't really want dinner? Did you have to ask again and again if dinner was ready, or were you always the last one to get to the table, as though you were resistant to dinnertime? Were others reluctant to come to the table? For example, did some members of the family have to be alerted again and again that it was time to eat? Did dinnertime feel more like a chore, like something you had to do, or was it a celebration—something like a nourishing homecoming to your togetherness as a family? Did one or both parents prepare it? Were both parents present, and if so, what was their food dynamic like together? Did one care, take their time, concentrate on creating a real meal, while the other did nothing? Did one parent eat slowly while another mindlessly wolfed down their meal? What was the family pace of eating? Did people ever put down their forks and take a breath, or a moment to drink in the atmosphere? Or were their heads down, their utensils steadily moving in shovel-it-in-mode? How long did mealtime last? Did you participate in food preparation? Did you like to? Was the food homemade or store-bought? How did it taste? Did you like it, or was it always just a little disappointing—or missing a nutrient you actually needed? Was there variation in your meals, or the same food on repeat? Did the people at the table enjoy their time together, or was there tension? How did people talk to each other at the table? Were emotions allowed? Did drama often ensue before, during, or after a meal? What were manners like, and were they enforced? Did you have to put your napkin on your lap, chew with your mouth closed, eat with your fork in the proper hand, or other rules? Were you scolded for the way you behaved at the table, or otherwise criticized just for being you? And most importantly, were you able to truly relax, or do you remember keeping yourself on guard? *Ready to explore and transform your long-held internalized relationship with your childhood memory of the shared meal? See Exploration 23.*

Whether or not you can recall the specifics of your early family mealtimes, see if you can get a body-based sense, a kind of internal feeling memory, of what it was like to receive nourishment. Try closing your eyes and sinking back to your childhood self. Now, ask yourself: When you took in the flavors, textures, and sustenance of food with the people in your household, how did that feel in your body? Did anyone bring awareness to the taste or quality of the food they were eating? Did anyone express thanks for the opportunity to feast together? In many ways, eating is one of the deepest spiritual connections we have with the energy of the Earth. How much awareness of this sacred, beautiful rite did your family have? Were meals memorable, or just a kind of set and setting for the dynamics of family drama? Did anyone at the table take time to recognize how sacred it was to share dinner together? How do you think your family or caregivers felt in their own bodies? Was there an energy of encouragement, of comfort, of creating a nest of coziness? Did eating feel safe? When you ate with your family, did you feel secure in your body and connected to a felt sense of well-being?

To take an example, perhaps there was hostility in the atmosphere where you ate as a family, and each bite you took felt like the ticking of a bomb before some inevitable explosion. Maybe rather than feeling hunger in your stomach, or the sensation of growing satiation, you felt nothing but nerves as you waited for the bomb to go off. Perhaps everything appeared calm, even loving, at your dinner table, but there was an unspoken look a parent would give you when you'd reach for seconds, leaving you feeling micro-monitored. Or maybe no matter how hard you tried to make sure dinner went smoothly, one family member would always disrupt the peace, and you'd find yourself forever back in the same situation—upset, unable to take another bite, or else emotionally burying your feelings in an extra helping of whatever would allow you to numb the discomfort in your body. And were you able to feel the difference between each family member's own, individual experience and your personal body, or did you feel the whole family's energy as an extension of your physical form? Were you able to separate self from other at the dinner table, and protect your own boundaries, or did your energy leak, leaving you receiving and reacting to others' thoughts, feelings, and sensations, self-collapsed and entangled? No two families are the same, but I have found that more often than not, those of us who struggle with our eating and food behaviors have some memory of disruption or discomfort related to our early years at the dinner table. It's not just that mealtime disruption is a root cause of our long-held dysfunctional eating patterns. Rather, it's that mealtime is a nervous-system activity that engages (or should engage) our senses (namely tasting and smelling), which we carry out ritualistically from the very start of our lives, and when our senses are engaged, we are more deeply able to embed memories. Family mealtimes also provide the archetypal setting (literally, since each family member has a place to sit, a visual location) for the family dynamics we've internalized. Examining our earliest family mealtime memories can help us to see how, as independent adults, we are often still operating under the influence of the behaviors and relationship dynamics we absorbed in our very earliest years.

For instance, later in life, we might find ourselves fervently collapsing into a habitual old friend—a bag of chips, a box of donuts, or whatever our particular numbing agent of the moment happens to be. We may do this for years, unsure where we learned this behavior, or which part of us keeps returning to it. We might think it comes from our gut biomes, or our brains, or some throbbing pain in our bodies. The truth is, our strange-seeming eating habits most likely don't come from just one thing. They are a coping mechanism, developed through a unique genius for keeping ourselves safe—a genius we have now, however, outgrown. So while we might not be able to unearth one single culprit as the root cause of our defunct behaviors, it's a good idea to investigate whether we're making up for missing parts of ourselves, developmental pieces that weren't nourished or nurtured during our implicit years.

Let's take the example of a client of mine; I'll call her Donna. Donna came from a family with a strong, outspoken, strict, and often explosive father figure. When heading into any interaction at all with her father, Donna could not predict how he'd respond, so she mostly tried to stay out of his way. When he walked into a room, he'd seem to fill the entire space, energetically. Donna never felt at ease in his company, even though he was her father and she did love him. He also had some great attributes, one being that he worked hard to provide for his family, and she respected how much he'd sacrificed, especially because she could see how stressful his job was. Because her father worked so hard and was the breadwinner of the family, Donna's mother made catering to his needs her first priority. It seemed the entire house walked on eggshells around him.

In these early years, if Donna had a need or request, or felt sensitive or emotional about something, she'd sometimes try to approach her father, hoping he might speak tenderly to her or make room for her emotions. But her bids for his gentleness never went as she'd hoped. Typically, he would become impatient and blow up in her face, or say something particularly hurtful. Donna told me about one time, for example, when she was about eight years old and she tripped on the top stair. She fell all the way to the bottom and hit her knee, which began to bleed. When Donna cried out, her father looked up from his paper, in eyeshot of his injured daughter. Instead of jumping up to come over to her, to tend to her wound or console her tears, he yelled from his seat. "Donna," he scolded, irritated. "You never look where you're going!" Donna continued to cry, holding onto her knee, feeling terrible. Still ignoring her injury, her father followed up with, "Stop crying! You look ugly when you cry." Though her swollen knee hurt, his words hit her harder, and she stopped crying immediately. She recalls right then and there consciously burying her sorrow deep down inside herself, as though she was vacuuming up her sensations and pushing them deep inside. She absorbed the tumult internally.

Not long after, Donna's mother called the family to the dinner table, and even though Donna limped toward her seat, no one asked her how she was. When she sat with the family, she felt emotional and physical pain. During dinner, the single directive she was given by her father was to eat everything on her plate. So, as she held back her tears and suppressed her felt sense of abandonment and multilayered pain, she was forced to chew and swallow food she had no appetite to stomach. As she made her way through the meal (which she described as a terribly dry pot roast and soggy green beans—her family's standard), any time she felt an upsurge of her stuffed-down emotions, she spoke to herself sternly. In many ways, her internal voice mimicked the tone her father had used to scold her. She made the part of herself that was tender as small as possible, and the part that forced her to operate without feeling became larger and louder.

Donna shared with me that this was only one of many family events she spent focusing on trying not to set her father off. I helped Donna see the correlation between this family dynamic and the way she struggled with food as an adult. As a full-grown woman, Donna operated under the firm conviction that she was "just fine"; she handled her many responsibilities well—her work meetings, her domestic life, and her friendships. Out of the blue, however, and without being able to put her finger on exactly why, Donna would sometimes feel a kind of switch. The switch *seemed* like hunger, but she came to realize it couldn't be, because she'd feel it even if she'd eaten a full meal containing an array of healthy ingredients, or even after eating a snack. And when she felt this hunger, it was often the case that it seemed to have no bottom, so a snack would turn into a whole bag of chips, or two bags, or even more; or she'd eat a whole cake or a gallon of ice cream. During these experiences, she would no longer feel her stomach, or even anything like hunger—so she started to wonder whether this "hunger" wasn't in fact about food. Rather, her "hunger," we came to learn, was a desire to be immersed in a comfortable space, to feel protected and able to relax into an energy of calm and care—to be nourished, from the inside out. The fluffy, spongy texture of a cake; the sweet, smooth glide of ice cream; or sinking into a warm cookie—all this was just a stand-in for the comfort she really sought.

The problem Donna wanted to resolve wasn't her longing for a cozy, comforting food—in fact, that's quite normal. It's in our makeup as humans to seek out warm, nurturing, and cozy food sources. (It's our first human instinct, after all, to seek mother's milk.) No: Donna's issue was that she felt she was being taken over, even bullied, by a force she couldn't control, a program that seemed to besiege her every thought. When she felt this hunger switch turn on, she seemed to have no choice and no free will. She'd go from being "just fine" to piling food into her mouth at great speed, often stopping only when she literally became physically sick. Eventually, after years of repeating this routine, the behavior itself seemed to signal to Donna that she was powerless, worthless, and should feel ashamed. I helped Donna to see that somewhere between her sense of operating in the world as "perfectly fine" and her coping mechanism of eating into oblivion, there was a part of herself that she'd never been allowed or able to acknowledge, develop, or deal with. This was the missing piece of her emotional process, the part she needed to consciously recover so that she could allow it to have emotions and a variety of expressions and responses. The piece she was now very much encouraged to feel.

Donna's parents did not model healthy empathy and emotional care. When she felt an emotion or sensation, it was not acknowledged or soothed. Donna thus internalized her parents' response to her feelings (namely, to ignore what she felt) as her own. As an adult, too buffered to recognize her own sensitivity, emotions, or sensations, Donna played out the dynamics of her deep needs with food. She didn't know any other way, because our self-soothing behaviors—whether healthy or unhealthy—are ingrained at such a young age, long before we learn how to tie bunny ears on our shoes. For Donna, there was a missing piece, a gap in her self-care behavior. She handled her life like a job to get done, limiting her feelings to a very narrow spectrum of just a few allowable states, such as being "fine," "stressed," or "tired." If something happened that upset her, she struggled even to put a finger on what it was, having trained herself to be numb to the causes and triggers of her emotional discomfort. She had never been shown how to have compassion for herself, because feelings were off-limits in her family.

Once we broke down some of Donna's complex response patterns, she saw that any time she experienced a forbidden emotional feeling or sensation (whether it was conscious or subconscious), the part of her that forced her feelings to switch off kicked into gear. Internally, her parents' fierce, threatening reactivity combined with her own inner-child's feeling of helplessness. With her nervous system both firing and freezing to extreme degrees, Donna subconsciously saw just one option—she had to leave her body, which meant shutting herself down. And so she let food, a legal and readily available numbing agent, become her emotional operator. Food helped her to push down any feeling that surfaced, just as she had at her childhood dinner table. She came to me because she couldn't stop eating cake, but together we came to see that liking cake wasn't the problem. The issue was that she was losing all connection to her self-worth, collapsing completely, and taking herself all the way out—and using cake to get there.

In our time together, Donna explored and ultimately transformed this outworn program. We opened new avenues in her physiology to enable her to cultivate patience with herself; we helped her learn to foster a sense of strength and self-connection so that she could stay present with her sensations. Donna had to learn that it was safe to feel her emotions. It seems simple, but for so long, and so deep in her psyche, she'd been running a story that whatever she felt was wrong, and that expressing her emotions was equivalent to risking her life. When she came to me, she'd reached the point where any slight hint of feeling would lead her to collapse her self-worth and integrity. Together, we slowed down the steps in Donna's learned behavior. We got the mature adult in her—the one who managed a large international company and handled major business deals—to come on board with her whole person. We had her listen to the part of herself she imagined she'd loathe meeting the most: the sad little girl inside of her who dismissed herself entirely, because she had never received the attention she deserved or felt that anyone really cared about her. First, she learned not to be scared of this little girl. Then she learned that when the girl began to cry, instead of canceling her out with a large quantity of sugary food, she could find something as simple as her breath. With that, Donna found, for the first time, the space to feel her emotions from the inside of her body, from her pelvis, her stomach, her ribs, and her heart. And in there she found a reservoir of tears; tears that felt, at first, like they might never end, though in time they did. She also had to learn to listen to her internalized voice of tyranny—the one that sounded just like the demanding, critical father who had yelled at the crying little girl still trapped inside her. I helped Donna to stay with her parts, allowing them to express themselves until, eventually, she found she knew herself better. As a result, she started to feel something new, something she called a "sense of semblance": an integrated voice that let her know she was okay—all the parts of her. The part that was aggressive and demanding and even mean to her inner-child—that part had served a purpose. It had helped her survive. And her little girl, the one that wanted to cry freely, to be held, rocked, coddled, and loved and listened to—it turned out that this girl's heart was as wide as the wings of a dove, and as Donna allowed her to take up space, she was filled with a new sense of tenderness and love. That little girl that she'd been shutting down day after day and night after night had held the key, the whole time, to the more passionate life that Donna deeply longed to live—the life that would fill her up far more than any food.

It's not easy to go through the process Donna went through. In fact, it's the heroine's journey.

Some of us can find sacred healing relationships that provide professional support as we move through these patterns—but some of us can't. This is one reason I built an app, also called Nourish: because I wanted to create an accessible approach for anyone to transform their relationship to food and eating, by exploring and transmuting the stories formed in their earliest, implicit family years. I wanted to help people like myself, who know what it's like to search for so long outside of ourselves, to see that *we* are the ones with the power to stop sabotaging our own lives through behaviors that don't support us. Creating my own relationship to nourishment, and defining for myself what it looks and feels like from the inside out, is the most promising path I personally have found to truly transforming my relationship to food and eating—and this is the underlying idea of the Nourish app. It's designed to help others discover the abundance of tools they already have. One of the most beautiful aspects of stepping onto the Path of Nourish is realizing that we are on this path together, as women—transforming inherited, personal, cultural, and collective patterns in order to find the whole-system way of our own wisdom. Whether we use an app; or work with somatic therapies; or find healing, nourishing communities to share in our processes, I believe that when we set and commit to an intention to accept ourselves, we can build the foundation for real transformation.

Donna learned to set a Nourishing Tone that allowed her to stay connected to her sense of value and worth. Since we started working together, I've seen Donna's life flower beyond both of our wildest dreams. She left a position she'd been in for decades to grow her own personal and professional life. She nurtured a version of herself that was able to access joy, live more deeply in the moment, and experience life as a creator of her own destiny, rather than living like someone just barely getting by. Along the way, she shed some relationships that no longer served her, which wasn't easy by any means. It required her to stay self-connected during challenging conversations, practice mindful communication, and take responsibility for her needs and boundaries. Donna also embraced some seasons of social loneliness, as she grew accustomed to her new, true-to-self mode of being, but she stayed committed to trusting herself and—even more—trusting that she could navigate the unknown. Ultimately, she became intimate with her own energy, her mystical core, her unscripted essence, and her feminine being. She learned to find love, even in the spaces she couldn't control or see clearly. I watched her grow uncollapsible. This doesn't mean she didn't go through moments of pain, of questioning, or even setbacks—but through them, she continued to gain greater self-awareness. From there she found an inroad, an internal door to self-compassion, which extended to having compassion for others.

As I often find in my work, helping Donna was in fact a great gift for me. I learned so much by watching and experiencing her transformation. She inspired me. Today, Donna guides women to empower themselves and others by healing the divide between their feeling and functioning selves, cultivating true self-compassion, just as she has done for herself. She teaches that self-compassion is foundational not just to personal empowerment, but also to cultivating the sense of safety, security, and possibility that our world is really hungry for. *Do you want to heal the divide between your feeling and your functioning selves? See Exploration 24.*

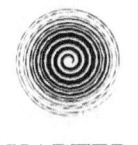

CHAPTER 6

Nourishing the Unknown

By recognizing that we have the wisdom to redefine nourishment for ourselves, we've reached a major turning point as women. We don't need external influencers dictating the size, age, or diet that is nourishing for our bodies, or encouraging us to strive for the goal they're selling—of appearing perfect, eternally happy, agile, and available for everyone else. No. We recognize that we can stop starving ourselves, controlling ourselves, and bullying our inner-genius. We realize that though we fear letting go of the stories we've inherited, the danger of doing so pales in comparison to the much bigger risk of never letting go and embracing our greatness. We realize that rather than using food to stuff our real feelings down and live feeling full, but numb, we can give ourselves permission to feel full of *the essence of who we are.* We see that there are so many things we can creatively feast on, and that we deserve to live in our felt sense of fullness now, having activated our joy and potential and, even more, our sense of security and safety in who we are as women, in the here and now.

In these pages, we've described a new framework for defining what "nourish" means to us, and we've traced the way the energy of Nourish connects to our brain activity, the intelligence of our bodies, our inherited physiological systems, and even the narratives we tell ourselves. Now, we get to look at a crucial component in our garden of nourishment—that is, our relationship to the unknown.

The French call it "*je ne sais quoi.*" It could be something little that you love but can't describe, or the invisible sacredness of a fleeting moment—a type of light that comes through the curtain, say, or even seeps into the cracks of our tired hearts. You could say "the unknown" is the greatest currency in the world. In it, all the possibilities of our desire live as potential, capable of being actualized—our loves, our wins, friends we've not yet met and places we've not yet seen. If you could market and sell the unknown, you would certainly make trillions—and, in fact, much of our commerce has taken this approach, whether in the form of life insurance or promises of major returns on investments. Preparing for or predicting the unknown is a major part of the economy and all other forms of organization—which makes sense when you consider that one of the greatest human fears is simply facing the unknown.

Many of us might define the unknown as the flip side of security; it's all the things we aren't sure of. The unknown, however, is actually the fabric of our whole lives. Though opinions vary wildly around the world, no one has ever been able to prove beyond doubt why we exist at all, where we come from, or where we're going. We have our beliefs, and some of us are committed to deep certainty in those beliefs, feeling we've cracked the code and know life's truths. But truth itself lives in the unknown. The luckiest, or most agile, or cleverest among us might seem to somehow land on their feet in moments of life's turbulence, but when major change is underfoot, it is inevitable that each of us will face events where the outcome remains unknown. There's no avoiding the fact that in life, whether we pick up our cards and sit at the table or stay on the sidelines watching the game, the unknown will win every time. So why don't we bet on her, devote ourselves to her, enjoy her constant hovering presence? Why do we find ourselves so scared of the unknown?

For many people, leaving the space of "knowing" is one of the greatest triggers to our unconscious or unwanted behaviors around food and eating. As soon as we feel something confusing, disorienting, or even familiar but unnerving, and we lose footing on how to respond, how to take care of ourselves, or stay present—we meet the unknown. Next, we might feel anxiety in our bodies, or our internal dialogue may turn self-critical, firing out phrases like, "I'm not enough to figure this out," or, "I don't think I can get through this." Rather than breathe into the unknown, we'll do the familiar: We'll pile up a stack of negative narratives until they're so tall we can't see. These tales of imminent tragedy then hover around us, creating a sense of dis-ease until we've no other option but to run to food like little children scared in the night—unwilling to confront the unknown.

In this state, we are apt to forget that we are made of the exact stuff that constitutes the unknown. We are running, then, from ourselves! We are made of magic and possibility, a one-in-seven-billion creative force that generates life and endless options. We are made of the tendency to connect, to bridge relationships, to transcend even the most difficult situations. We are built to grow in the cracks, to spring up verdantly; to leave legacies by surviving even the most difficult circumstances. We are mysteries masquerading as bodies that seem like physical matter but are composed of more than 70 percent water and atoms made of 99.9 percent space. And we are part of a human race that might seem substantial, but all of our human atoms packed together total just the size of a single dice. When we love, we play in the unknown, gambling with each beat of our hearts—and we have been doing this for millions of years, replicating the unknown in the mystery of birthing life. Looked at one way, life is nothing but a vast unknown, meaning it's our perception alone that allows us to feel safe in it—and better yet, willing to dance.

Through the lessons we learn and the journeys we go through, we each create a long-term relationship—a marriage of sorts—with the unknown. We often start our lives quite open to the unknown, dreaming of being magical faeries or explorers of the vastness of space. But by the time we grow up, we've often closed to the infinite possibilities that lurk in mystery. Rather than using our imaginations to explore the vast energy of the unknown with enthusiasm and excitement, we might find ourselves carrying around contracted beliefs like "I can't change" or "it's impossible"; "it's too hard to figure out," or "something bad is going to happen," or "it always ends up like this." The truth is, we really can't limit the vastness of the unknown, so we limit ourselves in relationship to it. The unknown is eternally filled with possibility, value, mystery, creative elements, resources, reconnections, reunions, and love. It is also filled with potential lessons for us, which can be painful, shocking, and heartbreaking. Usually, our minds are so preoccupied with trying to predict what lies ahead, in the unknown, that we forget the essential piece of information: that the unknown reflects to us precisely what we're made of—potential energy. Have you ever gone to an event for which you had zero idea what to expect, but felt good about it before you arrived, for no real reason—only to find that, minutes into the experience, you make a new friend, create a fresh opportunity, or have an unexpected conversation that ends up changing the course of your life? Or have you ever randomly decided to divert from your usual route someplace, again for no real reason, when, out of the blue, you encounter someone on your way who needs something that only you can provide? This is a direct reflection of the unknown that lives inside you, forever innovating—the part of you that effortlessly shows you all the time that you're equipped to handle uncharted experiences and even come out with something valuable. We can listen and respond to such mysterious calls from within because we come with a built-in feature, provided courtesy of the unknown—and it's called instinct.

It can take a lifetime to learn to listen to our instinct, and yet it's so important. In my experience, for those of us who have struggled with food and eating, overriding our gut feelings often makes us more susceptible to our mal-adaptive thinking and behaviors. For example, imagine you have an event to attend, but that night, something inside of you just doesn't feel like going. Say you already RSVPed, though, so you decide that it's easier not to offend the hosts. As soon as you arrive, something feels "off." Maybe the environment is uncomfortable, or the conversations feel exhaustingly empty, or perhaps you even get offended by something someone says. Irritated, you scold yourself internally, saying, "I should have listened to my instinct." By the time you leave the event, you feel ungrounded, unnerved, and triggered. Your agitation, programmed to catch like wildfire, escalates quickly. Before you know it, you're cussing out loud at the unknown, and furious you've once again put yourself in a situation you could have avoided. You can't logically justify why, but now your system feels maxed out, and the last thing you want to feel is that all-expansive, anything-is-possible, improvisational energy of the unknown.

So you try to shut the energy down with some corner-store cookies smashed up in ice cream, with a sugary soda to boot, consumed while locked inside your car. There you are, in a parking lot with your eyes glazing over like frosting that has lost its taste after too many bites in a binge. In this case, at least for a moment, it seemed much safer to repeat a pattern you've been honing for twenty-five years, rather than try to figure out how to stay present and connected to life and all the possibilities of the vast unknown.

We might ask ourselves again and again why we repeat our sabotaging, self-limiting behavior when we have fought so hard for success in our lives. We may have gone to great schools, earned significant sums of money, and forged professional careers, and yet we let ourselves get trapped by a vat of ice cream nightly. And while we might blame the ice cream, pretending that the whole problem starts with that tub, on some level we know there's something bigger beneath the dynamic. It's not about food; it's about the enormity of the universe and all those unknowns. It all feels too much, and so we condense all our overwhelm into ten tablespoons of sugar. The ice cream provides us with some form of safety in a universe with so much darn input and activity, and so many options to navigate.

See, your brain has these eighty-six billion or so neurons, and your body is holding at least 150,000 years of evolutionary history—nervous system stories about tigers, wild bears, intense storms, and seasons of food scarcity. On top of all that, you're living in a universe that's about

4.6 billion years old; 4.6 billion years of constant ebbing, flowing, vibrating, creating, and recreating. And here you are—a tiny speck, smaller than a single flea in the fabric of all this existence that ultimately emerges out of—mystery! So, say it's taken you twenty, thirty, forty, fifty, or more years to come up with a mostly functional means of operating amid this giant amount of enigma and complexity. If you're able to survive in this vastly unpredictable universe, and you've found some means of regularly getting yourself from point A to point B in the story of your life, but the methods you've found entail checking out, freaking out, or pigging out on food—is it really that bad? If you're paying your bills, getting your laundry done, keeping your job, taking care of your family—isn't it worth allowing yourself whatever slightly self-limiting behavior you've taken on to keep yourself from having to feel the overwhelming intensity of life? Should we really try to let go of the only control system that's worked for us, especially since it took us so many years to hone? What will happen if we let go of the ropes—with eighty-six billion neurons in our brains and thirty-six trillion cells in our bodies, in a world of seven billion people and two billion Instagram accounts—how will we deal with all the overwhelm in the world?

It's easy to rationalize our way out of change, especially when we consider what it takes to truly shift our habits and behaviors. When this type of rationale takes hold of us, it can return us in a flash to our same old food and eating behaviors, justifying them because they seem safer than braving real, inside-out change. In these moments, we're concerned that we don't have what it takes to live any other way, or the confidence to truly liberate ourselves—and when we surrender to those fears, we're forgetting something quite marvelous: that even if these patterns have been around since our first bites of food or our first birthdays, it doesn't have to take decades to rebuild different behaviors and ways of operating. When we begin to live out of our wisdom, it operates like a good investment: we get compound interest. And when we learn to start to let go of the continual failed attempts to live under control, and instead shift step-by-step toward self-trust, we find something miraculous: that a life can have more than a single season of seeding, sprouting, shooting up, budding, blossoming, fragrantly flourishing, and wilting. As spiritual teacher Mark Bajerski writes, "In the natural flow of life, a flower will lose its beautiful petals. In doing so, that flower becomes even more beautiful, ready for new life. Like the flower, let go and watch your life renew into the most amazing flower that life could bring." What if you had not only more flowers but countless gardens within you, just waiting to grow so you can experience and enjoy them? How much are your patterns of collapsing connected to your fear of letting go into the unknown, of putting yourself in unfamiliar circumstances, of letting yourself feel new things? How much do you trust that you have the skills, the tools, and the ability inside you to handle whatever happens on the outside—and how willing are you to create the space, patience, and room to let the unknown in? To what extent is your food-fixation story entangled with the energy of impatience, agitation, expectation, and control? And what might it entail to become friends with the unknown—to take some time every day to get connected, to reconnect, to the vast mystery? *Would you like to make a new friend named Mystery a.k.a. The Unknown? See Exploration 25.*

160

CHAPTER 7

Living Uncollapsibly

As we've seen, from our fingerprints to our brains, none of us are identical. There are no two people in the world—not even twins—who have the exact same needs, thrive in the exact same environments, and follow identical lifestyle protocols and diets. Sure, large studies have determined general guidelines for health and wellness, based on observations of thousands of people. Sleep, for example, is usually good for the brain. Excess stress, on the other hand, is usually not so good for us in the long run. But things can soon get confusing, because while there's inexhaustible science-backed data about human health, for every great study, you can typically find a contradictory one. For example, humans seemingly need vitamins derived from the sun—and yet we should also be wary of the sun, or even fully avoid direct exposure. Meanwhile, reports show that happiness is essential to longevity, and that humans thrive with ample healthy social time. However, this isn't true for all of us. Some of us produce our best work, do our clearest thinking, and settle into our strongest sense of joy with decreased social time, less external stimulation, and more time spent in solitude.

Considering that the seven billion humans on Earth are so infinitely varied, it's perhaps unsurprising that our species has created so many "personality typology" systems. In fact, a person could spend their whole life getting to know themselves through Myers–Briggs, Gene Keys, or genetic and microbiome lab tests. We might walk away from such self-analysis enlightened by the knowledge of our type O blood, ENFJ personality type, and position at number 7 on the Enneagram—but still find ourselves acting out in ways that harm our very nature. Simply knowing these data points doesn't necessarily help us to find true self-love or self-knowledge, or give us any clue about how to make impactful shifts in our behavioral health.

What if the very part of ourselves that can't be tested or assessed is actually our core component—the magnetic part that calls us over and again, like a tide rolling back in, to enter the inner-doorway to our own mystery. Through this inner-door, we can let go of both our set definitions of self and any fears we may have formed about ourselves in relation to others or our external environment. We get to tune in and attend to our internal world—and that can leave us speechless and even lacking a fixed idea of who we are! In this inner-place, we might not feel a need to put a label on ourselves; we might naturally surrender the need to know and instead simply embody our existence, discovering what nourishes us by attuning to our feelings. What if we don't need to *know* who we are at all—what if our real need is to *feel* who we are?

When we choose what nourishes us from the inside, it becomes easier to navigate the endless external choices in the world. We are bombarded all day long by a million ways to define ourselves as a route to knowing what we need, and even more conflicting opinions about what is actually healthy for us. To add to this complexity, we live in an ever-changing world, so inevitably these options and opinions will shift with time. For example, not so long ago, we were told in no uncertain terms that fat was bad, and this apparent fat fact was emblazoned on every bag at every store, all of them shouting on their shiny labels that this product was delicious and low-fat, no-fat, reduced-fat, or fat-free; that was the skinny on fat. Then, just one generation later, we discovered that "fat doesn't make you fat"—that on the contrary, we need essential fats, fatty acids, healthy fats, full-fat food—why, fat is where it's at, in fact! Carbs are on their own rollercoaster—sometimes considered the devil, then in some seasons featured as a "staple" of the Mediterranean diet (which of course, if you follow it, will bring you a long, healthy, and richly relaxing life, and make you look as gorgeously easygoing as the woman on the cookbook's cover). Some schools of thought will profess that cooked food has no nutritional value, and raw, unheated meals are the only way to go if you want to eat something enzymatically rich. But just down the street from that school is another that will contrarily quip that raw food is impossible to digest—that you can go ahead and eat your arugula salad and raw spinach if you want to be as bloated as a buddha, so long as you don't mind that it's also toxic unless cooked! If it's vitality and beauty you seek, this school says, it's cooked food that truly balances the body's system—and of course this school has its own cookbook too, complete with a gorgeous, perfectly easygoing, eternally youthful woman on its cover to convince you. Some health experts will tout that wine is bad, soberly pointing out that alcohol consumption can shorten our lives and promote neurodegenerative disease. Others (who might or might not be intoxicated!) preach that wine is, simply, divine, and its antioxidants increase one's lifespan—so drink away! Or take coffee: some say it dehydrates us, promotes excess cortisol, destroys our sleep quality, carves lines of age in our faces, turns our hair grey, and also harms our eye health by increasing the risk of glaucoma. Others insist that coffee is a superfood, fighting against neurodegenerative disease, increasing our physical performance and mental alertness, and even supporting eye health—by decreasing the risk of cataracts! All these opposing opinions and studies can literally leave us dizzy, drained, and feeling unwell. At least that's one place science does agree: data overload can create mental exhaustion!

It might feel frustrating to face so much contradiction in the health data available to us, but this wide spectrum of information actually signals something extremely useful to consider. As this book has reiterated on many pages, *nourish* is a word you must define for yourself—and even when you've done so, that definition must be flexible, accommodating change as your own life shifts and your inner-needs change. When it comes to deciding what physically nourishes you, the world is your oyster—and this can be intimidating. Add the continual hit of external ideals of the best life and the standard of beauty, and it becomes even more difficult to know what really feels right for us, and to take small steps—or even great leaps—in the direction of figuring it out for ourselves.

We can brave embarking on our own path of inside-out nourishment when we align with an ageless truth about our core nature as women: we are resilient. We are like the strongest medicinal plants in their natural environment: invincibly determined. If the wind pushes us down, and the inclement weather threatens to rip out our roots, we'll spring back again, season after season. By listening to ourselves deeply while connecting to the energy of our resilience, we will learn to trust ourselves to explore our options, and this way arrive at a deep sense of what's vital and life-promoting for us. We will learn to trust our own desire to empower rather than sabotage ourselves.

It can seem intimidating, that in this vast world you get to explore and decide what *nourish* means for you. You get to decide how you want to feel in your body, how you want to focus your mind, spend your time, optimize your potential, care for your wounds, exalt your genius, enlighten yourself, and engage with your world. More importantly, you get to decide what you want to believe about yourself. We must remember that we have many internal resources and we can commit to shifting into a mindset that is unlimited instead self-limiting. At any moment, you can simply ask yourself, "Am I limiting my life through my thinking right now?" Just ask and notice. Growing awareness is key to empowering nourishing change.

When we learn to trust that what we personally need might look completely different to what we see in our friend groups, our families, or on social media—we find freedom. In finding our core self, we soon discover that it's a place we can return to when we need to connect to what feels right for us—our truth. When we move from a place of self-connection, we can respect others' feedback, but we no longer shrink ourselves in the face of their opinions about us—whether projected or real. We learn to trust ourselves to make myriad turns on our paths, knowing that our routes will even include inevitable "mistakes" or "missteps," and that we will grow through these so-called obstacles. We might try a million ways and still not give up; in fact, this is what the most rewarding journeys often look like. We learn to reframe "failure" as a kind of strength training, like Thomas Edison saying of his journey to invent the light bulb, "I have not failed ten thousand times. I've successfully found ten thousand ways that will not work." It may be that we must seek the answer inside of ourselves ten thousand times—then, on the ten thousand and first attempt, we may find we have grown the wisdom to locate something profoundly effective for ourselves—our own "light bulb." Our so-called "failures" help us to harness our own inner-light and listen to her voice—and to grow the ability to return again and again to self-connection. And when we keep coming back to ourselves, we learn to allow ourselves to change along with our needs, to trust that we can let go of or evolve our outworn behaviors, because we know that listening within is our path to live, love, and heal ourselves. Through this gentle but deep dedication to our own path, we liberate ourselves from our negative self-narratives and cultivate uncollapsible self-confidence. We know that we are okay, we are inherently valuable, and—most of all—we are capable of beautiful transformation. *Do you want to learn, like Edison, to see your so-called "failures" as guides on your learning journey? See Exploration 26.*

I believe that each time we hear a story of a woman's self-exploration and transformation, we are elevated to embrace our own unique lives. In this spirit, I'll share a pivotal moment in the life of one of my clients—we'll call her Laura. For years, Laura believed she was "happy enough." She had lived in the Southwest for more than two decades, had long adapted to year-round sunny weather, and lived an athletic life, engaging with the great outdoors as much as possible. She enjoyed her job as a social worker, she felt comfortable in her home, and she was committed to keeping a grain-free, low-carb diet that she felt "worked for her." These were the staple points of her identity, and they seemed to support her quite well for many years—until something started to feel "off." That's when Laura came to me.

She told me that underneath her "happiness," she was lacking real energy and interest in things. She found herself frequently isolating from her community, and too fatigued to keep up with her previously highly athletic lifestyle. She was also secretly snacking on foods that had been on her no-no list for years. Her willpower, she said, felt like a leaky tank—no matter how often she refilled it with statements of her convictions, it quickly drained. And she felt guilty. She had a great life, so she "should" be happy—but instead, she carried a looming sense of shame and failure. As we dug into her belief system, she shared that she felt too old, too exhausted, and too locked into her life to make a true shift or try anything new. Additionally, because she found herself slipping, she believed she needed to buckle herself in aggressively, to force herself to act more firmly. She told me she wanted "more willpower," and that she hoped I could support her in getting "on track."

In our sessions, I helped Laura to see that her inner-self was not a Pandora's box, dangerous to open up and explore. No: it was key to finding out what her soul was really calling out for. By creating space to look within and bringing her gentle presence, Laura learned to get curious about her feelings; to hear what her whole being was calling for as nourishment for her mind, body, and spirit—rather than imposing rules and strictures on herself. In time, Laura began to trust she could shed her "should" attitude ("I should be happy, I should not complain, I should feel my life is enough," etc.), and connect, instead, to her psyche's subtle, symbolic, dreamlike expression. Here, in our shared, safe space together, we discovered that her sense that something was "off" was in fact an untapped, unheard potential energy ready to be turned *on*—ready to create change inside her. Rather than being frightened of this potential energy, or interpreting it as something exhausting, Laura became fascinated by the art of listening within.

We explored what Laura might need to feel truly connected to her life, rather than just happy on paper. When we opened the doors to the fortress of Laura's deepest desires, we found such a precious memory there from her girlhood years. She had spent a handful of her early teenage winters in her mother's homeland of Denmark. She recalled loving candlelit cafés and writing in her journal, spending time in *hygge* spaces—those places designated in the Danish and Norwegian languages as encapsulating a felt sense of comfort, coziness, and contentment. She remembered loving the warm atmosphere and the feeling of being tucked away in wintertime with candles, warm blankets, and soothing beverages, around other people also simply enjoying this artful space. She felt again how her body had relaxed in that atmosphere, and recalled how sure she'd been back then, as a young girl, that she would grow up to become a writer. In fact, she'd made a pact with herself that she'd spend a winter in Denmark writing away when she became an independent adult.

And yet, Laura hadn't been to Denmark since she began college. Her parents had died unexpectedly in an accident not long after her freshman year at university, and, in dealing with the trauma of losing them, Laura also let go of her connection to Denmark. It felt safer to relinquish her whole past and, in this way, grieve less, focus on her studies, move on, and—essentially—survive. She devoted herself to her studies and went on to ace college with honors, then create her own family, marrying a lovely man with whom she raised two children and built a family life in the Arizona des-ert. Fast-forward through a few decades of Laura's life, and we find she's created a successful career as a social worker, raised her two children to young adulthood, and amicably processed a divorce with her (now) ex-husband. Though thankful to have a wonderful group of close friends, a rich local community, a satisfying professional life, and even some love interests here and there, Laura still felt some-thing deeper calling her. When we gently explored her oldest memories, we found the still-unresolved shock of her parents' death. And beneath this pain, we discovered something more. There was a kind of lantern, a light still on, lit by Laura's younger self, who never stopped longing to return to Denmark to write and allow her stories to spill forth and be shared.

Laura had built rules and order as a sensible means of making her way in the world when faced with the tragic loss of her parents, which had left her feeling all alone. While her self-imposed rules were quite genius on their own and had helped her to achieve so much in her life, beneath this drive to create predictability was a beautiful, creative wildness crying out to let go—to freely explore and express herself. After so many years of relying on her fixed patterns, it made sense that Laura hadn't heard this part of herself—that she'd blocked out the creative wildness in her. And yet her inner-wildness still made itself known, like the beautiful creative source that it is—leading her to experi-ence out-of-control eating episodes and break all her own rules.

When Laura and I created a welcoming, warm space where she could give herself carte blanche to imagine what this part of her might want, she located a deep calling and, without further ado, booked a flight to Denmark. And so, laden with journals and her laptop, Laura set out into the dead of winter to write for two weeks, open to whatever came through her and without any agenda as to what this writing "had to be." She found a very *hygge* apartment on the very street her mother grew up on, right near the center of Copenhagen, and decided that for these two weeks, she would follow her instincts—which meant following the guiding light of her own inner–little girl. She'd let her instincts lead her to what nourishment really meant to her soul, with no fixed rules, only passion and curiosity leading the way. Being careful not to set any ideas in stone, Laura gave herself a gentle, general guideline for her time in Denmark: to create a daily ritual of listening to her innermost needs—trusting that even if difficult feelings came up, she'd stay committed to herself. She'd use her own tools and hone self-love, continually returning to a felt sense of self-connection. For extra support, we envisioned her granting herself a deep permission: that it didn't really matter which foods she chose to eat. What mattered was that she'd choose her food from a place of self-connection, and commit to truly tasting, appreciating, and slowly reveling in her food, whatever it might be. She would eat not only for her body's need for nutrients, but for her body, mind, and soul's deep hunger to savor life. She'd select foods that felt loving, that filled her with a sense of deliciousness, and invite herself to appreciate the moment, celebrate her aliveness, and remember that she's welcome to take up residency in this great life. This ritual would allow Laura to learn on the somatic level that when she eats, she is creating a sacred rite, and that eating is a holy practice and a time both to receive the gift of sustenance, and to give thanks for that gift.

Though it was an outward adventure, Laura's trip to Copenhagen was also a symbol of the internal work she had committed to. It marked her willingness to step into the unknown, give herself permission to access her deep desires, and allow her intuition to lead. This wasn't easy. She'd been gripping tight to her self-imposed rules and identity for so long, seeking the sense of safety they seemed to promise. And in fact, her fears surfaced the night before she was scheduled to depart for her trip. She called me, her voice firm with conviction as she said, "I can't go." But after spending about ten minutes trying to talk herself out of her travels with familiar old patterns of self-control and outside-in rationale, she remembered. She had created her travel plans from the depth of her heart, and in her heart, she knew she was going to Denmark on a quest for self-love, because her inner-voice was calling her to come to life.

The next morning, Laura boarded her plane. She sent me a text before takeoff, saying, "I have been repeating this to myself since last night: 'I listen within. Step by step, I create safety and security for myself. I am my own home.'" The unexpected miracle is that Laura returned from her travels with an entire novel—written in two weeks. She reported that she'd learned something profound about what she had been calling "willpower." She realized she'd been using "willpower" as a sort of external control, but her rules and willpower had never encouraged her to step deeply into the moment, had never asked her to let go, listen in, and feel with her heart. She'd always recognized the value of will-power, of course. She had created her long-standing proto-col with her own best interests in mind—but it wasn't flexi-ble to the inevitable changing of her own seasons. Instead, her willpower often insisted she override the rhythms of life, out of commitment to some intellectual construct—but life is about change. In an attempt to stay safe, secure, and "buckled in" to her plan, her self-will had kept her from feeling fully alive; from going into the unknown with her heart wide open; and from being receptive to the magic, circumstances, mysteries, and potential relationships that lived there, in the mystical unknown. The storyline of Laura's book—which, in fact, she channeled from the un-known—was about finding a lost land that lived in another dimension, intricately layered within a historic European city. Her protagonist was a woman much like herself, who was brave enough to explore this hidden dimension and, in so doing, ultimately discovered an untapped power and sense of beauty inside herself. This female-driven fantasy novel secured Laura a book deal, and she is now working on the follow-up full-time.

Laura's life reflects a theme of letting go and embracing the unknown. She's found a new and very different form of security, which she calls "step-by-step safety." She traded in willpower for learning how to care for herself, listen within, and trust her own ebb and flow. This doesn't mean that Laura lives in a state of unfaltering happiness every day; of course not. Like all of us, Laura is susceptible to discomfort, unsettling emotions, and unexpected events. However, she has cultivated a way to be with life more fully, to engage with its potential, taste its flavors, be with herself in the moment, and work with life as a cocreator. She sees that attempting to control life actually cuts herself off from all the energy that lives in the unknown. Now, when events go in a direction she didn't plan, her first response is not to try to force or control things, but to dial in even more deeply to her unwavering sense of self-trust. She's confident that when she's connected to herself, she is strong enough to not only engage with the unknown, but befriend it. By

nourishing her inner-world, Laura has learned to impro-
vise with each day as it unfolds, and, as a result, transform
her whole relationship with the art of living—creating a life
filled with joy that is bigger, bolder, and braver than she'd
ever dreamed possible.

Shifting Gears from Willpower to Resonance

Conceptually, "willpower" makes sense; it's understand-
able that it's gotten a lot of airtime throughout history.
Willpower helps us impose structure on ourselves—a
structure that's ideally built from our best intentions, our
drive to become our best self and so live a great life. However, it's worth considering that, as a construct, willpower
has come hand in hand with the idea of "rightful" conduct. Willpower has been a talking point since about the
dawn of the written word, revered in fields from religion
to philosophy to psychology. It's prominent in Aristotle's
foundational discussions on ethos and self-control, and
in the thirteenth-century theologian Thomas Aquinas's
famous doctrines on will and religious moral responsibility. Anthropologists view willpower as key to human
survival, noting that it's the quality that has made certain
tribes powerful. Consider, for instance, the willpower of a
leader who could bear to brave fighting the wild and sac-
rifice themselves for the sustenance of their community.
Today, the field of psychology emphasizes the importance
of willpower as a means of coping and of managing our
animalistic impulse control. Willpower is even embedded
in our science, since it's integral to the self-regulation of
our nervous systems, namely the way we tend to our internal responses, take responsibility for our perception,
maintain healthy boundaries, and handle life's storms. It's
directly linked to how much we value ourselves and how

well we have refined our primal urges and controlled our addictive personalities. We use willpower every time we handle our own self-sabotaging tendencies, stay committed, keep calm, and maintain a steady tone. When you look at it this way, it makes sense that our society reveres willpower—that it's right up there with the golden rule.

However, from the perspective of self-nourishment, it takes more than willpower to truly activate our internal compasses; to learn to navigate by our own deepest desires and create liberated lives. Therefore, I'd like to introduce a new, nourishing spin on willpower, replacing the concept's old outside-in orientation—where achieving "rightness" means living by certain externally imposed constructs—to an inside-out, self-nourishing orientation. This internal connection, which I call "resonance," allows us to discover the most self-aligned sense of being and action available to us, by prioritizing our ability to feel, listen in, and connect with the life inside ourselves. Through resonance, we don't prioritize a rigid set of exercises we need to check off our to-do lists in order to have willfully created our days; rather, we emphasize cultivating self-connection. From a self-connected space, we grow trust in ourselves. We create a felt sense of security and safety within ourselves and in our environments, which supports us to operate from a place of self-love, greater presence, and awareness. We recognize that the more presence we can create in the moment, beginning with a sense of deep embodiment, the more we feel we belong to our lives. From here, by attending to our deep well-being and learning to trust ourselves more than the external controls we had been enforcing, we begin to move with a sort of organic, self-connected sanity. To illustrate: willpower may reinforce an idea of rightful etiquette, appropriate behavior, and external concepts of the correct choices to make—but resonance invites us to let go of what we believe we "should" do, and instead discover what we actually need. And in the moments when we lose "willpower," we often feel shame and a sense of failure, whereas when we lose resonance, we are invited to reconnect with ourselves through self-compassion and personal inquiry. Rather than belittling and diminishing ourselves until we fit into a compressed, collapsed space of self-loss, with resonance, we remember we can always reset and find our Nourishing Tone.

It might sound like we can only build resonance if we are already functioning in a way that feels positive, or already in a pleasant space. If we are summering by the shore, lazing on a lounge chair, our toes dipping into warm sand, being served a strawberry margarita—sure; why not feel resonance with life?! But on the level of practice, resonance is situationally agnostic. This means that, whether we're in a beautiful place and feeling fantastic, or in physical pain or discomfort, we can still trust in ourselves as our safest source of grounding and presence. We don't have to feel our environment is "right" to resonate with our own ability to navigate it. Navigating our inner-world and dropping in to find self-connection, while also growing our felt sense of connection to the outer world—this *is* the art of resonance. In fact, the simple act of turning inward and allowing ourselves to be where we are already grows our sense of resonance.

In this way, our work is made much simpler. Rather than striving for perfection, which is often the goal of willpower, we are invited simply to listen within. In the same way we might intuitively learn to care for a screaming baby, we learn to patiently listen and tend to ourselves. We learn to rock our inner-infant, to feed her and coddle her—or at least to stay present with her when she wails all night. Resonance is a humble, beautiful path of remembering that, as powerful as each of us might be, somewhere inside, we all still carry infants, and that this part will always be vulnerable and need our attention at times. When we learn to be with this gentle part of ourselves, we see its enormous potential for creativity and joy—in other words, how powerfully it can help us to create resonance with our lives. Resonance reminds us to ask ourselves, "How do I create peace with myself now, and (again) now, and (yet again) now?" It is a moving peace pilgrimage, this path of finding resonance!

When we tend to our internal space, we grow self-trust, which forms the core of the resilience we'll need to stay present with ourselves in those moments when we feel our old patterns getting triggered. By listening within, we hear the parts of ourselves that didn't trust they were okay or good enough, and we stay with those parts, reaffirming that we are valuable just as we are, and no one can take our power away. It seems rudimentary to reinforce this to our highly accomplished, butt-kicking, name-taking, and genius selves, but we must do the groundwork of patiently going inside and listening to our tenderest parts, and reminding ourselves that we belong, we're enough, and we're valuable.

And by the way, taking time to reconnect with the energy of resonance doesn't always have to be a grand gesture. Sometimes we might catch ourselves collapsing into our environments in the subtlest ways—and then there it is: the opportunity to apply our tools and return to self-connected self-care. We'll see such micro-acts of resonance play out powerfully in the story of a client I'll call Christine, who found an opportunity to strengthen her sense of self-connection in the midst of a triggering moment.

Born in Argentina, Christine was "discovered" as a model in her late teens while working at a shopping mall. By her twenties, she'd traded in her college plans for a lucrative and exciting career in the world of fashion. Traveling the world for over a decade, Christine lived a far grander life than she'd ever imagined, and it all seemed to unfold like a day at an amusement park, filled with exhilarating rides and endless adventures. Then, as is often the case in the modeling industry, by the time Christine hit her midthirties, the work opportunities began to slow down. It so happened that she was ready for a change, so at age thirty-five, Christine enrolled in college. She set out to study medicine, and was too fascinated by her studies to pay much attention to the fact that she was more than ten years older than the majority of students in her class. By her early forties, Christine had graduated with honors as a physician's assistant, and after years of success, she went on to teach university-level classes. By the time she neared her fifties, Christine had a powerful track record of success in fields that had nothing to do with her physical appearance. She'd excelled as a teacher, a published scholar, and a well-loved friend.

Yet even with her strong sense of personal empowerment, Christine experienced moments in which her sense of self-worth would unexpectedly falter. This frustrated her, because these moments were usually triggered by self-criticisms related to her physical appearance. She wanted to believe she was far too wise to let her self-worth be impacted by thoughts she traced back to years of focusing on her outer appearance in the modeling industry.

One Sunday morning, for example, Christine went to write at her favorite café next to the university where she taught. As she organized her notes, she noticed a young woman walking through the door with a tall, handsome man trailing behind her. The couple sat close enough for Christine to overhear their conversation. The woman was quite stunning, and hearing her describe her budding career to her companion, Christine realized she happened to be a model. Christine wanted to focus on her work, but instead found herself getting sucked into the nearby conversation. Before long, she noticed her own mood shift; where she had been in a good mood, now, negative self-talk began to take over. Without realizing it, she'd begun to compare herself to this woman—a stranger she didn't even know. Her psyche was now throwing out self-critical thoughts like, "Who am I to feel I belong anywhere in the world?" She suddenly felt "frumpy" and "old," and as she listened to the young model—who seemed so energized, youthful, and vibrant, with her whole life ahead of her—Christine shrunk herself. She made herself smaller and smaller until she basically disappeared. Seemingly in an instant, Christine collapsed her whole sense of being and self-esteem. Everything she'd worked on in the last decade, everything that had seemed important to her and formed her identity, had dissolved—just because she had overheard a random conversation between two people she didn't even know. Christine caught herself feeling horrible, unlovable, even hideous! Even worse was her embarrassment at being triggered by something that seemed so unimportant.

After ten or so agonizing minutes, Christine decided to gather up her books and laptop and abandon her mission to write for the morning at her favorite café. Instead, she felt she needed to go home and hide, tuck herself away somewhere no one could see her. She was so ashamed of comparing herself to another woman, and that she was wasting her time feeling unlovable and unattractive when she knew there were so many more important things happening in the world—and that only made her sink lower. Then, as she left the coffee shop with the intention of heading home to dissolve into despair in privacy, she paused. She noticed that as she stepped outside into the open air, the sunlight touched her skin—a stark contrast to the dark, shrouded feeling she was carrying. This slightest shift in her awareness, provided courtesy of the sun, allowed Christine to let go and *receive*, for just a moment. And in that moment, she was reminded of something bigger than the hamster wheel spinning in her mind: nature's generosity. That was when something remarkable happened. Christine followed the sun's cue and decided to take a detour, stopping to sit on a bench to gather her energy. Guided by the sunlight, Christine took a deep breath. She closed her eyes and used her inner-eye to go within—to feel into her body, right there, experiencing the day, in that very moment on the park bench. She realized how triggered and wrapped up in her own mind she'd been for the last thirty minutes. With compassion rather than criticism, she saw how the quality of her thoughts had absolutely wiped her out—and that, moreover, these thoughts she had been battling weren't even true. In fact, more than anything else, they were just plain mean. They were biting thoughts, and her internal dialogue had been speaking to her more maliciously than she would speak to her worst enemy. Christine saw how she'd gone from feeling excited about the cozy day ahead of her, from feeling empowered to write on a leisurely weekend morning, to being emotionally tanked. The woman she'd overhead in the café had evidently triggered something Christine hadn't been allowing herself to recognize. In fact, the trigger had nothing to do with the young woman herself; it was all about Christine's own deepest fears. Despite all her hard work to create a life for herself, and despite the outer markers of success she really had achieved, inside, she still carried a fear-informed story that she had somehow failed. Simply because she was no longer twenty years old and valued primarily for her physical beauty, she believed, somewhere deep down beneath all her success, that she was no longer a candidate for love. She wasn't worthy of being loved.

By bravely turning inward and tuning in to hear her vulnerable inner-voice, Christine was able to gently tend to this internal self-saboteur. She listened to this part of herself and heard its full story. Then she asked herself, could she make room for more self-compassion? Could she realign to her own perspective, and remember that these external constructs that have for so long dictated what is valuable, beautiful, and worthy, aren't even what she herself chose to believe? By taking this time, Christine was able to reconnect to her felt sense of resonance and her presence in the world; to the energy and power of the spirit of life—and the value of her own life.

With just a little bit of sunlight and self-compassion, Christine noticed that her sensations were able to shift. By giving her inner-world just a little attention and time, Christine saw that the trigger she'd experienced had led her to cut off her felt sense of resonance between herself and world—and that allowing herself to simply feel what was happening inside her with no forced agenda of fixing the situation had enabled a deeper transformation. In short, her trigger had become an opportunity to transform. Now committed to simply surrendering and receiving, Christine put her hand on her heart, closed her eyes, and turned her face toward the sunlight, to allow herself to explore her sensations and let the so-called "broken part" of her share its wisdom. As she listened, she saw that the part that had seemed broken wasn't, in fact, broken at all—it was the same part of herself that was constantly inviting her to discover who she authentically is in the world.

When Christine opened her eyes on that park bench, she found a much different world than she'd experienced only moments before. Everything was so vibrant. She saw people young and old walking down the street or pausing outside storefronts. Whatever they were doing, everyone was engaged with life in their own way; each with their own mood, their own reality. Christine observed her surroundings as she remained connected to her own sense of safety. She'd created a kind of "safety network" that came from within herself. It filled her own form, and it also extended outward. This warm web resonated all around her, allowing her to feel woven into the world while remaining uniquely her own individual entity—part of the web. She took a deep breath with mindful awareness, recalling the kind of "mental trip" she'd just brought herself through, and welcomed the grounded reality she'd returned to—a reality she could connect with, participate in, and experience in the present moment. She had self-regulated, strengthening her nervous system. She had successfully shifted from a state of self-collapse to one of self-connection. She was able to see that the thoughts that had made her feel so wretched were outdated notions deeply ingrained in her since girlhood: the distorted idea that in order to have value, she had to be eternally beautiful in some externally prescribed way. By making room to listen in and feel what was happening inside her, and then receiving the warmth and light of the sun, Christine had created resonance for herself. She had shifted her energy in a way that supported her to feel present and resourced in her own body and in the world.

Rather than a doctrine of willpower, Christine had decided to give herself an invitation to love. She had used love as a source of guidance. Instead of setting rules for herself, Christine decided to cultivate trust in herself, listen in, and respond to her feelings and thoughts with compassion. *It's okay you think this, or feel this, or worry about that. You are safe.* It seemed almost funny at first, that as a grown adult she'd benefit from coddling some part of herself with tender words—but she'd accessed something essential to self-nourishment. There is a part in all of us—no matter how successful, smart, well-adjusted, or mature we are—that needs to be patiently loved. It needs to be gently coached toward remembering how capable we are of braving life's real or imagined discomforts. *Are you ready to create real nourishing resonance in your life? See Exploration 27.*

To connect to our own, ever-changing flow of Nourish means we listen in, and we allow ourselves to adjust, transform, and shift. This is how we build our boundaries: by returning to our felt sense of self and growing our ability to experience life from a state of self-connection. From here, we feel secure enough to cultivate rich relationships with others—because we have cultivated a rich relationship with ourselves. We can allow life to flow, shift, and change as it always does. By cultivating resonance, we nurture the energy we want to experience in the world. We prioritize trusting that we are *already* enough, just as we are; we have enough, and we give enough. We let our own natural grace move us, however that looks, without trying to fit into anyone else's shoes. We start to cherish how darn adorable we are, because we've let life in to move through us, and it feels joyful. We allow ourselves to feel alive. When we're unsure, we listen within in a spirit of inquiry, and in that very moment we learn what it means to nourish our felt sense of safety and security. We continually check in, gauging how to create security within ourselves and reciprocity with our world. The more we befriend ourselves, the more we get to recognize other people's feelings and internal processes. We see, more and more, that things aren't only about us. We expand and open to the world both within us and around us, and step more fully into interconnection, all the while taking care of our inner-worlds and maintaining our healthy boundaries. *Interested in creating an empowered way to respect your boundaries in the world? See Exploration 28.*

Nourish as a Lifelong Practice of Divine Self-Companionship

At the start of this book, I shared that for years I let the story of "not enough" hold me back. I wasn't skinny enough, healed enough, smart enough—basically, flawless enough to pursue my desires. It was easier to keep my emotions at bay using food to numb myself, or let food fill up the places where I felt lacking. In ways, my eating behavior kept me held back in familiar patterns that weren't comfortable, but at least they were safe, because I'd repeated them for decades. I knew what it was like to go from feeling interested, curious, and even confident about my future for a fleeting moment—only to tank my ambitions and faith in myself with a sugary week or two in snack-food hell. I was aware this pattern I had with food wasn't the most vibrant choice, but at least I knew how to do it—whereas I wasn't so sure how to create the kind of unlimited success I wanted for myself. I wasn't so clear on how to show up to my life every day with the energy of self-belief and self-love. So I kept up the pattern of self-collapsing and used it to ignore all the places we've covered in these chapters—the places inside me and inside each of us that are hungry for real nourishment, for awareness, for presence, for compassion, and for attention. By using food as a way to shut down my own energy, I avoided deeply nourishing my mindset and my mental health and cultivating a sense of feeling safe in my body. I even avoided making friends with the unknown, and stayed locked in a pattern of alternately attempting to control reality or losing my grip on it altogether. When I finally surrendered to the need to turn inward and truly feel my internal world, I slowly learned to stay with my body and grow a sense of self-connection. Over many years, I continued to gain insight about how to nourish my life by my own standards. I know now that all the expansion, abundance, and actualized joy my soul and spirit long for is right here—in tending to the parts of myself that need to be met. The more I heal my own life, the more I have to share with others—and the more I can help them to listen to their own unique being.

In case you're wondering whether you're ready to live your greatest life and start to share it with others, I want you to know that you absolutely do not need to have arrived at some externalized point of "enoughness" before you can share your story. You are credible just by being your incredible self, and I am certain—with every bone in my aware, present body—that you have all you need to live your own truth. And, too: you are allowed to falter, in big ways or small. Remember: faltering is key to the learning journey. The beauty is that on your Path of Nourish, you gain the skills to pick yourself up, gently. You will begin to prioritize acknowledging whatever is happening inside you, and over time you will realize that, in fact, the riches you seek live in the process of self-acknowledgment. Even when your inner-tyrant attempts to belittle you, roaring in its intimidating voice, "How the heck are you still grappling with this stupid issue?"—you will stay present and curious, until, over time, you learn to love even this voice—and in loving it, you set it free to transform.

Just this week, for example, a moment with my own inner-bully gave me an opportunity to move from trigger to transformation. I had committed to performing in a dance competition. Now, dance is one of my major loves; if anyone asks me what I'm passionate about, I immediately start gushing about my love of all things dance. I love to practice multiple times a week, rehearse new choreography, learn the various traditions of movement from around the world, and find self-expression in this ageless art. Dance is a safe place for me to feel my body, to connect to rhythm, and to resonate with the world, and I've been doing it for years, even performing in handfuls of competitions. And yet, even with all this enthusiasm and experience, I still found myself overwhelmed on the day of the competition. I'd been practicing intensely, but rather than feeling excited for the event, I was having an existential meltdown, convinced that my performance would somehow result in utter embarrassment, and I'd leave feeling like an eternal failure and shunned by my dance community. I spent hours ruminating on the myriad ways I'd surely be doomed if I danced that night; I simply could not talk myself down from the ledge. I also felt angry at myself that I was freaking out, responding with such fear to something that should be a no-brainer. No matter how I tried, I couldn't seem to get it together! In the past, I probably would have called in sick, canceled the event, or somehow found a way to create an actual emergency, so it would be physically impossible for me to get to my own show on time. Then, instead of getting on the dance floor, I'd have found my way to a corner store. I'd have piled up a "consolation" kit to consume in my car, comprising a collection of snack bags and sugary, doughy, creamy treats to drown my sorrows and my eternal sense of failure. I'd have trashed all evidence of wrappers and empty bags before I got home, as though wiping clean any evidence of my entire day of tumult. Energetically shut down, I'd likely have gotten under my covers, turned on a movie, and soon after, passed out. That would have been the path of my older, habitually responding self. In fact, some part of me still thinks that plan sounds pretty good—like a cheaper version of a beach vacation. A chance to get away.

It may seem like a small accomplishment, but I am so grateful that after years of repeating that pattern, I chose the path of self-nourishment instead. I found a way to pause and be with myself; to find resonance. I created a quiet environment, and I sat down and felt into my own body. What I was feeling in there was not pleasant, to say the least. I was a mess of internal signaling and disorganized thoughts. In fact, it was hard to locate exactly what I felt, because at first, I couldn't even "find" myself. Settling in and being with my feelings felt a little like asking a child to jump into an ice-cold ocean in the middle of a hailstorm. And yet, despite my resistance, I found my breath. I put my hand on my heart, and as hard as it was at first, I spoke to myself like a little child—out loud, and lovingly. I asked myself what I was feeling, and I told myself I would just listen. And then I was led within—I was granted entry. I listened from a place of holding space for myself, a place of self-guardianship, a place of bearing witness. I asked myself what was really going on, and then I simply watched the show. I saw my fear.

I feared that I wouldn't remember any of my dance moves (even though I'd been working so hard), and that I'd feel stupid for being lost on the dance floor after all of my practice. I was sure that I would appear fat and foolish in front of the audience. I imagined my whole sense of confidence taking a nosedive, and that I'd never recover from the humiliation. And then I did something I would once never have done. Instead of collapsing, I called a close friend, and I let her know that I needed some support.

She heard me out, letting me voice my fears that I would absolutely fail that evening. Despite my pessimism, my friend smartly asked me a question that turned my mind around. "Isabel," she asked. "What do you love about dance?" I told her that I love being swept up in the movement of music, and I love the costuming. I love the opportunity to learn a structure that feels supportive in my body and that I can stay with. I love how dance allows me to feel life moving through me, and somehow lose myself while finding myself. And I love the fact that I'm in my sixties and just now giving myself permission to feel alive and connected to beauty, vibrance, sensuality, and, essentially, a body-centered form of self-esteem. With her question, my friend helped me connect to the expansive, joyful resonance with life that I feel through my dance practice.

Then I had an idea: What if, rather than being focused on my external state—wondering if I looked okay to others or had my steps straight—I let my dance be an offering? What if, that night, as I moved my body, as I allowed myself to feel, I offered my movements up as a gesture of hope for all women to feel liberated to express their grace, their worth, and their exquisiteness, however they wish. I wanted my dance, whatever it looked like, to set a seed of intention that women all over the world can recognize themselves as beautiful—not because they'd put on a dress that they thought was appropriate or pretty, but because they could value themselves—just as they are—from the inside out. By listening to the tenderness in my body, I had discovered a long-held pattern of believing it was actually dangerous to feel joy, and that I shouldn't be allowed to be in my vital body. Rather than trying to force this pattern to turn off, or convince myself it wasn't true, I let it be a guide. I didn't judge myself for feeling emotionally triggered. Instead, I asked this fragile part of me what she was about, what she needed, and how she might feel welcomed here, into reality, with me—to dance with me that very night.

At that moment, I created the opportunity to transform—and this is how we create a life of resonance, step by step, moment by moment. By the time I showed up to dance that night, I honestly didn't care what people had to say. I knew I wouldn't collapse myself into anyone or anything, because I felt connected to my joy, my purpose, and my dedication. I'm not sure if I "nailed" all my dance moves, or if I made it through without a major mess-up, but I felt exquisite, as though I was moving like silk. Life lit up through me, and it felt truly nourishing. I danced differently that night, because I wasn't just dancing with my partner, I was dancing with life itself. I felt the beat of the music through the center of my body, and I breathed with it. I resonated with my environment, and in finding this newfound ability to really give myself to that resonance, I knew that I was giving others permission to do the same—and *that* was more rewarding than any medal I could have won. (Though I will say, I do love collecting those medals!)

The Path of Nourish isn't about cutting off any part of ourselves because we think it's spiritually, mentally, or physically wrong to inhabit our full size or our full spectrum of expression. Nourish reminds us that we do not need to shrink ourselves physically or energetically to fit any externally imposed standards. Nourish is about letting ourselves be full, and fully committed to all of who we are. It is from this place that we can make radical transformations and achieve something greater than even stepping on the moon: we can reach true self-trust and self-love, and step deeply into ourselves. *Do you want to learn how to love the most tender aspects of yourself? See Exploration 29.*

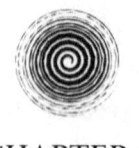

CHAPTER 8

The Essential Vitamins for Inside-Out Nourishment

F ood has long been linked to vitality. For example, Ancient Greek philosophers such as Hippocrates and Galen noted how diet directly influenced health. In Egypt, nutrition was originally a spiritual, mystical practice; a way to explore the connections between our physical bodies, our spirits, the Earth's resources, and the energy of life itself. By the nineteenth century, science had begun to make the correlation between disease and nutritional deficiencies, and dietary sustenance became an important part of living "rightfully"—almost a religion in its own right. Methodologies and regimens sprung forth, replete with pronouncements on the right ways to eat each day, as well as fixed doctrines stating that certain foods were either "good" or "bad." In the early twentieth century, the term "vitamin" began to be used to describe the essential "vital" elements that sustain life. Vitamins are usually associated with the food sources or elements of nature that provide us with these essential nutrients, but if we want to truly receive these vitamins, our emotional state is as important as the items we ingest. If we're not nourishing our sense of well-being from the inside out, it's more likely we won't absorb all of the goodness in the food we consume. In fact, certain medical conditions, such as "malabsorption syndrome," inhibit the body's absorption of nutrients—and chronic stress can be a primary cause. Hoping to emphasize the key role of emotional well-being in our absorption of life's nutriments, I've created a Nourish-oriented essential vitamin list, which includes the key phrases that remind us to find resonance within, prioritize self-connection, and consider "health" or "nutrition" as more than some external protocol. In this way, vitamins become a symbol of our deep interconnectedness with nature and all of life, of the ways we nourish our spirits and our emotional well-being, and of feeding not just our physical forms, but the essence of what it means to truly live.

Vitamin A is for cultivating Awareness, growing Acceptance and Appreciation, and Actualizing Abundance. Vitamin A is associated with vision and immune function. It's found, for example, in carrots, sweet potatoes, and spinach. When we're in emotional tumult, it can be harder to absorb this essential vitamin. To support our relationship with vitamin A, we can practice becoming aware of how we're feeling. From here, we practice patience, grow self-acceptance, and cultivate appreciation for our own and others' gifts, as well as appreciating the ability to live, learn, and actualize a mindset of abundance.

Vitamin B1 is for Balance, Believing (in yourself), and Boundless Beauty. Vitamin B1 (a.k.a. thiamine) is related to our energy production and nerve function. It's found in foods including whole grains, beans, and pork. When we're in a perpetual state of anxiety, it can be challenging to absorb B1. To fully absorb, receive, and nourish yourself with life's gifts, be a B1 queen! This means recognizing that balance is not fixed, but ever-changing, and so we must drop in, go with our flow, reconnect, and recommit to believing in ourselves. From here, we define what it means to be boundlessly beautiful on our own terms.

Vitamin B2 is for Boundaries and Bravery. Like B1, vitamin B2 (a.k.a. riboflavin) is related to energy production and the health of our skin. It's found in foods including yogurt, cheese, asparagus, broccoli, almonds, oats, brown rice, and mushrooms. When we live in prolonged states of stress, our B2 levels can deplete faster than they can be replenished. To absorb vitamin B2, we can focus on building boundaries that respect our deep needs. Do we need a certain bedtime? Do we need a quiet night versus one with lots of activity—or vice versa? Do we need to move more or less? We listen in and respond—and from here, we access what we're really feeling inside. We can then delineate between our own and others' needs, and make sure we are taking care of our ourselves rather than showing up for everyone else. This isn't always easy, as we've been conditioned for so long to tend to everyone else before considering what we want or need to feel nourished. By prioritizing self-care, we become more available to receive nourishing energy—including the energy of vitamin B2!

Vitamin B3 is for Becoming Bedazzling. Vitamin B3 (a.k.a. niacin) is vital for digestive health as well as maintaining our skin—our largest organ! It can be found in chicken, tuna, and avocados. Sadly, living in a state of prolonged depression can impair our B3 absorption. Depression can be a cue to investigate what it will take to find our joy, listen without judgment, and tend to our inner-spirit. When we learn to nourish ourselves from the inside out, we get to claim the things that capture our fascination and attention in the world. We recognize the true fortification that comes from inviting our senses to awaken, from letting ourselves feel passion. From here, we can step into a life where we allow ourselves to become all that we are. No longer hiding our power, we can fully embrace how bedazzling life is—and allow ourselves to dazzle, as well!

Vitamin B5 is for Bounty. Vitamin B5 (a.k.a. pantothenic acid) supports our energy production, hormone synthesis, cholesterol management, red blood cell production, and liver detoxification. It is found in eggs, avocados, sunflower seeds, lentils, salmon, sweet potatoes, beans, and beef, but high stress increases our body's usage of B5, and can lead to deficiency. One way we can shift out of a stress state is by slowly but surely developing an unbreakable sense of self-connection. When we cultivate feeling safe in our bodies and secure in ourselves, we are more able to transform stressful moments into opportunities to connect to life and tap into the energy of bounty.

Vitamin B6 is for your Brilliance and Breath. Vitamin B6 is connected to our neurotransmitter synthesis and immune health, and is found in foods like bananas, salmon, and potatoes. When we are perpetually stressed, we increase our metabolic demand and deplete our B6 reserves—meaning it's a good invitation to look inside and listen. We can ask ourselves how we're taking care of our mental health, then attend to our cognitive health by simply connecting to our breath. Through deep breathing, we can balance our bodies' chemicals to support the creation of new neural pathways, which will activate our most brilliant lives.

Vitamin B7 is for living Big. Vitamin B7 (a.k.a. biotin) supports our metabolism, healthy hair, skin, and nails—basically, all the things that let us feel luscious. It's found in egg yolks, spinach, peanuts, almonds, cheese, cauliflower, mushrooms, and sweet potatoes, but when we undergo periods of emotional distress, B7 absorption is hindered. When we learn to live in rich connection to life, reality, and the moment, we let ourselves live big, transcending our emotional duress by embracing all that we are. We understand that when we feel upset, we are not defined by this momentary emotion, and rather than collapsing into a concept that is self-limiting, we let ourselves live big. We let our energy grow as large as we want, taking care of our boundaries, our bodies, our minds, and our soulful expression.

Vitamin B9 is for Big Heart. B9 (a.k.a. folate) is essential for DNA synthesis and repair. It's found in leafy greens, citrus fruits, and beans—but anxiety can interfere with its absorption. To support receiving B9, we can practice self-kindness. Connect with yourself, and recognize that this self-connection is the seed of love. The heart, that portal that connects the head to the stomach, encourages us to trust opening to our own lives, connecting to the world around us, resonating, and living in love.

Vitamin B12 is for Brightness and Bliss-Following. B12 is connected to nerve function and blood cell production. It's found in meat, dairy, and fortified cereals, but when stress impacts our stomach health, specifically, our B12 absorption is impaired. When we cultivate nourishment from the inside out, we create the conditions to, as they say, follow our bliss. We let go into the mystery—the mystical. We let go of unnecessary attachments that cause stress and anxiety, recognize the power of life at large, and are strengthened by our ability to feel spiritual magic and connect to the sacred seed of life source inside us.

Vitamin C is for Courage to Connect. Vitamin C supports immune defense, stimulates the production of white blood cells, enhances nutrient absorption, acts as an antioxidant, and is crucial for skin health and collagen production. It is found in oranges, strawberries, bell peppers, broccoli, tomatoes, kale, and snow peas—but even if we're consuming these vitamin C–rich foods, emotional distress can rapidly deplete our vitamin C levels. When we feel triggered, rather than enforcing some harsh mandate on ourselves, we can drop in, reconnect, and return to a felt sense of resonance—remembering that we have an internal healing source that's always available to us. This practice gives us access to our truest sense of self-companionship. And even when we're not "triggered," we can develop a regular self-care protocol of nourishing our core connection to self. See, vitamin C absorption is supported when we courageously commit to riding the ebbs and flows of our own rhythm, and that means finding the practices and resources that nourish us—whether it's a hot bath, a needed pause, a committed morning ritual, a regular sitting or walking meditation, a good therapist, practicing dance, or any other activity that allows us to support our inner-self.

Vitamin D is for Daring to Deepen your Desire and Devotion to Deliciousness. Vitamin D, which is synthesized through our skin and naturally obtained straight from the sun, helps us to feel energized and positive, and supports strong bones and immune function. When we feel depressed or have irregular sleeping patterns that keep us from receiving the day's generative sunlight, it might be a sign of vitamin D deficiency. I believe that as women, we are fortified not only by sunlight, but by our own internal light—and also the rhythms of the moon and its pull on the tides. When you feel the sunlight on your skin, remember the internal light inside you, whose energy is every bit as central to the beauty of the world. Can you dare to let your light shine? Can you live in the energy of your desire?

Vitamin E is for Essential Energy and Enoughness. Anti-inflammatory vitamin E is essential for protecting your cells, and specifically for keeping your endothelial cells (the cells that line blood vessels) healthy, while supporting your skin, eyes, nails, and hair. Vitamin E is found in nuts, seeds, and vegetable oils—but even if we get lots of the good stuff, states of high anxiety increase oxidative stress and keep our bodies from getting enough vitamin E. To support our intake of E, we can breathe in a reminder to ourselves: "I am enough" (as in, "I am vitamin E-nough!"). Consider how much time you spend on your appearance every day. What would it be like if you devoted as much time to taking care of your energy as you do to your physical appearance? Vitamin E reminds us to find energy by seeking self-connection rather than external stimuli that will ultimately drain us. It invites us to locate our inner-essence, reinforcing our deep commitment to loving ourselves. We relieve ourselves of external stress, letting go—even if only for a moment—of our self-imposed to-do lists and all the things we believe we need to become in the world just to be "enough" in our own or others' eyes. We remember that we are already way more than enough!

Vitamin K is for Kinship, Kindness, and Knowledge. Vitamin K is necessary for blood clotting and bone health, but stress can disrupt our K production and absorption. Vitamin K is found in leafy greens (kale, spinach, collards), broccoli, brussels sprouts, soybeans, chicken, and prunes. One of the first things that happens when we're stressed is that we forget about the most sacred kinship we have: our lifelong relationship with ourselves. We may have an aggressive inner-monologue, bullying or criticizing ourselves.

When we regularly practice kindness, we are much more able to receive true nourishment—the kind of nourishment that comes from being connected to ourselves and, in this way, accessing a major reserve of knowledge and wisdom. Next time you feel stress, consider your bone health and your blood function—the vitamin K in your state of "I'm okay." Recall your kinship with self and the kindness you can express internally, and always remember that your own knowledge is often the very wisdom you seek.

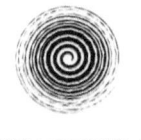

CHAPTER 9

Epilogue and Explorations

The Path of Nourish invites us to reframe personal growth and self-development. For so long, and especially as women, "working on ourselves" has too often meant trying to get closer to perfection—frequently at the gym or by joining a new diet trend. This idea that we should forever be striving toward the end goal of a picture-perfect version of our lives, a moment when we're finally "good enough," creates a chronic inability to be present in the moment and celebrate all that we are. Of course, we will always have room to grow and heal. That is, in fact, the core truth of our nature: our physiology resonates with healing energy. And yet though there is always room for growth, the Path of Nourish is not a path of arduously, painfully starving ourselves. Rather, it's a path of true self-fulfillment. On this path, we get to let go of the behaviors around food and eating that might not serve us, as well as other patterns that aren't supporting our full life expression. More than just one or two practices, Nourish becomes a mindset that is unique to our personal life path. What nourishes you will not be what nourishes others. Your Nourish is one of a kind! Nourish won't strip away parts of you from the outside in so you can become "flawless." Rather, Nourish will deeply befriend you on a soul level, reflecting the love you already are. Nourish will remind you that your goal is not to "fix your problems," because you do not need to be "fixed." Instead, Nourish will invite you—with a gorgeous, gold-sealed, personalized invitation—to deepen your self-connection. And rather than trying to "fix" you, Nourish will enable you to liberate yourself, showing you that you are not weighed down with problems, but rather filled with the endless energy of opportunity.

As the energy of Nourish spreads through your whole life, the following explorations will help you to deepen your sense of self-connection and your ability to listen within, and, ultimately, create a life that nourishes your mind, body, soul, and spirit. Note that the following explorations are all linked to specific passages in the pages of this book. If you are working with these explorations as you read the text, flipping to these back pages as you go along—great! Alternatively, if you are checking out these explorations consecutively—that works, too! Feel free to return to any exploration at any time. They are offered to support you in developing presence in your body, in your relationships, and in the world at large. The Path of Nourish is all about connection. It is about embracing ourselves and learning to share our unique expression in the world from a place of self-connection, dialed into the energy of appreciation and generosity. As powerful women leading the way for powerful women in the generations to come, I believe we owe it to history, posterity, and ourselves to really Nourish our existence in this lifetime. It is with honor and an eternal "beginner's mindset" that I share the contents of Nourish, and the explorations that follow, with you. If ever you have any questions, thoughts, or feedback on your Nourish journey, you are always welcome to connect with me and my work at **www.isabel-chiara.com**. That's also the place to learn about my personalized activation sessions and Nourish app, featuring engaging written and recorded processes designed to support you in exploring and transforming any outworn behaviors around food and eating, in order to live a truly nourished life.

$\mathcal{E}$xplorations

EXPLORATION 1:
What's Your Food Thing?
In this exploration, we'll gently create the space to understand your personal pattern with food.

First, prepare your space. Make sure you feel comfortable and safe, and that you won't be disturbed. Read through the exploration in full before you begin.

Next, set a timer for five minutes. As it is often not comfortable for us to put our mind consciously on our dysfunctional eating patterns, knowing this exercise (after you read through the steps) has a set duration can be helpful. Light a candle if you have one; otherwise, find a still point in the room to focus on. Keep your eyes open to stay present, connecting to this exploration.

In this five-minute exercise, you'll envision yourself eating in a way that feels like a problem for you. This can be any behavior where you don't feel aligned or connected to your body. You will see yourself going through all the steps and simply notice the pattern, working to observe rather than judge.

As you watch the steps of your dysfunctional eating, it can be helpful to adopt the compassionate voice of a caring parent watching a child. Speak to yourself in a kind tone, gently saying, for example, "I hear you," "I see you," and, "It's okay." Then ask yourself tenderly, "What do you really need?" Listen for the answer. Next, ask, "What are you feeling inside?" and listen again. Finally, ask, "How can I support you?" and, "How can I hold you?"

When your five minutes are up, cross your arms and stroke your hands downward from the upper biceps toward the elbows, as though you are brushing off old energy and soothing your own being. Now let go of all that you've been experiencing by envisioning a blank canvas and breathing into it. Visualize a light inside you, which begins at the top of your head and moves to your feet, spreading its clear brightness as it goes. Exhale with a sound or sigh, and place your hand on your heart, sending yourself some grounding words. You might say internally, "I am here," or, "I am with you."

Now listen to yourself again. Do you need something, such as a glass of water, a nap, a shift in posture, or a series of deep breaths? Maybe you just want to stay still for a moment. Ask yourself out loud, "What can I create for you? Is there something you need in order to feel safe?" Does your need in this moment show you a practice you can regularly create for yourself to nourish your internal world? Listen, and if you hear a response, write it down.

Remember, it is in little steps toward self-awareness and cultivating nourishing care that we begin to shift our old, outworn patterns and find safety inside ourselves. The goal of this exploration is simply to gain awareness of yourself. There is no fixing, only "being with."

Returning to this exercise daily or weekly will support you to better understand your patterns with food and eating, and gradually, compassionately make transformative shifts.

EXPLORATION 2:
How Do You Do "Collapse"?

In this exercise, we'll take a moment to journal about self-collapsing.

Write a story no more than one page in length about your personal experiences of collapsing your felt sense of energy, presence, physical grounding, or emotion. Let the story include your first memories of collapsing in this way, as well as any more recent occurrences and the "typical" circumstances of this type of collapse. Make sure to describe how it feels in your body.

If you need a little assistance, consider the following prompts:

Do you ever wake up feeling strong, vibrant, and connected to the energy of beauty—a sense that you are part of life? Do you ever experience true felt presence, the kind that seems to stop time and fill you with an awareness that feels like permission to be as expansive as you are, just as you are?

Have you ever then gone into the world and encountered a different atmosphere, or had an interaction with people, and noticed your physical sense of self-connection dwindling? Suddenly, you are disconnected from that grounded, secure presence, or some part of your body seems to grow or shrink; maybe you even feel yourself floating out of your physical form to hover somewhere in the room, or losing sensation in your limbs. In this state, you might not be able to tell where your energy or body ends and someone else's begins.

This is one of many illustrations of what it means to feel "self-collapsed." On the psychological, spiritual, physical, or emotional levels, we can dislocate from "self," so that we are no longer inhabiting our lives, our reality, or the moment. This then impacts our behaviors (for instance, how we eat) and our sense of engagement with ourselves, as well as how we relate to everyone and everything we interact with. Self-collapsing skews our perception, so that we are no longer grounded in reality, and it greatly diminishes our ability to grasp our agency and reach our creative potential. It can send our energy spiraling downward, into a negatively reinforcing concept of self.

What sparks *your* moments of self-collapse? Are there certain environments or conditions where you feel more prone to losing your sense of self-connection?

And on the other hand, in which circumstances are you *least* likely to self-collapse?

When you've finished writing your story, make a list of twenty adjectives (yes, twenty!) that describe how you feel in your body, mind, soul, and spirit when you are *not* self-collapsed—when you're feeling connected to yourself, clear, strong, capable, and empowered in your place in the world.

Once you've finished writing this list, take some full breaths, working toward a specific breathing rhythm. You'll count four beats on the inhale and seven beats on the out breath (creating a longer exhalation). At the bottom of your exhalation, count eight beats (with your lungs empty), and then repeat. This breathing style will calm your nervous system to a parasympathetic rhythm. Work on breathing this way for a total of 10 breathing cycles, and while you do so, invite the adjectives you've written down to enter your felt sense of being. Breathe in this energy—an energy your body already knows—of how it feels to be uncollapsible.

When you reach your tenth breath, choose just one word from your list, and select a simple gesture to go with it—perhaps a finger snap, a pat on your shoulder, or putting your hand on your heart. The combination of this one word and gesture is now your personal protection mantra.

Whenever you transition from one space to another, or move from one interaction to another—from being alone, for example, to being present with others—you can use this word–gesture mantra to stay self-connected. Remember, you *can* take care of yourself.

When we are raised in an environment where our caregivers aren't able to give us ample presence, patience, attention, or time, we can carry the sense of lack into adulthood. It may take some practice to slow down enough to hear our own process and learn what's happening inside of us—and then soothe our sensations and support self-connection. However, with real dedication, we can transform our patterns of self-collapsing.

It is important to remember that no matter who anyone is, there is no reason—ever—to collapse your sense of self into what they think of you, or their vision of reality, or any other source of downward-spiraling judgment. Collapse happens specifically when we begin to judge ourselves or others. Stay in a space of taking care of your own business, and you will foster your uncollapsible sense of self-connection.

EXPLORATION 3:
Naming Our Nourishing Needs: Body, Mind, Soul, and Spirit

You have the power to decide for yourself how to define the word "nourish" in your own life. Let's explore a full-spectrum sense of what "taking care of yourself" looks like for you.

Below, you'll see four central components of what we'll call your "personal temple"—areas of your body, mind, soul, and spirit that make up the composition of who you are and how you live. Here, we differentiate "spirit" from "soul" as follows: Spirit describes the life energy you allow to move through your being. It is the wind under your wings that allows you to take flight, reminding you that you are part of life; the energy that connects your own felt sense of life to the life that runs throughout the world. Soul, on the other hand, is the essence of your personhood—a gift that you alone possess, and which informs your life journey, helping you, always, to evolve. Through the gift of your soul, you learn lessons in this lifetime and, ideally, express your soul-gifts in the world.

In each of these areas, I want you to take a moment to reflect on the questions below (or even to write your thoughts down). Give yourself time here to really feel into what nourishes your body, mind, spirit, and soul—as defined by you.

BODY

- Which activities do you do regularly to take care of your body?

- Do you ever let yourself take a break from these activities, and if so, how do you feel? Is it easy to return to them? Do you let yourself shift and change in response to your body's needs?
- If you listen to just your body (not your mind's directive), what does your body "need" now to feel radiant, joyful, energized, connected to the world? Are some of these needs related to creating specific relationships in your life? Are some of them about cultivating your direct relationship with your physical being? (Such needs might include needing to get your heart rate up more, or get more sleep, or eat more slowly, or relax and put your work down.)
- Do you eat to feel a certain energy, or not to feel a certain energy (such as anxiety or sluggishness)? What do you want to feel in your life at this moment, in this season, and which foods tend to promote this feeling in you? Does variety work for you to a certain degree, or do you tend to keep your food choices rigid and consistent? If you listen to your body, what do you think it wants in relationship to food? How easy is it for you to listen to that desire? If it's difficult, what overrides your body's needs? How can you support connecting to your body, mind, soul, and spirit through the act of eating?
- What do you need to put in place in order to eat in a way that feels resonant?
- Do you ever override your body's desires with "shoulds" (for instance, you should do this, you should not do that)?
- What do you believe about your body that you'd like to shift or let go of?
- Which words or ideas or beliefs could you take on that would let you feel more physically "nourished"?

- Do you believe your body should look a certain way in order to be beautiful?
- Do you think you have what it takes to let go of external ideas about what your body should look like, and really listen in to what it tells you from the inside?
- Is your physical self-care regimen fixed, or does it contain a giant trove of options? Do you trust your body to try different ways of eating, moving, or living, so you can learn what works for you?
- Do you trust the strength of your body's constitution? Do you think she's on board with wanting to feel healthy and vibrant? Is there anything getting in the way of her living her best life? Which beliefs could you shift in order to gain greater love and acceptance for your body, just as she is?

MIND

- How do you take care of the content of your mind? What do you do regularly to create a state of mental peace— and what have you done in the past to strengthen your relationship with your mind?
- To what extent do your mind and body feel connected? For example, do you naturally remember to check in with your body, or do you find your mind racing off with a list of things it wants to accomplish, or a handful of ways to rebel against the intended task at hand?
- Do you criticize your own mind for thinking certain things? How do you speak to yourself?
- How easy is it for you to hear what's on your mind? Do you ever override your own thoughts in order to prioritize others' ideas or thinking?
- Do you give your mind freedom to explore ideas?

- How patient are you with yourself when you need time to "figure things out"?
- When you feel an uncomfortable emotion or sensation that you don't really understand mentally, do you sometimes try to force your mind to shift, to get over it?
- Are there ways you're gruff with your mindset, rather than really nourishing? What could you do to make your mind feel loved and cared for?
- What does your mind believe about your selfhood? Does she say that you are enough? Does she feel safe? Does she trust that no matter what happens, you can take care of yourself?
- What fears does your mind hold? Is there anything helpful these fears can tell you to guide you toward ways to nourish your life?
- Have you ever considered that your mind's fears are actually just guides to your own long- and short-term safety? Have you ever gently questioned your mind when she's fearful, and tried to understand more about her concerns?
- How could you befriend your mind more?

SPIRIT

- To what extent can you feel the energy of life moving through your body?
- When you wake up, which aspect of your existence do you become aware of first? Do you feel your energy mentally or physically? Do you have a sense of connecting with your internal state, or do you find yourself reaching outside of yourself for "energy"?
- Where do you think your energy comes from? Do you sometimes find yourself reaching to external energy sources like food, your cell phone or other screens, people, or shopping?

- How do you tap into your own energy? Does it entail doing something physical, or can you connect to your energy without physically moving?
- Can you bring energy into your body, or does it exist mostly outside of you?
- Do you feel your spirit through your body?
- What would you need in order to trust the feeling of the "spirit" of life moving through you?
- Do you ever notice a part of yourself keeping spirit from fully flowing through you? If so, why do you think you'd keep the feeling of life from fully expressing itself through you? How would it serve you to play small?
- What do you want from your sense of spirit?
- What would nourish your spirit more fully?
- Have you ever felt the spirit of life moving through you? This might have felt like a surge of energy, or a feeling of well-being, or a sense of connection with the world that may have been exciting or safe or even cozy.
- What's your earliest memory of connecting with the energy of life?
- Are there places in the world where you let yourself feel life's energy more than other places?
- Do you tell yourself stories about your relationship to life's energy? Do you ever feel that you "take on too much energy" from others, or that you can't "manage your own energy"? What do you think would nourish your own energy, and how can you describe that shift in your own terms?
- Is there anyone you know who seems to take very good care of their energy? How does that express itself in their life?

- Who was your role model in the realm of energy and spirit? Did anyone teach you how to respect or take care of your own spirit, and if so, what has worked?

SOUL

- Do you feel you have an "essence," or something that makes you unique—something you might call a "soul"?
- If so, how much time do you regularly give to listening to your soul?
- Do you have a relationship with your soul that feels strong and solely your own? Is there a part of you that connects to the "universe," or something greater than your individual life, allowing you to tap into the vastness of existence?
- Simultaneously, can you feel the way your soul dances, its steps ringing out in your whole being and the stories you play out in this lifetime?
- What does your soul long for?
- Do you long to rise to the potential within you? Do you long to stop getting in your way?
- Do you have any stories you make up about yourself that limit the power of your soul?
- How often do you ask yourself, "What does my soul want now?" Can you ask yourself this question right now? Can you give yourself a few minutes—or even longer; perhaps an hour, a day, or a week—to listen closely to what your soul wants?
- Does your soul speak to you in words, in feelings—or both, or neither? How do you know your soul?
- Have you ever connected directly with another person's soul? Have you ever felt that someone knows you on a soul level, allowing true intimacy—that all of who you are could be seen and accepted?

- How often do you take time to settle into your body and connect with your soul?
- Do you find your sense of soul in your body, or does it feel beyond your body? What would you need to feel your connection to your soul inside your physical self?
- If your soul could name a few qualities it would like you to cultivate, to give it room to express itself in your body, what would they be? How does your soul wish to connect to your body now?

After you've considered the questions above, giving ample thought to each one, take a moment to define nourishment by your own standards. For example, you might express the Path of Nourish in your own words as: "I nourish myself through the actions I take and the presence I possess to feel grounded and alive and able in my body. Nourish, to me, means cultivating connection and coherence in my thinking, so that I can respond to my ever-changing needs while connecting to the greater life force, and, within it, my own powerful uniqueness." In this way, your definition of Nourish can be supportively informed by your answers to the questions in the table above.

Now, equipped with a fully fleshed out sense of what Nourish means to you, you have a faithful inner-compass to support you in each choice you make throughout your day, helping you determine what will most nourish you and what you need in that moment.

EXPLORATION 4:
Acknowledging and Appreciating Your Old Behavioral Patterns

First, take a moment to settle in. Take some deep breaths, and give yourself permission to pause, and settle and find center in your sense of being, here in the moment.

Once you feel ready to begin a self-query, ask yourself the following: "Can I recall a time when I felt I 'lost myself' to a behavior that felt out of control? Do I have a memory of a specific time when I collapsed part of myself?" Beyond just the physical action (say, eating something you think you shouldn't have), try to remember how you talked to yourself in the midst of this maladaptive behavior, or the visual or energetic sense of self you slipped into during the episode. Where do your feelings of self-confidence, faith in life, safety, security, and connection to the greater world go when you're in a pattern of collapse?

If several instances of self-collapse or outworn behavior suggested themselves to you, now zoom in on the one that feels most vivid to you, whether it's recent or from the past. Think about it for a moment or two, and then ask yourself, how are you looking at this pattern? Do you think it's "horrible" or "disgusting"; that it makes you less capable or beautiful than "everyone else"? Does it make you feel like you "can't do life" as well as those you see around you? And what does the pattern or behavior feel like? Is it a heavy weight you long to be free from, but which keeps you enslaved, like a tyrant or thief of your free will? Take a good look at your relationship to this pattern, in the same way you might observe any other relationship in your life. Notice your negative judgments about it. Are you, in fact, treating the behavior as though it's not part of you at all, but more like some jerk you're married to that you really hate? What kind of negativity or detachment are you projecting onto this entanglement?

Now I want you to pause and try to let go of your negative perspective for a moment. Instead of judging, try to get curious about your behavior. Ask yourself, "How has this pattern actually helped me? How was it protecting me, or soothing me?" It might also help to ask, "Did this pattern offer me some internal sense of organization at times when I couldn't organize my feelings? Was this behavior a way to 'clear the whiteboard,' or reset my sense of overwhelm to zero? Did this pattern turn off the chaos in my brain? Did it quell my nerves?" It might even go deeper than that: maybe this pattern kept you alive, or maybe you inherited it from your family because it kept *them* alive, way back.

To answer these questions, it will help to break the pattern down to its simplest drive. Those drives might include:

- The drive to survive. Are you reaching for food out of a survival instinct, because you're living in a state of life-and-death fear? If so, can you take a moment to thank the pattern, and yourself? Thank the food for the comfort—for helping you to get through moments you felt you might not. And thank yourself for your genius in finding this way to cope when there were no other resources available. This might feel strange; it might even feel like thanking an enemy. All the same, take some time to feel your gratitude for the invaluable lessons this pattern has presented for you to learn about yourself.
- The drive for companionship, during lonely moments when you couldn't be around anyone else, or you felt no one could understand what you were going through. Consider how much this behavior "understood" you, helped you when you couldn't find a way to deal with the risks or the challenges you were facing.
- The drive for financial security or physical comfort. Did this behavior fill in the gaps when you were hungry for worldly safety?

213

- The drive to soothe yourself while reeling from shock, or having to rebuild everything in your life from the ground up.
- The drive to escape the pressure of being asked to carry someone else's stress—and to escape, too, the feeling of not knowing how you'll ever get out of a situation.
- The drive to escape or manage the stress of your own out-of-control to-do list, piled higher than a skyscraper and threatening to topple down on you.

These are just some of the potential drives that might be at the heart of your eating behavior. Whatever the core instinct was for you, consider the ways the pattern released or eased your discomfort, even if just for a moment. It could be that the feelings inside your body were too intense to feel. Over time, the effort of trying to deal with these feelings and sensations became too much to bear—and this behavior stepped in as a surrogate for your breath. At times when you weren't able to breathe into your feelings, this behavior helped you cope, or gave you a reward you could count on in a world of unknowns.

See how the behavior allowed you some relief—or at least the idea, the notion, that relief was possible. The behavior was your brain and your whole entrained physiology, reaching out for some alternative to living with overwhelming pressure. In the interconnected network of self and other, your self reached to the behavior as the other, crying out for relief at a time when perhaps there was nobody else to call out to—or at least, nobody who would respond as consistently and fully.

As uncomfortable as it might be, can you see how this behavior helped you get by? Can you, in fact, give thanks for its complex intelligence?

Now that you know what your true need was, and that this behavior was simply the best response available to you at the time, you are ready to open to a new perspective, a new pattern that can begin to honor and meet your deepest needs. Next time you feel this outworn behavior begin to arise, thank it. Talk to it like a parent to a babysitter. Tell it that you appreciate its availability, you see how it's shown up and how creative it has been in taking care of your inner-girl. Then let the behavior know that from now on, you can take care of your sensations, emotions, and feelings. Write out a list of multiple other actions you might take rather than repeating this old behavior, and keep it on hand. On the same list, write out how you'll feel about yourself if you do repeat this outworn behavior, noting the negative or limiting consequences of your old pattern. The goal is to get your mind, body, soul, and spirit on board in a new way, so that, rather than making yourself wrong for having needs, you find a newfound respect for your whole process.

If you'd like to take this exploration even further, take some more time here to consider other outworn patterns or behaviors you still find yourself acting out—anything that doesn't fit into your full vision of who you are and how you want to be in the world. Use the following table as a self-exploration guide. What's essential here is that you now have the opportunity to thank these behaviors. I suggest speaking to them aloud, or recognizing them in whichever other way feels complete for you. Finally, you have the beautiful opportunity to think about what you are calling in for your *new* lifestyle. Which behavioral patterns will you create consciously, using self-compassion and love to transform your self-limiting and outworn behaviors?

215

Area	Need	Stuck feelings about yourself in this area	Behavior(s) that have helped you cope with discomfort in this area	How did this coping mechanism help you? How can you appreciate it?	What does your adult, higher-self call for now? How can you grow self-compassion and become accountable for your feelings?
Friendships					
Body image					
Your ability to create opportunities					
Sense of identity in the world, feeling of belonging					
Intimacy					

EXPLORATION 5:
Safely Exploring What "Trauma" Means for You—A Body-Based Practice to Create Presence with Your Whole Being and Truly Nourish Your Physiology

The following is a gentle self-practice which you can do as often as you wish. In fact, the more often we check in and work with our own energy and the stories we're telling ourselves about our lives, the better! This practice helps us to gently turn inward, recognize our power, and reinforce that we are able to tend to the parts of ourselves that may be holding old patterns rooted in our past.

Before you begin, it's important to note that working with trauma can bring up a lot, so please take extra care in this exploration. Make sure to listen to your needs and modify the practice to whatever version feels safe for you. One way to track whether you feel "safe" is to note whether you are able to stay connected to your breath and your physical sensations. In this exercise, you may tap into parts of your physiology that have been holding energetic or emotional blockages. Though the concept of trauma has gained much popularity in both psychological and cultural settings, remember that every person experiences trauma differently. Your deep-held patterns and unprocessed emotions or sensations might be personal, inherited, or even cultural, and it can take a lot of bravery and delicacy to be present with our deepest patterns, memories, or stored sensations. As I mentioned at the start of this book, I am not a medical professional, and I always suggest that anybody who is doing deep inner-work might find themselves best supported by a highly trained trauma or medical specialist. So listen within and take good care of your journey as you explore.

This exploration is designed to invite us to recognize how trauma—big or small—impacts our personal lives, in support of our growing self-awareness. Remember, implementing even the simplest practices on a regular basis can help to shift long-held trauma patterns that may be holding the reins of our lives.

Grab a journal and find somewhere quiet where you won't be interrupted—a safe space that feels cozy and comfortable.

Take a moment to arrive, and to create a nourishing atmosphere. If you have a candle, feel free to light it, or to change your space in any other way that will help you feel connected to yourself, to life, and to your spirit. Next, sit or lie down in a relaxed position and bring your awareness to your breath. Just notice where in your body your breath is naturally residing. Next, begin to lengthen your breath, inhaling deeply through your nose and exhaling through your mouth. With each exhalation, let out any distractions or sensations from the day, so that gradually, you become more present to the activity at hand.

Next, we'll take an inventory of our bodies.

If it's comfortable for you, close your mouth and start breathing in and out of your nose only. Nostril breathing is more focusing, and can be more supportive for neurocognition and physiology. Continue to lengthen your breath, feeling the way your inhales and exhales move through your physical form. Let the body relax and soften, so that the breath itself is leading the movement.

Close your eyes, and begin to visualize your breath as light. With the pure, bright light of your breath, scan your body from the crown of your head slowly down through your whole energetic being, or your chakra system, if you're familiar with it. Scan very slowly, feeling the light of your breath moving from the top of your head, to the center of your forehead, to the throat, to the heart area, stomach region, pelvic floor, and down through the legs to your feet. Feel the length of your spine, connected from the top to the bottom of your body. With the help of your breath, notice any areas of tension, discomfort, or numbness. Are there places where the breath moves through more comfortably, and others it skips over, or where you have less sensation, or that feel just too tight to let the breath in? Without ever forcing it, keep allowing your body to soften, simply feeling what's there. What sensations (or lack of sensations) do you have inside your tissues? Where is your physiology "flowing," and where does it feel stuck? Don't try to change your physical state; simply notice with a compassionate awareness.

Once you have a full, rich sense of how your body feels in this moment, gently call to mind a situation, event, or relationship that has felt stressful, whether now or in the past. It may feel most sensible to choose a less-intense source of distress, something that feels intuitively safe to explore, so that you can support yourself in this practice. When you bring your mind to this specific challenging or triggering situation, notice whether you're holding onto it or resisting it anywhere in your body. If you're not sure how to read your bodily sensations for any stress they might be holding, you can simply ask yourself whether any of the sensations or feelings in your body are linked to stress from past or present experiences.

Now, sense into your body for any general feelings of unease. For example, can you feel a pressure to get something done, or a fear that you aren't going to be able to meet your goals? Notice whether, beyond the event that might be triggering a physical response, the ecosystem of sensations and feelings in your body also contains limiting underlying beliefs about yourself.

To further hone the skills to better connect your body, mind, and feelings, bring your awareness back to something that's causing you stress or discomfort. This time, choose something that's distressing you in the present moment. And remember, let your own body and awareness be your guide, and if a certain situation feels like too much, listen to your body's cues and take care to protect your well-being. Remember, it can often be best to work on our triggers in the presence of a professional or trained guide.

As you bring your awareness to this challenge in your present life, notice what happens to your breath and how your body responds. Do you want to move, change gears, do something else? Do you feel physically weighted down or de-energized, like you could go to sleep? Or do you feel something fiery inside, as though you're ready to defend yourself in a physical fight? How much energy is moving through you—or, alternatively, how depleted does your energy feel? Run your awareness again from head to toe. What are you holding? Do your shoulders feel tight? Do your bones or joints feel strained or achy? Do you feel a knot in your stomach, or pain in your lower back? Does any part of your body long for relief? What's going on inside?

There's now an opportunity to go even deeper, into the past—if you feel comfortable. Before proceeding, always remember to respect your own limits and needs. If you would like to take this investigation further, bring to mind a specific difficult aspect or incident from your earlier life. This might be a chronic source of distress, or a specific injury or event that felt shocking, painful, or life-changing. For example, you might recollect a particularly bad breakup, the loss of someone you love, a car accident, a financial loss, or growing up in a verbally abusive or impoverished household. Whatever you choose, advance slowly and listen carefully for any warning signs of acute distress in your body. Remember, if any exploration ever begins to feel like too much to access, take pause and prioritize tending to your physiological needs. This might mean that it's safer for you to either not explore these early memories on your own, but rather with the support of a trained therapist.

As you continue with this exploration, try to stay with your breath and your body's response, rather than your mind's incessant chatter. How does your stomach feel? How does your pelvic floor feel? Your heart? Can you connect to the energy of love or light moving through you? Notice your breath.

Staying with this challenging memory, now fill your sense of being with the energy of life, of self-connection, of appreciation for your vitality. Say to yourself, internally or aloud, "I trust myself now. I am okay now. I did the best I could. I can take care of myself." How does your body respond to these self-affirming phrases? If you notice intellectual resistance, keep reciting these phrases until they sink into your tissues and you feel them in your body, rather than just responding to them intellectually.

Now, as you remain in this energy, take a few notes on how you feel, describing your sensations in your own words. In your journal, write briefly about the physical sensations, memories, connections, or insights you've made during this exploration.

When you've finished writing, remind yourself that you are not in that space any longer; rather, you are exploring the experience in order to transform, heal, and create greater nourished joy in your life. Connect to your breath again, or feel your feet on the floor, or if you've lit a candle, look at its flame to remind yourself of the warmth and connection available to you now.

When you feel safe and grounded, review your words. Do the descriptions of what it feels like to recall that trauma seem familiar to you? Are these feelings you often notice yourself having in response to other, unrelated situations, or, for example, when you feel stressed or frustrated? Are these common ways your body begins to close down and keep life, opportunity, energy, and curiosity from coming in? Might your reactions to life's events sometimes be distorted by past traumas still playing out in your nervous system? How can you bring more awareness to the sensations that arise when you feel triggered, so you can notice if an old pattern is repeating? And how can your body help you navigate so that you learn from the past and create a life that feels safe?

Remember, we want to simply notice these connections, without making judgments about ourselves or deciding that any of our feelings are "right" or "wrong," or that we need to change ourselves. Greater self-awareness is the only goal of this exercise—because, in fact, self-awareness is the essential first step toward shifting and transforming our outdated patterns.

To close our exploration, let's amp up the energy of self-compassion and reassurance. When we go to these places in the past that have informed our current behavior, we're often working with parts of ourselves that are suspended in childhood, parts that have been "sent away" and not allowed to feel or express themselves. When we deal with these tender parts, we want to be extra kind to them. Treat yourself like a gentle guardian would treat a baby—softly, and with soothing kindness. Place your hand on your heart, take a deep breath, and listen in to hear which self-nourishing words might support you now. Now, say those words to yourself, silently or aloud. You might say something like "I am safe," or, "I am valuable," or, "It's okay to feel this way." These might be words you never heard when you were younger, or words your soul needs to hear but which were never honestly spoken. Take this time to parent yourself now.

To close, visualize a safe place, real or imagined, that brings you a sense of security and peace. This is a space where your body feels calm, supported, and relaxed. Remind yourself that you are a creator and can build any world you wish for your inner- and outer-states. You can create the inner- and outer-resources to live at peace with yourself. Spend a moment basking in the feeling of safety and comfort you can create for yourself. Practice letting go of all other responsibilities beyond simply being in this moment and feeling exactly as you are. If you wish to journal further, go ahead!

Try repeating this practice a few times a week for a season, to help you integrate past experiences and gain self-soothing skills and a greater sense of felt presence. Over time, you may notice that your emotional responses or your patterns of tension change, and that you're more skilled in responding with self-compassion when you feel emotionally or physically triggered.

EXPLORATION 6:
Visualizing What "Feeling Safe" Means for You
In this exploration, we'll follow some simple steps to find a sense of what "safety" means to your whole being.

In a world where we are so often encouraged to "be strong" and "take action," we can sometimes override the tenderest parts of ourselves—the parts that have strong emotional responses or sensitivities. In this exploration, we get to unpack what "safety" means to us on a physiological level, in our nervous systems and also our spirits and souls.

Feeling safe allows us to create boundaries and a sense of self-respect, and ultimately is key to embracing who we are, which we can only do when we feel safe to be ourselves. Learning what safety feels like for us enables us to prioritize building safe relationships with others, with our work, and throughout all areas of our life.

Step 1: Visualize and Connect with Your Strength

- Find a quiet space to sit comfortably, close your eyes, and take a few deep breaths.
- Now, imagine yourself in a powerful moment when you felt incredibly strong and accomplished. It could be at work, with family, or at the moment of a personal achievement.
- See the details of the scene. Visualize where you are, what you're doing, and how you feel. Notice the inner-energy and power that you can connect to in this moment.

Step 2: Visualize and Connect with a Felt Sense of Safety

- Now let's shift focus to the energy of safety. Imagine a safe and nurturing environment where you feel completely secure. This might be a place from your past, or an imagined space that feels comforting.
- Engage your senses. Notice the sights, sounds, smells, and textures of this safe space. Feel the warmth and protection it offers.
- Notice how the energy of safety feels in your body. Allow this energy to fill you up and nourish your whole being.

Step 3: Combine Strength and Safety

- Bring your powerful self to this safe space. Picture yourself as the strong, powerful woman you visualized earlier, now standing in this safe and nurturing environment.
- Notice how your strength and your sense of safety can coexist. Feel the balance between your powerful self and the comfort of the safe space.

Step 4: Define Safety for Yourself

- Ask yourself, "In this nourished state, what does safety mean to me?" Allow any thoughts, images, or feelings to arise without judgment.
- Create a symbol you can bring out of this exercise and into your life. What shape, color, or object comes to mind when you feel into your sense of safety? What symbol comes forth, to embody your unique sense of security?
- See the symbol glowing. Picture this symbol of safety glowing and integrating into your powerful self, reinforcing your inherent strength with a sense of safety.
- Any time you feel triggered—whether you're anxious, concerned, feeling negative, short of breath, or physically uncomfortable—this symbol can support you to take inventory of your sensations, listen to your body, and create safety for yourself—whether internally or externally.

If it feels helpful, take some time to draw your symbol or write about this topic more in your journal.

EXPLORATION 7:

Healing the Story of Unsafety

In Exploration 6, we focused on tuning in to the value of feeling a sense of safety in our bodies. In Exploration 7, we're ready to heal the stories we may hold about not being safe—and specifically those stories that were seeded in our very early years. Again, this exploration should be done with the most ginger care. It can often be more helpful to do deep early-childhood processing in the presence of a trained professional. Listen to yourself pristinely and proceed mindfully through this practice. At any point during this exploration, if you have the sense that you feel overstimulated or uncomfortable, take pause. This may be a sign that it is safer for your body and being to do this work in the supportive space provided by a trained professional.

Ideally, it can be best to try to work with our earliest memories in this exploration, as they are often the most deeply seated in our self-perpetuating patterns. Perhaps it might be best to pick something simpler, a general moment where you may have felt uncomfortable or concerned as a young child. This could be a single memory, or something that happened repeatedly. For example, perhaps you felt scared of the dark, so you hid under the bed or under the covers, or ran into your parents' room at night. Or perhaps you remember a time when you suddenly began to second-guess your environment, or felt uneasy around someone. We can experience unsafety as a physical, mental, or emotional sensation, or even as a behavior that emerges as a coping mechanism. However the experience was for you as a child, this exploration will focus on a memory you would like to heal.

Before we begin, it is important to again stress that accessing frightening or lingeringly difficult memories from the past can be triggering. If you begin to feel distressed, it is advised to seek the support of a health professional rather than dive deep into uncomfortable sensations on your own. Listen to yourself wisely.

Step 1: Ground and Connect

- Find a quiet space where you won't be disturbed. Sit or lie down in a comfortable position, close your eyes, and take a few deep breaths.
- Stay with your breath and ground yourself by imagining roots extending from the base of your body down into the Earth, stabilizing you. Now, imagine those roots sending a bright white light through your feet into the core of the Earth. Concentrate on growing the felt sense of a deep, energetic connection to the Earth, and the ground beneath you.

Step 2: Visualize and Connect with Your Strength

- Connect with your strongest, most empowered energy by calling in either a time when you felt powerful, confident, and accomplished, or the energetic power of your greatest sense of self-confidence. In this vision, picture a vibrant energy emanating through you from the inside out.
- As you picture yourself, absorb the energy of your strength, even if it feels foreign to see yourself this way. Allow the vision and the energy to fill you up, seeing yourself glowing with empowerment. With the support of your breath, cultivate the felt sense of confidence and power within you.

Step 3: Connect with the Unsafe Little Girl Inside You

- In your imagination, travel back through time until you reach your oldest memory of feeling "unsafe."
- Welcome that little girl in your mind's eye, as the younger version of you or even a part of you that hides. Connect to her more deeply by inviting her to take part in this experience with you now. Reaffirm to her that you are with her now, and that she is okay; you are safe. Gently acknowledge this part of yourself. You might say internally, "I see you, and I am here to listen and support you."

Step 4: Recognize Your Unsafe Little Girl as Your Teacher

- Ask the little girl what's happening for her, and what she needs to feel safe. Listen to her and accept her feelings, just noticing. Allow any thoughts, feelings, or images to arise without judgment.
- Compassionately reassure her that you're with her, that you won't leave her, and that you have her back. Let her know, "You are safe now. I am here to protect and nurture you."
- Appreciate the gift your unsafe part is giving you by showing up and sharing with you now. Recognize her as your teacher.

Step 5: Integrate Your Empowered and Vulnerable Selves

- Now integrate your vulnerable self with your empowered self by imagining these two vital parts of you connecting. Remember they are both extremely intelligent and valuable.

- Take a moment to absorb the energy of them reaching to each other. See them embracing and merging into one empowered self: your nourished, full, felt sense of self-connection.

Step 6: Absorb the Integration of Your Vulnerable Self

- Affirm your experience by taking a few moments to absorb what has happened. Tell yourself, "I am safe. I am whole. I can be both strong and vulnerable. I can transition into my life and through the moments of my day trusting that I can let all of myself be present, and that, together, all my parts work for my greatest safety and most nourished life."
- Breathe the energy of joy—the deeply nourished, spirited sense of love—into your body. Which sensations do you notice when you bring the energy of nourished joy into your body? Which qualities do you notice? How does your skin feel, your belly, your heart? Allow these feelings to energetically imprint in your being so that you can locate them whenever you need to feel nourished and self-connected.

Step 7: Record This Experience in Your Journal

- Take a moment to journal about any insights and feelings that came up during this practice. Recording the experience will help reinforce the connection and understanding of your need for safety.

By recognizing and embracing both your strong and your vulnerable parts, you can create a more integrated and balanced sense of safety in your being and in your life. This practice allows you to honor your need for security while also celebrating your strength and resilience.

EXPLORATION 8:

Love—A Neuroplastic Opportunity to Nourish Our Lives

This practice is designed to support the activation of new neural pathways in your brain; it can take just one minute, or expand to take as long as you wish. Integrate it daily at random or regular intervals to create a state of well-being that's nourished from the inside out.

First, bring one hand to your heart and the other to your belly. Now repeat the following mantra five to ten times, aloud if you can, but internally works just fine too: "I am in charge of my mental experience. I accept whatever I'm feeling. I am capable, and I love myself."

Keeping your hands on your heart and belly, check in with your body. Can you access the feeling of safety in your body right now? What about the energies of inspiration, passion, joy, and interest?

Now ask yourself two questions:

- How do I feel in my current immediate physical environment?
- How do I feel in the town or city I'm in?

If your system tells you that you are in true physical or psychological danger in your current environment, that is your signal to change your setting and seek a more inviting, safe-feeling space prior to proceeding with this exploration. Otherwise, take this opportunity to notice the abundance around you and what is working for you in this environment. Allow your awareness to rest on these gifts. Remember that even if you habitually hold frustrating beliefs or feelings about your environment, you are in charge of how you perceive your reality. If you so choose, you can shift your perspective at any time and change your relationship to the space around you—at no cost!

To facilitate an expansive mindset shift, connect to your breath. Begin by simply noticing the breath, then start to lengthen it, feeling it fill your body and move more fully through your being. Notice any sensations you can let go of on your exhalations. The transformative power of breath makes it possible to shift even a physiological state that might have felt hard to shake.

Now envision the breath as light. Visualize your breath as a light that spreads first through your body, then into your physical space, for instance the room you're in. The expansion of the light is seamless, safely connecting your full, well-bounded, well-protected, embodied self to the energy of the space around you, the town or city you're in, and even the whole Earth. See that you are protected and that you have the power to take in only what nourishes you. Notice that you can soften your resistance to the space around you and receive the love it has to offer. Trust that you are stronger than whichever negative stories you might make up about your physical self and your environment.

Now, cultivate the energy of love in your body and in the space around you. First, seek the energy of love within you, using the breath as your guide. Even if the energetic sense of love feels muted or small at first, breathe it into your body, into the space around you, and into your greater environment.

Now ask, out loud or internally, "What would it take for me to feel more love right now? And how can I dial more deeply into the expansion of love?" Notice any places you tend to make yourself small in your own body and in your relationship to the environment. Notice any ways you're conditioned to either give up on or refuse receiving the energy of love, collapsing yourself into a story of failure or unworthiness, whether in your relationship with your body, with your immediate space, or with the greater environment you reside in.

Now tap more profoundly into the energy of the universe, which wants you to receive deep, divine, universal love. Feel that invitation. Feel the natural energy of love that is available to you. Tell yourself again, out loud or internally, "I have everything I need. I trust in what I have. I trust I can be generous with myself and others. I trust I can receive love. I trust that there is no end to love—and I can safely connect to its endlessness."

Having repeated these phrases, turn your attention back to your inner-state. Can you feel any shift? Notice that, just as you can stretch your body in the morning, you can stretch your mind to let in more life, more breath, more light, and more love.

EXPLORATION 9:
Nourishing the "Normal Task"—Bringing Awareness to the Way We Habitually Address Ourselves

In this exploration, we'll create more self-awareness around the ways we treat ourselves in our daily habits, as well as the ways we treat our environment and our relationships. The Path of Nourish is truly about how we relate—and since the "mundane" aspects of life are where most of our days unfold, it is a powerful place to learn to nourish ourselves and our relational styles. Nourishing the normal task allows us to create greater presence and awareness in our daily habits, which helps us grow the energy of appreciation and gratitude—in turn, allowing us to feel nourished and make nourishing choices.

Give yourself about ten minutes to explore the following steps.

Step 1: Reflect on a Daily Task

- Think of something you do every day—something that feels like a simple, mundane responsibility, like washing dishes, sweeping a floor, folding clothing, brushing your teeth, or organizing work meetings.
- Reflect on how you usually approach this task. Do you show up already only semi-present (for example, looking at your phone, or with your thoughts elsewhere)? As you begin the task, are you already rushing to get to the end? Is your impatience physically uncomfortable? Do you tell yourself that this "thing" is just not fun, and there is no joy for you to feel in it? What do you tell yourself about your life or your abilities as you complete the task? Is there any underlying storyline that you "always make a mess" or "just can't slow down"; that you're "always disorganized" or you "never do this right"? While you're completing this task, do you focus on something you dislike in your environment, or alternatively tell yourself there's something you can't even bear to look at? Or do you tell yourself that something about you, yourself, is hideous? Do you have a hard time being fully present, because that would mean having to look at yourself, and that would be uncomfortable? Do you believe something is disgusting or dissatisfying about yourself or this task?
- As you imagine this task, try to notice and familiarize yourself with the thoughts and feelings that might be robbing you of enjoying all you are and all you have.

Step 2: Bring Mindful Awareness to the Task

- Now see yourself pausing before you start the task, taking a deep breath, putting your hand on your heart, and offering yourself whichever of the following mantras feels right to you:
  - "I take great care of my life and I can perform this activity as though it is a choreographed dance with the universe."
  - "It is an honor that my spirit gets to interact with the physical world."
  - "Taking care of my life is a gift I get to give myself."
  - "I trust that I can organize my energy to be present and connected to this moment."

- Now envision yourself performing this normal task, and as you watch, take a deep breath, feeling the air fill your lungs. Tell yourself on repeat, "It's okay." Whatever discomfort you often bring to this task, it's okay, you're okay, and your life is okay!

- As you continue to envision yourself completing this task, invite yourself to become more present by fully inhabiting one or more of your senses. For example, if you're imagining brushing your teeth, notice the taste and feel of the toothpaste. If you're making tea, focus on the scent of the tea leaves as they steep. If your senses settle into a story of displeasure (for example, that you don't love the way the dishwater feels on your hands or how it feels to stand on your feet while you clean), practice neutralizing this sensation and taking the big story out of it. This way, you can simply be present to reality rather than bringing a negative internal narrative to activities in your life.

Step 3: Infuse the Task with Appreciation

- Make a plan to create a positive intention next time you engage the task you're envisioning. For example, before setting out to do a chore, you might say, "I appreciate this moment," or, "I bring my whole self here. I can settle into this activity. This is part of life," or even, "I will bring joy to this activity."
- Make a plan to find your gratitude for the opportunity to participate in this task. For example, if you set out ten minutes to prepare a quick meal, rather than feeling irritated by being called away from whatever you were doing, reflect on your good fortune in having food abundantly available to you. Think about how hard everyone (including yourself) has worked to bring this food to you.
- Next time you engage your chosen task, connect to the energy of gratitude, recognizing that this mundane activity (even peeling carrots, for example, or cleaning the stovetop) is a high spiritual homage. Consider running grateful phrases through your mind, such as, "I am grateful for the chance to take care of myself," or "I appreciate this moment to nourish my well-being."

Step 4: Reflect and Appreciate

- Create a plan to pause and reflect after completing your task with gratitude and presence. Take note of any changes in your mood or energy levels. Notice how a simple task can either decrease or increase your sense of well-being. Take your power back from any negative idea or relationship you've created around this task and, instead, thank it as a teacher. Take a moment to thank yourself for the genius ability you have as a creator of your attitude and actions.

When you mindfully engage with your tasks in this way, remember that the goal is simply to do your best. Even if you don't think you did a "perfect" job of loving your activity, recognize the beauty of the steps you took and anything you were able to observe. Silently or out loud, acknowledge the effort you've put into performing your task mindfully. You might also find it helpful to notice any areas you'd like to place more awareness next time—but even in these instances, make sure to accept yourself in full, just as you are. Appreciate the ways this simple act contributes to your well-being and daily life.

It's important to remember that even the most brilliant movers and shakers in the world can struggle to change their most basic habits. Be tender and give yourself time. Trust in yourself! By bringing mindful awareness and appreciation to your daily tasks, you can transform mundane activities into opportunities for joy, connection, presence, and appreciation. This practice helps you nourish your mind, body, soul, and spirit, fostering a deeper sense of fulfillment in your everyday life.

EXPLORATION 10:
Accessing the Higher Self

Grab a journal for this exploration! Here, we will work on cultivating the space to regularly ask ourselves the profound question, "What would my higher self do?" This question alone has the power to help us shift out of behaviors that do not nourish our whole sense of being.

First, identify and write down something you'd consider a "non-nourishing experience." This could be any habit or pattern that you engage in despite knowing it doesn't nourish you on a body, mind, spirit, or soul level. It could be something like negative self-talk, overworking, not having compassion for yourself in a specific area of your life, moving too quickly in general, feeling impatient, or reaching for unhealthy foods when stressed.

Once you've written your non-nourishing behavior or pattern down, ask yourself, "How does this behavior really make me feel?" Take a moment to reflect on this, and on any negative self-concept this behavior enforces. When you go to this behavior, or after enacting it, does it make you feel guilty, ashamed, or unworthy? Does even thinking about it make you feel bad about yourself? Write down your feelings. Even if the behavior itself seems minor and inconsequential, if it brings with it a giant feeling of dis-ease, personal failure, or sadness—and if it makes you feel bad about yourself and your life—then it is a behavior worth investigating.

Next, let's work to understand the origins of this non-nourishing behavior, by asking yourself, "When did it start?" Think back to the first time you remember choosing this behavior. What were the circumstances? Was there a particular event or time in your life that triggered this pattern? Did you see this behavior modeled around you? Was there a period when things were confusing, for example, and you internalized the confusion—and it became this behavior? Or was there a period of high pressure when you felt a need to escape the discomfort—and this was a way to quell your feelings? Or did you feel bored, limited by the people or environment around you, or that your imagination wasn't being met—and this behavior became a way to fill up your sense of emptiness or boredom?

It might be difficult to discern exactly why this specific behavior arose, but write down any thoughts that come up. For example, did the behavior seem entertaining? Or rewarding? Did it give you something to do? Was it physically comforting? What made your subconscious select it as a habitual pattern? What did the behavior help you cope with? How did it provide temporary relief or comfort?

Now let's consider which stories about yourself the behavior was perpetuating. How did this behavior, at the same time as offering relief or escape or comfort, stimulate a negative self-concept you already held, such that this also became part of the cycle? What's familiar about that perpetuated negative self-concept? For example, if someone in your family left you feeling confused, and you turned to food, then you noticed that afterward you felt less clear, energized, or even good about yourself—then was your behavior playing out that relational self-degrading pattern? Whatever discomfort you feel your behavior initially answered, do you still feel that discomfort in your life? Does this pattern still help you with that discomfort—or is it just an empty habit that doesn't do much for you anymore? Answer these questions in your journal as fully as you can.

Now, close your eyes and drop into your body. Connect to your higher sense of self—the part of you that is here to be of best service to your spirit and soul's journey; a part of you that is rooted in love for yourself and others. This higher self is the part of you that never disconnects from your own deepest needs and resonance and is inherently connected to the universe, always respecting life deeply— especially your own life. Ask this higher sense of self for support here. Ask her to help you visualize a different choice you can make in the same situation—or ask for some words that will help you to align with what you really need.

Ask your higher self now, "What do you need to feel grace, to feel life's beauty and love? What do you need to feel valuable? How can you fill up on love instead of hurting yourself with maladaptive behaviors that enforce a negative self-concept? What are you really craving? What do you need to know about yourself or life in order to create a more nourishing inner- and outer-environment?" If you don't know what you need, ask your higher self for support now, so that you can begin to hear your own deeper needs.

Feel what it's like to sit with your higher self—as though your being is literally nested in her light and presence. Then, together with your higher self, imagine engaging in a nourishing activity that supports your well-being. This might be anything from resting in meditation to moving, from taking care of your body to a more expansive activity that lights up your spirit and feels soul-connecting. Just ask what you need, and see what comes up.

Staying with this vision and your connection to your higher self, feel into your whole being—your body, mind, and spirit. See how connecting to your higher self helps you to feel safer in your body; more relaxed, connected, and capable. Absorb the positive emotions and sense of fulfillment that come from choosing a nourishing path. See how this nourished life is safe to connect to—see how you deserve to feel good! You can live your life choosing the things that make you feel more alive, and overcoming your self-limiting beliefs and behaviors.

Now, write down up to ten ways you can nourish yourself—things that will support you to transcend your non-nourishing behaviors. These nourishing choices could be activities that bring you joy, relaxation, or a sense of accomplishment. It might mean calling on an expert in the area where you often find yourself collapsing, and asking for help or insight. This might mean integrating activities into your life that will build you vibrance, for example, making time—no matter how hectic life may feel—to take a walk, have a call with a friend, or practice deep breathing.

These little nourishing moments might include meditating, reading a book, enjoying a healthy snack, taking a long hot shower, curling up to grab a catnap, listening to music, doing a creative activity, or simply wandering into the day without a plan, but with a vision for adventure and fun.

From your list, choose just one activity to practice. The next time you find yourself tempted by the non-nourishing habit, consider this activity instead. Work with your higher self and, with her support, commit to giving it a try. And remember that it's always important to listen within, to hear what will nourish our unique physiology at any given moment. Life is change, so naturally, what nourishes you will change.

Each day, you can set an intention to recognize and shift non-nourishing patterns. Remind yourself that you have the power to make choices that support your highest self. It can be helpful to dedicate five minutes at the end of each day to reflect on the choices you made that day, and how nourishing they were for you. Did you choose activities that ultimately made you feel better or worse about yourself, and why? By engaging in this exploration, you will cultivate greater self-awareness. From here, you can transform non-nourishing habits into opportunities for growth and self-care. This practice helps you align with your highest self, fostering a deeper sense of empowerment and well-being in your everyday life.

EXPLORATION 11:
Making a Breath Altar of Self
This practice to deepen your relationship with your breath can take just five minutes, or you can expand it to take as long as you like. Practicing it regularly will help

you to enter into a more aware relationship with the most constant activity in your life: breathing.

First, find a quiet, comfortable place where you can safely close your eyes, undisturbed, and check in with yourself mentally and emotionally. Once you feel you have dropped in, take an inventory of how you're feeling right now. On a scale of one to ten, rate the level of stress you're currently feeling, with one being the lowest stress and a state of calm and focus, and ten meaning you feel significantly stressed out. Write this rating down somewhere.

Next, find a comfortable position, either sitting or lying down, and begin to connect with your breath. Spend about three minutes cultivating your awareness of your breath. When done regularly, focusing on the breath in this way helps us to nourish our whole state of being.

Take a moment to dial into a rhythm of breathing: Inhale deeply through your nose for a count of four, hold for four, exhale for four, and hold the breath out for four. You may have encountered this pattern, often called "box breathing," before. It nourishes us by activating the sympathetic nervous system when we hold the inhale, increasing alertness and focus. The exhale and holding the out-breath then support the activation of the parasympathetic nervous system, which helps to promote relaxation and reduce stress. Being able to flow between these states with ease can support the overall health of the nervous system.

Repeat this cycle for a few minutes.

After box breathing, we'll shift to a second pattern, which supports the parasympathetic nervous system, our "rest and digest" function, and our capacity for feeling both self-connected and connected our lives. You'll now inhale for a slow count of four, and when you get to the top, don't hold; instead, exhale for a count of seven. At the end

241

of your exhalation, work toward holding the breath out for eight counts. Take five breaths in this manner, resting your awareness on staying with your breath.

Notice how you feel after breathing this way. Can you feel a deeper sense of relaxation and calm?

Anytime you start to feel triggered, you can remember to implement this breath, 4–7–8. Give yourself the gift of breath to support your mental and emotional state. It's an unbelievably effective tool for behavioral transformation—and even better, it's extremely simple, and it costs nothing.

EXPLORATION 12:
Choose a Small Commitment for a Big Outcome

In this exploration, we'll observe how making small commitments can have significant long-term benefits for the body, mind, soul, and spirit.

Start by connecting to your breath and body. Notice what your breath is like now, and begin to elongate your breathing. Take five to ten breaths, allowing each one to connect you more deeply with your sensations. Notice how your body expands as you inhale and relaxes as you exhale. Simply by breathing, you are already reducing stress in your body and enhancing your brain function.

Make a list either in your mind or (better yet) in your journal noting ten simple, small, and achievable activities that you think would holistically support you to feel healthier, more energized, more positive, and more connected to life. Some examples might include reading a book before bed instead of using your phone, taking a daily walk, drinking a glass of water first thing in the morning, practicing gratitude by writing down three things you're thankful for each day, or stretching for a few minutes after waking up. Or perhaps, for you, the most powerful changes would include less screen time in general, meditating for five minutes daily, listening to calming music, letting go of irritation about something you can't control, creating more time to prepare a nourishing meal, journaling your thoughts and feelings, spending a few minutes in sunlight, or having a tech-free meal.

When you have your list of ten small, simple changes, consider what it would take for you to integrate each of these habits into your life. You might ask yourself why it has been difficult for you to do things differently; to integrate little, supportive acts of self-care. Have you experienced some resistance to introducing these changes? Think about how your current lifestyle and behaviors make you feel, and which energies you might invite into your life if you introduce some new, nourishing activities. Ask yourself what has held you back from making choices that support your inner-nourishment, and what you might need in order to choose your personal well-being.

Commit to making one small change—something that feels achievable rather than intimidating or unrealistic. Create an accountability system, so you can regularly check in and make sure you're staying committed. For example, you could find a goal-setting partner and update them regularly on your progress, or make daily notes and create a reward system for yourself, or set reminders on your phone. Speak your commitment aloud or internally! Even better, look in the mirror and speak your commitment while gazing into your own eyes. Finish by saying to yourself, "In just a few minutes, I can make small commitments that have significant long-term benefits for my body, mind, soul, and spirit. This is how heroes live their lives, and I am my own hero." Consider yourself the parent of your behaviors, supporting yourself to create small steps in the right direction.

Consistently taken, your small steps will lead to substantial positive changes in your overall well-being. Notice what happens when you introduce just one new commitment to your life and integrate it into your day, your week, or even your month. Make sure to celebrate any steps you take toward behavioral change, as this will positively reinforce their effects.

EXPLORATION 13:

Recognizing Beauty in the Core Areas of Your Life

Can you remember the last time you felt the kind of joy that comes without any pressure to get somewhere or achieve a goal you set for yourself? If so, when was it? What were the circumstances? And if not, would you like to increase the joy in your life? This exercise is designed to help you recognize and appreciate the beauty in core areas of your life, through a simple, five-minute daily practice.

Choose one core area of your life to work with each time you do this exploration. For example, you might choose your personal relationships (with your family, friends, or partner); your relationship to your work or career; your personal growth or hobbies; your health and well-being; your home environment; or any other area that matters to you.

Next, find a quiet space where you won't be disturbed, and bring your awareness to your breath. Let your breath elongate and fill your whole body. Take five full breaths in and out, focusing only on following the breath.

Now, call to mind the core area of your life that you've chosen to work with. Reflect on any beauty you recognize in this area—and specific memories or general qualities of this area that bring you joy and appreciation. Despite any challenges you've felt or any feelings of lack you might have, think about the positives in this area of your life. Reflect on what makes this part of your life meaningful to you, leaving any negative associations aside for just a few minutes. Do you have a wonderful sibling, for example, or a friend who is a great listener? Maybe you have a neighbor who is particularly helpful, or a job that engages your most effortless gifts, or perhaps a physical stamina that has always come effortlessly to you. Whichever area you've chosen, contemplate what is working for you there.

Staying connected to your body and breath, see if you can more deeply access and even expand any feelings of gratitude and joy you have about this part of your life. Let these feelings expand within you.

Next, silently or out loud, express appreciation for this core area. For example, you might say, "I am so thankful to have family in this lifetime," or, "I appreciate the opportunities my work brings to me," or, "I'm so thankful I've been able to grow and learn as much as I have."

After you've grown your sense of appreciation and gratitude, take a moment to notice what you're feeling on the physiological level. Do you feel lighter, more energized, more stimulated in your body?

Set an intention to return to this feeling and this gratitude throughout your day. Notice how your thinking starts to shift when you carry this sense of appreciation with you. You could even commit to a five-minute gratitude and appreciation exercise daily, focusing on a different core area each day or before bedtime each night, connecting lovingly to this energy, and journaling about the experience if you choose. This practice might seem simple, but a felt sense of gratitude has been proven to transform health and help in the cultivation of joy and connection.

The more you can recognize and appreciate the beauty in the core areas of your life through this simple practice, the more positive transformation you will invite into these areas.

EXPLORATION 14:
Cultivating a Check-in Time with the Body
In just five or ten minutes a day, this practice will help you to check in with your body to support you to feel a greater embodied presence in your life.

Step 1: Set Aside Time

- It's important to commit to a regular time to pause and check in with yourself. It could be first thing in the morning, during a lunch break, or before bed—whichever feels most likely for you to truly commit to.
- Think of this time as a gift to yourself; a moment to turn your attention inward, away from distractions, and focus on your internal state.

Step 2: Tune in to Your Body

- Sit comfortably and close your eyes. Bring your awareness to the length of your spine and take some deep breaths, following any sensations in your spine with your breath as a guide. Notice any areas of tension, relaxation, discomfort, or ease. Acknowledge these sensations without judgment. Simply observe how your body feels in the moment.
- Notice how your current thoughts or your mood are impacting your body's sensations, and how the breath and energy moving through you also impact your mind and body.
- Check in with your whole being to notice the connection between your mind, body, and spirit—the energy

moving through you. Tune in without trying to change anything; just observe.

Step 3: Reflect and Respond

- After scanning your body, stay with your breath and ask yourself how you are feeling emotionally and mentally. Listen for whatever surfaces.
- Stay with the breath to create an energy of acceptance. Rather than reacting to the feelings that arise by intellectualizing them, or responding with agitation, concern, worry, or the need to "rescue" or relieve your feelings, simply breathe and invite a sense of trust into your body. Settle into the feeling that you deeply trust yourself.
- Envision this energy of self-trust and self-connection as a light. As you breathe and stay with your sensations, run a brightening light of trust in yourself through your body, staying open to anything you notice and relating to your body the way you would listen to a dear friend, simply interested in whatever she has to share. Note any stressors that might be influencing your state. You might even get a "download" here about how you can best support yourself. Use the awareness you've cultivated to guide your actions for the rest of the day, remembering what it feels like in your body to be self-aware and connected to your sensations. By cultivating presence, you can access a greater felt sense of joy—and experience firsthand that self-compassion is your greatest ally.

EXPLORATION 15:

Let the Body Answer the Question "Is This Nourishing?"

On the most primal, bodily, and energetic level, we are constantly asking ourselves, "Is this safe?" The Path of Nourish might seem like a series of choices about "what we want," but on a fundamental level, we are actually feeling into our sense of trust. In order to make choices and safely navigate our environment, we need to learn that we can trust ourselves.

One of the best ways to naturally create healthy boundaries and strengthen our self-care is to learn to pause before making a choice. When we pause, we can feel into our inner-wisdom to discern whether an experience, relationship, or opportunity will be truly nourishing for us. When we practice listening to the body's responses, we are apt to make choices that nourish our lives while increasing self-trust, setting in motion a positive cycle that reinforces the belief that we can rely on ourselves.

But how do we cultivate a practice of regularly dropping in to hear our own best judgment? Here's a small exploration that will help.

Begin by finding a quiet space, ideally sitting or lying down comfortably. Connect to the divine guide of the breath. Breathing with awareness, invite the body to relax and settle in. Allow the breath to fill you with awareness from your head to your feet, relaxing more and more into the moment, trusting that you can let go of everything except your commitment to listen inwardly.

When you have fully settled in, bring to mind a specific situation where you feel you lost your sense of self-connection, or where your energy was negatively impacted. This might be an event, a relationship with a particular person, or even a place that had a detrimental effect on you. Notice how your body feels when you bring your awareness to this situation. Does your chest feel light or heavy? Is your stomach relaxed or tight? How is your breathing—deep and smooth, or shallow and erratic?

As you notice your reaction to this person, place, or event, ask yourself, "In this situation, how can I stay aligned with my need to feel safe?" Feel into what comes up for you.

Take time now to remind yourself that you are protected, you are safe, and you trust yourself to stay connected in the moment, even in situations that challenge you. Remember, challenging experiences aren't things we need to avoid; rather, they invite us to practice self-connection and presence even more intentionally. Remind yourself that you can continue to hear yourself whenever you engage with others or in your life experiences; that you have what you need to navigate situations while staying true to yourself.

Take a moment to reinforce your commitment to staying self-connected, telling yourself, "I prioritize myself. I will not collapse myself in response to any expectation another may have of me, or anything I think I need to do. I am already enough, just as I am. I trust myself to make the best, most nourishing choices for myself. I am valuable, I am protected, and I can protect myself."

EXPLORATION 16:
Broaden Your Emotional Vocabulary

It's often the case that we find it easier to extend our empathy to others than take the time to recognize or value our own feelings. For example, have you ever found yourself being able to advise a friend through a challenge, only to struggle to navigate the same challenge yourself? Or similarly, have you ever been able to seamlessly understand what a friend is feeling, but then found yourself mystified by your own emotions, leaving you feeling overwhelmed or stuck?

The power of our emotions combined with the seeming complexity of knowing what to do with them can lead us to disconnect from our emotions rather than sort them out. Instead of processing what we're feeling, we end up opting for familiar phrases like "I'm tired" or "I can't." But to truly grow, we must connect more deeply with ourselves, which makes it essential to broaden our emotional vocabulary. It's also important to create tolerance for our emotions without judging ourselves as "crazy," "hopeless," "worthless," or whichever other criticisms we have handy. And creating true self-trust and internal self-awareness also means learning to listen to our emotions without trying to solve them.

To practice exploring your own emotional bandwidth, check out the table of emotions below. This table is not meant to be exhaustive; it's simply a good place to start. Find a quiet space to sit or lie down comfortably. Connect to your breath and allow your body to relax and settle. Stay with your body's sensations, noticing the feelings that arise as you look at each of these words. As you read through the list, define each emotion in your own terms. See if you can connect to your own experience of this emotion, whether from a specific event or a general sense. As you work through them, aim to expand the range of emotions you can name and understand in your own life. Over time, this practice will help you develop greater self-compassion and resilience, as well as remind you that sometimes one emotion, such as anger, might be hiding other feelings, because just like every other part of our biology, emotions work together in a complex and beautiful ecosystem.

Emotion Chart

Happy	Sad	Angry
Excited	Fearful	Anxious
Confident	Frustrated	Content
Curious	Disappointed	Grateful
Guilty	Hopeful	Hurt
Jealous	Lonely	Proud
Relaxed	Relieved	Resentful
Stressed	Surprised	Uncertain
Vulnerable	Worried	Embarrassed
Ashamed	Envious	Overwhelmed
Inspired	Motivated	Bored
Annoyed	Peaceful	Nostalgic
Secure	Insecure	Elated
Devastated	Melancholic	Ecstatic
Optimistic	Pessimistic	Compassionate
Indifferent	Euphoric	Apprehensive
Detached	Empowered	

Remember, regularly identifying and acknowledging a wider range of emotions helps you to foster a richer understanding of your internal experience and build a more compassionate relationship with yourself. In this way, your emotions can be your teachers. If you reframe emotions as energy that wants to move through your body and mind to support your spiritual growth and help you claim your soulful gifts in this lifetime, you will begin to see that emotions provide information and offer insight. In fact, it is often the case that when we allow ourselves to feel into what we are experiencing—or, alternatively, when we can no longer tolerate ignoring or resisting our feelings—we create the conditions for change. It might take some time to get to know your emotional self, but connecting to our emotions rather than shutting them out directly supports us in creating nourishing lives, rather than lives filled with behaviors we use to numb out.

EXPLORATION 17:

Are You Resisting Your Body?

In this exercise, we'll explore any chronic patterns we fall into when listening to and interpreting our bodily sensations. This is a writing exploration, so grab a journal, find a comfy place, and dive in to the following investigations.

Getting Started

How would you describe your relationship with the self-care area of physical movement and exercise? What are your beliefs about this relationship? Think about how you take care of your body and how your body takes care of you. Which stories are you telling yourself about the way your body operates?

Self-Limiting Beliefs

Do you believe that your body is limited? Do you believe you are "not enough" in some way—not strong enough, athletic enough, coordinated enough—that keeps you from connecting to your body's needs or waking up a full range of expression in your body?

Body and Mind

Do you believe that your body and your mind work well together? If you aim to engage in a body-based activity, movement, or exercise, does your mind support your intention, or does it ever interfere with your body-oriented plans? And does your body keep up with your mind?

Energy

What is your body's relationship with receiving? Do you feel it can truly take in life's nutrients—the energy available to you in the form of sensations, feelings, and experiences? Does your body connect to the energy of your own "essence" as a resource? Does it welcome feeling spirited and open? And how does your body relate to change? Does your body leap before you look when it comes to new opportunities, or does it shudder in the face of transition? Does it sometimes move too fast or too slow, out of sync with your brain?

Recognizing and Understanding Your Fixed Beliefs about Your Body

In journaling about this topic, you may have identified some fixed beliefs about your body that may be working against you. Do these beliefs keep you, for example, from taking on new physical activities, or do you sometimes find yourself quitting before you begin, telling yourself you don't have the energy or enthusiasm to get into a particular sport? Do these beliefs keep you from loving yourself just as you are?

However, it's also worth considering the ways these body-oriented self-limiting ideas or behaviors might be working for you, strategically. For example, do you use any of your self-limiting beliefs as a way to relieve yourself from pressure, from the need to keep growing and taking risks, or even from accepting the responsibility of self-care? Do you find yourself saying, "I would do so-and-so, but there's something wrong with my body and I simply can't"? Do you blame your metabolism, your height, your legs, or your complexion for "holding you back"—while also secretly using these apparent "body issues" as a way to stay hidden, or avoid having to put yourself out there? Does your negative body narrative keep you from feeling happy, and so give you an excuse for feeling disappointed when something "inevitably" lets you down?

Learning to Listen to Your Body's Real Cues

Having investigated some of the negative or limiting beliefs you might hold about your body, now we'll begin to investigate what it would take to listen to your body's ever-shifting needs in the moment.

Consider these questions in your journal: How much do I pause to listen to what my body needs? Do I connect with my body by trying to control it? Do I ever let my body lead the way, asking it what would bring it the energy of true, inside-out joy? How spontaneous do I let my body be—letting my improvisation and creative energy move through my body? What might I fear about following the cues of my body? How willing am I to feel my physical sensations—especially if they are uncomfortable? Alternatively, do I let my body's sensations dictate my life? Am I constantly scanning my body, asking what's wrong and then trying to fix every sensation? Do I expect my body to work under my command at all times, like a slave to my mind?

Do I translate all of my bodily sensations into hunger cues? For example, do I soothe my physical discomfort, my energetic upset, and any emotional irritation or chronic pain with food, rather than moving energy through my body? Or do I use food to create physical energy that fuels my emotional upheaval? Am I trying to control my own feelings and resisting my natural feminine flow of energy through my body? Do I believe that my body works for or against me?

Calling in Your Own Listening

To close this exploration, we will investigate ways you can begin to shift your self-limiting beliefs about your body, and learn to really listen to its wisdom.

In your journal, consider the following questions: How might I create a way to listen to my body right now so that I do not feel defeated by my mind? What do I need to bring in greater support? Are there resources or people who can help me on my journey? How can I integrate small acts of self-care into my daily routine? For example, can I commit to specific times when I will connect with my breath, stretch, or offer my body something that nourishes it?

Finally, we'll identify some solid support that you can bring in to connect to your body regularly. Inspired by what you've learned in the course of this exercise, write some affirmations that are specifically for *you* and the way you want to connect with your body in the future. Examples might include, "I am worthy of self-care," "I am prioritizing listening to my body's needs," or "I have the strength to choose behaviors that empower my body."

Write your affirmations down and read them daily. Tape them to your mirror, your door, or anywhere you can regularly absorb them deep into your psyche.

With regular self-reflection, you can begin to shift your relationship with your body and make movement, exercise, and self-care integral and enjoyable parts of your life. Recognize that your body and you are in this together, and nurturing this relationship is the path to self-acceptance and self-love.

EXPLORATION 18:

Eating Is Sacred—Cultivating a Sacred Connection to Food

This exploration allows us to investigate any potential conflict or tension in our relationship to food. We all know that in relationships with people, it takes two to tango, and the way we show up to the relationship—the version of self that we bring—has a huge impact on the relationship's success. Equally, we all know that some relationships just seem to bring out the best or worst in us.

The same is true in our relationship with food. Sometimes, we might find ourselves in a chronically dysfunctional pattern with food and the way we eat, struggling to find a way to approach food without losing our integrity or getting lost in frustration, irritation, and even confusion. Specifically, we can observe how, when we connect with food, we bring our beliefs about who we are—just as we would to any other relationship. The way we relate to food exemplifies what we really believe about ourselves.

For example, no matter how successful we might seem on the outside, if, on the side, we believe that we are undeserving, impoverished, emotionally starved, or never getting what we really want—we will show up to food with these feelings. That's because food is a receptive space. It receives us, but it doesn't have a mind or the means to talk back. It's passive; it will never tell our secrets, and it can take all our blows—and of course, those blows are really aimed at ourselves. Simply put, our behaviors around food reflect our sense of self.

So let's explore. To start, think of a specific relationship, past or present, where you didn't feel that great about yourself. Maybe you felt ugly, unwanted, too much, or not enough around this person. Maybe you felt shut down, or on the contrary, always exploding. Perhaps you wanted to be calm and patient, but you found yourself impulsively responding with hurtful words. Maybe no matter what they said to you, everything felt like an attack. Or perhaps you wanted to like this person, but somehow, you could never relax around them. Consider the ways this relationship impacted you. For example, did you ever catch yourself in the mirror just after having an argument? What did you see then, and how did you feel about yourself? Or did you ever notice that, after an upsetting interaction with this person, you felt physically heavy, out of control, or drained?

Now think of a relationship, or even a single moment with someone, that felt truly nourishing. Maybe this person is in your life now, or maybe they're a distant acquaintance. Whoever it is, consider how your body felt around them when you felt the nourishing connection. Did you feel settled in their company and comfortable in your body? Did your connection simply feel organic? Was it easy to give your attention and be present? Maybe you shared a moment together that felt evocative, filled with wonder or awe. Perhaps you felt full of love or excitement. Think about what you believed about yourself in that shared space. Maybe you felt more confident, truly supported, and that you could accomplish whatever task you set out to do. Maybe things felt lighter, simpler, or clearer.

Now, let's consider how you feel when relating to various environments. For example, how does your relational energy shift if you are somewhere uncomfortable versus somewhere you find very welcoming? Imagine, for example, that you're at the Department of Motor Vehicles—or a place where you personally might not love the atmosphere. How does your body feel? What are the sensations of light and color that pass through it? How do your muscles feel?

Is there tension anywhere in your body? Now, by contrast, imagine that you're somewhere that feels spiritually alive for you—it could be anywhere from a dance space, a yoga studio, or a sacred place of worship. How does your body feel in this space? Are there any parts that feel especially open? Are you filled with any colors or specific sensations?

Now, in the same vein of inquiry, we'll consider how you feel when you relate to food. Imagine yourself approaching a meal. Do you feel about yourself the way you'd feel with a foe, or a friend? Which parts of yourself do you let come out? Supposing that food is abundantly available and always accessible to you—how do you treat this secure, ever-welcoming relationship? Does your shadow come out? Are you mean to food—wasteful, ignorant even? When you eat, do you forget about where your food has come from? Do you stop before you eat to appreciate the weeks, seasons, or years it took to cultivate the food you're eating? Do you believe, when you go to food, that you "need it," that you "have to have it"—do you find yourself grasping or letting yourself be a little greedy?

Do you let go of your appearances, of any formalities, in your relationship with food? Do you allow a less "put-together" version of yourself to play out in your relationship with food? Is there some part of you that's so exhausted by having to be perfect and do things "right" that you take out your overwhelm on a bag of chips—even though it ultimately just means beating up your own body? Is food your punching bag, or your silent therapist? If you feel bullied by food—as though you can't get enough, or that it always wins—how do you play into that relationship? Finally, do you have ravenous desires that you only allow yourself to express in your relationship with food and if so, in which areas of your life do you keep yourself from feeling or showing desire?

As we investigate our relationship with food, it can help to get creative. Ask yourself, if you were watching an action movie starring you and food in an entangled relationship, what would happen in the scene where you and food meet? Would you bump into food at a dirty saloon, with cowboy boots on, ready to kick butt and let food know who's boss? Or would you meet at a roadside bottomless buffet, where no one knows your name or has seen you before—meaning you can grab seconds, thirds, and fourths and keep eating until you can't move? Would you meet food at the center of an intense fire ceremony and consume it scalding hot from the flames, ignoring the pain as you burn yourself, eating like a primal animal?

Or maybe your food-movie is more of an emotional drama. If so, can you imagine the theme? Would you and food be in a serious makeup then breakup cycle? Would you be the abusive partner in your relationship but blame food for never being enough? Would you be exhausted, wishing you could end your marriage to food because your problems feel unresolvable, but stuck in a dysfunctional entanglement, because you can't stop relying on it? Would you be bitter because you couldn't get out of the relationship? Would you feel guilty because food provided you with so much and you just consumed it without giving anything in return? Maybe you'd star as the seemingly loving wife who secretly plotted rebellious acts of anger, scheming revenge on your life partner—food—for always having the final word. Or maybe it would be a slow burn—a film about your lover, food, who didn't care that the thrill was gone, who didn't really want to know what you felt or what you needed, because food knew you'd never leave.

Now that you've thoroughly investigated how you show up in your relationship with food, take a moment to think of a place that feels safe, secure, and deeply spiritually connecting for you—whether it's a place in your real life, or an imagined safe space. Visualize yourself there now—in a place where you can wholly surrender to deep spiritual connection, and attune to your body, breath, integrity, and life energy. How would you sit in this place of reverence? Where would you place your attention? How would you settle in? Notice your reverence for what's around you, and the self-respect you carry here.

Now consider that food is, in fact, this "holy" space. Food is the place and food is the connection that allows you to access your utmost respect for life. Food is royal and noble, wise and honorable, and approaching food is like going to your own personal place of worship. When you take care to respect both yourself and food, you heal your relationship to life itself, as well as the other relationships in your life and your connection to your environment.

Take some time to journal about how you can bring this attitude of reverence into your daily interactions with food. For example, can you sit down for a meal? Can you be more present with the food before you? Can you treat your food as if it were your total net worth? Can you be gentle, careful, and appreciative in the way you engage with food? Can you listen deeply to food itself, and let it help you decide what you really need? Can you make sure to take no more than your body needs in the moment? If you wanted to let food know how much you trust it, would you stockpile a five-year supply, or allow yourself to be in a greater flow with its abundance? How might you create a space of complete respect, and also respect your relationship with your body when you eat? How might cultivating this respect allow you to grow more appreciation and joy in your life?

Bringing your awareness to the nature of your relationship with food will help you to shift from internal judgments that you're "right" or "wrong" in the way you "do" food, and engage instead from a place of reverence for life and respect for yourself. Through the simple act of noticing, you will begin to slowly hear more clearly, every day, how you can remain connected to the essential sacredness of food, and so heal your relationship with it.

EXPLORATION 19:
Strengthening the Uncollapsible Self, Cultivating Awareness and Presence

Becoming more present with ourselves and where we are does not necessarily mean we'll immediately feel great about our lives, or even that we'll stop feeling resistance to whatever we're experiencing in the moment. In fact, it is often the case that when we become more aware of what we're experiencing, we grow more attuned to how uncomfortable we are, or how much we are rushing or keeping ourselves from truly embracing our lives. However, the beautiful thing about growing awareness and presence is that we begin to see the stories we carry—stories that are sometimes embedded deep in our physiology.

For example, perhaps you've built a whole project from the ground up. Maybe you're managing a team, or launching a product or program, and you have work to do! For some reason, however, you feel some resistance to getting started. You'd rather do a million other tasks (including cleaning your already-clean bathroom, retiling your floor, or organizing your sock drawer) than start on this important project. It seems that every time you sit down to do the work, you feel something unsettling. Within twenty minutes, you're overwhelmed and compulsively reaching for a snack, or your phone, or anything else, any other activity that will take you away from your desk.

Often, underneath our resistance and impatience, we're holding stories in our bodies that have nothing to do with the project we're doing now; rather, they are old beliefs about ourselves that keep us from engaging deeply with our lives. It's often the case that when we enter a moment without enlisting our awareness or presence, we bring with us the imprint of long-held patterns, expectations, or associations carried over from other times. This means that becoming more aware or present isn't only about being grateful and receiving love, but also about recognizing the negative constructs we're bringing into our lives—and how easy it is to feed these constructs.

In this practice, we'll use presence and awareness to look at our resistance and the story or stories we're telling ourselves.

Visualizing a Shift

Take a moment to tap into your highest vision of self. Open your inner-vision and connect to your felt sensations.

Picture your body and your whole being right now, just as you are, and see if you can concertedly visualize yourself as "a complete work of fine art." Rather than scrutinize our bodies as we often might by some critical standard, take a moment to appreciate your being as you would a beautiful expression of art in a fine museum. Notice the meticulous details of this unique expression that is You, just as you might marvel over revered artwork. As well as seeing yourself as artform, feel the sensation of your artfulness from your head to your toes. If you find it supportive, run your hands from the top to the bottom of your body, feeling the quality of your skin, the dimensions of your physical self in space, the movement of your breath and your pulse in the here and now. Feel, too, the space that's around your body. Notice the ether that's touching your physical form, and any materials that are in contact with your body. See and feel these aspects of yourself as richly delicious. Give yourself to this experience and the physical sensations of your sumptuousness, even if it feels exaggerated, or an unusual way to experience perceiving yourself—as a work of art.

Next, envision an energetic bubble protecting all of who you are, all of the sacred sensitivity you possess. See that this protective bubble extends far beyond your body, allowing in anything you need to receive while filtering out anything that doesn't serve you. Take some breaths as you sit with this vision and feel its truth. Breathe in this atmosphere of protection as though it's your very own "queendom"; a place where you are deeply celebrated. Feel how the space around you supports you as it makes contact with your body. Envision how freeing life is in your queendom: your reign also liberates you as well as everything and everyone else in your life. Expanding from your heart center, feel the environment around you. Feel how, expanding fifty feet in every direction, is a circle charged with the crystallized energy of your uncollapsed, expansive self.

See and feel yourself standing effortlessly in your center, with your own life energy powerfully protecting you and extending that protection into the environment around you. And now see how your self-protected energy, its grace and light, can expand further, for miles—energizing any place where you put your attention. Feel your destiny and the energetic opportunities that await you. This circle of light and potential now expands through the region where you live, across the country, the globe, and into the cosmos.

Envision and feel the abundance of resonant, generative offerings in this universe, waiting for you to receive them.

Now, select a quality from the garden of the universe—a quality you seek to embody, which is available for you to pick from this garden like an eternally blooming flower. Name the quality—it might be love, for example, or tenderness, or grace, or power, or vitality, or anything that speaks to you. Name it, and bring it deeply into your heart and the energetic circle of potential you are now occupying. Say to yourself, internally or aloud, "I possess and carry, receive and emanate this amazing quality." Let this affirmation shine through your whole being, from the top of your head, through your mind's eye, your throat, your heart center, and your stomach, down to the core of your pelvic floor, and finally through your feet.

Take time now to absorb this feeling, knowing that at any point, you can light yourself up in this way and listen deeply to your needs, and from there, choose how you want to move through life. Write down anything that might serve as a daily reminder of your highest self's journey in this lifetime, in mind, body, soul, and spirit.

Once you've completed this practice, you can consciously create a habit of regularly asking yourself, "Can I thread self-love deeply through the core of who I am right now?" With the guidance of our breath, self-compassion, and self-connection, we learn to trust that we can transform our obstacles into opportunities and create expansive unlimited energy for ourselves. We step into the awareness that no matter what we encounter in life, we never have to leave ourselves—we can stay self-connected and build uncollapsible self-trust.

EXPLORATION 20:

Beauty Constructs—How Much of Your Energy Are You Giving to External Beauty Ideals?

Grab your journal as we're going to dive in and do some writing. In this exploration, we'll contemplate the ways we've internalized societal constructs about beauty and self-worth, and how we might be using these externally imposed ideals to limit our sense of self, value, and potential. Then we'll explore ways to gently transform these constructs, recognizing our intrinsic value just as we are, and choosing to feel beautiful from the inside out.

Take some time to consider the following questions in your journal:

- How do you personally define beauty? Internal beauty? External beauty?
- Where do these definitions come from? Who has molded your ideals?
- How do you feel about your own physical body and appearance?
- How much time and energy do you spend trying to adhere to external beauty standards? (To note: these behaviors are different from ways you connect to your body to feel beautiful and celebrate your life. Here, we're considering the kind of actions and behaviors you might take to try to fit into a certain image, or aspire to some external idea of perfection.)
- Do you ever allow your well-being to be impacted by externally imposed ideals about your physical appearance? Do you ever give your power over to critical thoughts, scrutinizing or valuing yourself from the outside in?
- Do you hold any limiting beliefs that keep you from feeling connected to your own beauty and self-worth?

For example, do you believe you need to be a certain weight, or fit into a certain size to be attractive? Or do you believe you were only attractive in the past, when you were a certain age or a certain shape? Have you ever felt "beautiful"? Do you believe that you must look young, or meet some other standard, in order to be valued? Do you believe your looks keep you from getting the love you want?

Once you've taken time to recognize your existing limiting beliefs about your physical appearance, you have an opportunity to challenge those beliefs. Let's begin by looking for evidence that contradicts your long-held ideas. Try journaling on the following questions:

- Can you think of people who have found deep, true happiness despite their age, appearance, or weight? Do you know any people who are loved, cherished, adored, and admired, who might not appear "attractive" by social norms, but who radiate an inner-beauty and profound quality that is infectious and alluring?
- How do you think these people feel about themselves? Where do you think they put their time and energy?

Continue to seek out evidence that stretches or disproves your specific limiting beliefs, looking for examples among friends, your community, or in the media. For example, if you feel you need to look a certain way in order to be successful, seek examples of people who have found great success without being overly fixated on upholding a beauty standard. Recognize the qualities that make them strong, capable, and successful.

Now, let's take a look at just how limiting your beliefs are. It can be easier to overthrow ideas that no longer serve us when we fully appreciate the ways they hold us back. Take a moment to journal on the following questions:

- How much time and energy could you reclaim if you didn't adhere to these limiting beliefs?
- What would you spend your time bringing into the world if you weren't tied up with trying to meet external beauty standards?
- Who would you get to be if you didn't feel you had to look a certain way in order to be accepted? Who would you be if you prioritized what made you *feel* good instead of what made you *look* good?

Beauty is a powerful energy that we each possess in our own way; we can each tap into our own unique form of beauty, anytime. This individual form of beauty transcends all external constructs and is always specific to our own being. To tap into your own unique beauty, close your eyes and take a few deep breaths. Envision yourself free from societal beauty standards and the limiting beliefs you've uncovered above. Feel in your body that you are inherently worthy, beautiful, and powerful just as you are. See yourself moving through the world with this sense of self-acceptance. How might your daily routine change if you embraced this view? How might you carry yourself as you engage with others?

Take a moment in your journal now to write down any affirmations that reinforce your intrinsic worth and beauty. Examples might include, "Self-love makes me feel beautiful." "My attitude grows my sense of beauty." "I am more than my appearance and my worth transcends my appearance." "I embrace my unique beauty." Whichever affirmations feel right for you, once you've written them down, breathe them in and out of your body, repeating each phrase ten times. You can incorporate these affirmations into your life in many ways. For example, create a practice of placing your hand on your heart and repeating them to yourself before you start each day, or before you fall asleep. See how your energy and attention shift.

Tapping into beauty defined on our own terms also means making time to celebrate ourselves—just as we are. What do you find truly fun? What sets your mind at ease? How can you bring these experiences into your life regularly? In your journal, think of one to three ways you can connect to the feeling of joy and vitality this week, and make a plan to put them into action!

Finally, take a moment to see how far you have come. Think about how you treated yourself when you were younger. Who did you think you had to be? And how have you changed in more recent years? Thank yourself for all the positive changes you have made. Recognizing our achievements, including our achievements in self-care, is an important part of feeling beautiful from the inside out, because it gives us more momentum to share our many gifts with the world.

EXPLORATION 21:
Confirming Self-Worth

This is another journaling exploration, so grab your favorite pen and journal—and a timer—and find a quiet space to sit or lie down. In this exercise, we'll be tapping into our intrinsic sense of self-worth.

Make yourself comfortable, connect to your breath, and give yourself a few minutes to settle into your body. When you feel focused in the moment, ask yourself, out loud or internally, "What is valuable about me? Why am I worthy of creating the life I want?"

Now, set your timer for five minutes, and write down any and every aspect of yourself that confirms that you are plenty, just as you are. Make a list of all the qualities you possess that make you valuable.

After your five minutes are up, you'll have a list of qualities—all the things that make you beautiful from the inside out. Now, we'll create ways to celebrate these qualities, using the following sentence structure: "I celebrate myself for _____ by _____." For example, you might write: "I celebrate my perseverance to overcome challenges." Or, "I am proud of the way I can return to the energy of love and forgive myself and others." Or maybe it's: "I celebrate my bravery by trusting that I'm going to be okay when I feel stressed," or "I celebrate my independence by returning to my own energy when I feel I have given my power of thinking over to another person or situation." This exercise allows you to celebrate how valuable you are to yourself, using your own standards and rewards, rather than externally imposed ideals and achievements.

Come up with five sentences from your list of valuable qualities, reinforcing and reaffirming the wonderful attributes you already have. Place these sentences somewhere like an altar, or even taped onto the mirror or doorway, so you can regularly remember your powerful gifts.

EXPLORATION 22:
Allowing a Trigger to Transform You
This exploration is designed to help you identify triggers that often lead you to spiral downward in an escalating negative reaction, until you've created a sense of "tragedy." Once you've identified them, you can begin to reframe those triggers as teachers—opportunities for your own transformation.

Take anywhere from ten to thirty minutes to go through the steps of this contemplative visualization, and return to it regularly to strengthen your ability to transform your behavior.

Step 1: Identify a Trigger

Think about something that happens often in your daily life that brings up a negative emotional response. It could be receiving a particular comment from a colleague, a task at work, a challenging situation at home, or even a recurring thought about yourself.

Step 2: Reflect on Your Reaction to the Trigger

When you encounter this trigger, do you feel anger, sadness, frustration, anxiety, or a mix of many emotions? Consider your physical sensations, too. How do your muscles feel, and what about your heart—does it start to race? Does your stomach knot? What happens to your felt sense of being in the world when you are triggered? Do you feel disconnected from your environment, from others, or from your sense of self?

Step 3: Visualize a Different Response

In your mind's eye, see yourself encountering this trigger—but this time, instead of allowing it to take you down, you will see it as a profound invitation. Envision that the trigger is a request, asking you to stay committed to yourself despite your discomfort. When you encounter the trigger, you are being asked to listen in to your internal self and connect to your amazing inner-resources to feel and accept your emotions—to accept yourself. Which negative self-concept is this trigger asking you to transform? What do you need to shift? How do you need to express yourself? If this trigger is a teacher who guides you with the energy of love and connection, what is it asking you to notice? What does it want you to see or learn?

Step 4: Create a Trigger Mantra

Now see your trigger play out in your mind's eye, and imagine that you are attaching an audio recording to it. Every time you experience this trigger from here on out, you'll hear the phrase, "How can I call my energy back to myself in a compassionate capacity? How can I transform this experience into a gentle, loving opportunity for growth?" By regularly returning to these questions at moments when you used to self-collapse, you will begin to use your triggers as catalysts for positive change. This is how we become more resilient: by using our triggers as a strength-training protocol.

Step 5: Thank Your Triggers

Take a moment to thank your triggers for consistently showing up and giving you the opportunity to grow. You might even want to take the time to write a letter of appreciation to your trigger, addressing it as an ancient teacher who gave you all she had, patiently handing down her wisdom to help you see the opportunity for your own transformation, again and again.

Step 6: Make Room to Accept Others' Triggers

The more we practice compassion for other people's triggers, the more we can be tender with the parts of ourselves that are still learning and growing. How do others' triggers feel for you? Do you find yourself collapsing into them? Where and when could you be more mindful and tolerant of them?

In fact, beyond simply tolerating others' triggers, over time, we can begin to change the way we look at experiences happening in our lives. We can begin to see these experiences as opportunities to create more grace and growth. In this way, we cultivate the energy of mindfulness and compassion—which are the core components of self-connection and inside-out nourishment—and are able to connect more richly with the people we meet. This work isn't easy, but if we practice transforming our triggers when we're less activated, over time, we can learn to stay with our feelings and welcome our triggers as a call to growth and transformation.

EXPLORATION 23:
Shifting Long-Held Negative Memories of the Family Meal and Creating Your Own Self-Nourishing Food Culture

The following exploration will support you to let go of outworn behaviors by accessing implicit-year memories of what eating was like in the company of your family. In this journaling exercise, we let go of the past and its impact on us by taking more responsibility for the energy we bring into our bodies, minds, and spirits around food and all things nourishing.

Take anywhere from ten to thirty minutes to complete this three-step practice.

Step 1: Recalling the Past

Find a quiet, comfortable place where you can sit and reflect. Close your eyes and take several deep breaths, settling into your body. Now, bring to mind an early memory of the set and setting of your family mealtimes. If the memory is fuzzy, allow yourself to sharpen the details by focusing on the environment. Can you recall the table, the chairs, the people present, and the food? What do you recall about the moods of the people around the table? How did you feel around them? For example, were you anxious, uncomfortable, or closed down, anticipating some unpleasant event or other? Or did you feel open and safe to be vulnerable? Was there tension or criticism between any members of the family, or was it a time of connection and warmth? Notice how bringing your attention to this memory impacts the feelings in your body. Are your muscles tensing? Is your breath shallow?

Write about this memory in your journal, describing what you've recalled and how you felt. You could even write a small screenplay of the scene, about a little girl (you) having a meal with her family. As you write, notice any physical sensations that arise. Are you feeling tightness, heaviness, impatience, or unease? Breathe into these feelings, reminding your body that this memory is from the past and you no longer need to carry this story.

Step 2: Infusing Your Memory with the Energy of Love
Now, imagine walking through a doorway—a magical, transformative, mystical doorway. It brings you into that same dining space you recalled earlier, but this time, everything is infused with light and warmth. The table is beautifully set, perhaps with flowers and candles, or anything else that makes you feel calm and peaceful. The atmosphere is appealing to all of your senses, and you feel your whole body fully welcomed in the space. Your family members greet you with love and appreciation, their faces soft with warmth and smiles. Their energy is open and loving. They radiate ease, health, and comfort in their own bodies. Now, they begin to offer you and each other kind words. Everyone is celebrating each other for exactly who they are, just as they are. See yourself taking a seat at the table, and notice that it is set with your favorite dishes and utensils. The food is prepared with care, tailored to your tastes and needs, and it looks and smells delicious.

Now, you begin to eat with presence, letting yourself savor each bite, while around you the conversation flows easily. Everyone is present and attentive. You are surrounded by love, and the food you're consuming embodies the love of the moment. You are taking this love into your body. As laughter and pleasant conversation fill the room creating a harmonious and supportive environment, notice how warm and comfortable your body feels—relaxed, safe, and free to be yourself. Breathe deeply, taking in the feeling of deep calm in this environment.

In your journal, describe this new, transformed memory. How does the atmosphere feel different? How do the interactions with your family members change? Which emotions do you experience in this new memory? As you write, focus on the physical sensations in your body. Do you feel more relaxed, open, and at ease? Breathe into these positive feelings, letting them fill your body and remind you that you can create new, nourishing experiences.

Step 3: Creating and Integrating a New Narrative

As you breathe deeply, feel your body relax into this new, nourishing memory. Notice how your muscles soften and your breath steadies. In this safe space, you can fully enjoy the meal, gratefully savoring each bite. Imagine the warmth of the food and the love from your family nourishing you from the inside out. Reflect on the difference in this experience—how it feels to be supported, seen, and valued. Internalize this new narrative, letting it replace the old, negative associations. Remind yourself that you deserve to feel nourished and loved at every meal.

Open your eyes and bring your awareness back to the present moment. Feel your feet grounded on the floor, and feel your seat supporting you. Take a few more deep breaths, and with each breath, bring the positive energy and feelings from your transformed memory into your current life. Imagine carrying this sense of nourishment, love, and support with you, allowing it to influence your relationship with food and your overall well-being. Each time you sit down for a meal, recall this new memory and let it guide your experience, turning mealtime into a moment of self-care and connection.

To further support healing your earliest memories of shared meals, in your journal, write about ways you want to integrate these new feelings of nourishment and support into your daily life. How can you infuse your mealtimes with a sense of love and connection? How can you create a positive, supportive environment for your meals? What kind of culture do you want to create around food? Which small changes can you make to enhance your sense of well-being and connection during mealtimes? Breathe into these intentions and focus on your bodily sensations, allowing yourself to feel the shift toward greater nourishment and self-care.

EXPLORATION 24:
Mending Habitual Divides Between Your Feeling Self and Your Functioning Self

Are there ever times when you plow over your feelings because you "just don't have time" to take care of your emotions, or you fear that giving in to your sensations will take you down a rabbit hole of darkness? Do you try to shut your feelings off because you can't deal with your overwhelming sensitivity? Do you tend to give yourself orders? Here's a meditative exploration that can build a bridge between the part of ourselves that experiences big feelings and the part that would prefer to avoid having feelings altogether.

Set aside ten to thirty minutes for this exercise.

Step 1: The Director

Begin by finding a quiet, comfortable space where you can sit without distractions. Close your eyes and take a few deep breaths, allowing your body to relax. In the following visualization, remember you are always invited to open your eyes, come back into your safe and calm space, and connect with your breath. Listening to your physiological needs is always key when you explore. You're in charge here!

To begin, tap into a visualization of your inner-world. Activate your visual sense and imagine the physical landscape filled with color and energy that exists within you. Perhaps it's a place with lots of activity, excitement, and thrills, like a fairground, or maybe it's more like a serene spa. Take a moment to visualize this inner-world space.

Now, visualize that somewhere inside your inner-world, there resides a character we'll call "the Director." See this Director and give them features: an energy, a personality, a level of tolerance, and behavioral traits. Remember, the Director is a part of *you*, so allow them to carry an energy that emerges naturally in your psyche. Notice, too, the atmosphere around the Director: the colors, the energy, the environment they create when they move. You can even hear their voice; how do they sound? Do they speak evenly and sternly, or do they scream? As you move your awareness around different parts of your body, does your sense of the Director's presence change? Does the Director, for example, take up a lot of energy in your stomach, or leave a trail of fire in their wake? How do they handle your heart?

Step 2: The Emotive Self

Next, envision another character who lives inside you, called the Emotive Self. As you begin to visualize this

276

character, take the time to listen in and learn about them. Does she have a name? How does she sound? How does she move? What does she feel? Do her feelings have great range, or does she predominantly feel one thing? Is she young or old—or ageless? What does she look like? How does this Emotive Self feel about herself? Notice how she feels in various parts of your body. For example, how does your pelvic floor feel when you envision her? Do you have more or less sensation in your throat when you bring your Emotive Self's energy through you? What is her agenda? Does she have one? Is there anything she longs for? Is she an optimist or a pessimist? Does she feel recognized?

Step 3: Integrating the Director and the Emotive Self for Embodiment
Bring the Director and the Emotive Self together and see how they interact. Watch their dynamic. How does the Emotive Self feel around the Director? What happens to her felt sense of being when the Director comes around, and vice versa? How do the desires of the Director and the Emotive Self differ? How are they at odds? How are they similar?

Now, focus your attention on the Director. See them making a plan, and, as usual, executing their demands through you. "Do this, go here, make this happen—now—in fact, get it done yesterday," the Director might scream. Notice how your body feels in response. Now, widen your focus and reintroduce the Emotive Self to the scene. See the Emotive Self having a need, something to say, or a feeling—something the Director may not like to deal with. Watch their interaction unfold, and see how it feels in your body. This interaction—and your response to it—is key to understanding the pattern you follow when your self-direction and your emotions engage. What happens? Do you get tired? Do you want to check out? Do you feel like you "just can't get it done"?

Now we'll create a strong, integrated new vision for these parts of self. Call the Director into your awareness and watch them having an idea. Now, notice that instead of blasting you with an agenda, the Director goes to the Emotive Self and asks for some support. In fact, the Director asks the Emotive Self how the two of them could collaborate to make the plan or vision work better for *you*. Now, watch as the Emotive Self responds, and the pair begin to get to know each other better, realizing that they aren't so different. See them realizing that if they learn to listen to and respect each other, they can create more power and love for *you* than they ever could on their own. See them realize that they need each other.

Continue to envision these parts—your Director and your Emotive Self—working collaboratively. Notice how your Emotive Self feels when she's really heard, and how the Director might calm down and, in fact, make greater and more graceful progress by allowing their actions to be informed by the energy of the whole self.

Feel free to write down any realizations you might have around these parts of yourself, staying present with them while recognizing that they are simply aspects of your whole, integrated being.

End your exploration by imagining a new possibility. Envision a typical situation where you might let a plan of action override your emotions. Instead of trying to ignore how you feel or turn off your feelings, think about how you can get curious. Imagine pausing and asking yourself what's really happening inside. Remind yourself that whatever you feel, you will survive it, and that there is room for your whole self to be accepted and heard. In this way, we

278

can nourish ourselves, deepening our felt sense of love and presence.

EXPLORATION 25:
Befriending the Unknown

This ten-minute exploration invites you to bring awareness to your relationship with the unknown elements of life, and to connect to the unknown as a source of self-connection and presence in the moment.

Find a comfortable place where you can sit or lie down without distractions. Bring your hands to any part of your body that would be supported by extra grounding, warming energy. Connect to your breath, elongating your inhalations and exhalations. Hold your out-breath before you take a new breath in, supporting you to let go of tension or stress held in your body.

Using your breath as a guide, explore the energy of your physical body. Fill the breath with awareness, and let it scan you from the top of your head to the bottoms of your feet, taking in the sensations of being just as you are, living your life.

Now, let's turn our awareness to the unknown. Bring to mind something you care about but cannot ultimately control—which, of course, means most things in life. You might consider an opportunity that is currently available to you, a work project, your financial standing, your own or others' health, or the well-being of your friends and family. While it's likely uncomfortable, I want you to feel the energy of uncertainty that surrounds this thing. Give that energy contours, texture, color, even a persona. What does uncertainty look like? What's the feeling tone of this energy—the energy that says that no matter how much you prepare, life can always find a way to surprise you? How does it feel to sit with the inevitability of unpredictability? What is the first feeling you can locate in your body? Is it fear, resistance, or even anxiety that arises when you consider the energy of the unknown?

Now, let's gently shift our focus. Keeping your attention on the energy of the unknown, allow the visualization to begin to transmute and transform. See the colors of the unknown become more warm, bright, alluring, and engaging. As you watch, the unknown becomes a richly welcoming place that gently chants, "Yes! Yes! Yes! I love you!" Feel its energy transform into that of an amazing friend, someone who delights you and always brings you wonderful presents. The field of the unknown becomes an energy you wholeheartedly welcome, a beloved that you are thrilled to host and care for. You notice that she is filled with vast potential and energy. She offers a vision of all your dreams, already come true, and beckons you to join her and effortlessly delight in the joy of life. You fill with respect for her as a master artisan—a magician, even, alchemizing all your challenges into jewels of opportunity and growth, and carving out new experiences and unexpected joys. See how she loves to celebrate those who have put their heart and soul and determination into their passion, and see how she showers inspiration on you, asking you to trust your desire as a way to navigate her.

See the unknown now as she holds out her hand—open, warm, and dazzlingly bejeweled. In it is a golden seed that she wants you to have. See yourself reaching out to her, and feel that when your hands meet, her gift of a golden seed flows from her palm to yours, then to your heart. In your heart, this seed fills you with the warmth of self-love and connection to all of life; to yourself, to others, and to your environment. Hear the unknown laugh lightly, whispering a secret into your ear. She says, "The source of infinite potential and the greatest gift of joy and vitality is within you. Trust yourself. Open yourself to the unknown. Listen as you go."

Returning to your breath, come back to the physical space around you—the known world. Feel the transience of all things, and remember that uncertainty is a natural part of life—that in fact, it is only in the unknown that we discover new facets of ourselves. As you come back into your current reality, bring with you the awareness that you can choose how you relate to the energy of the unknown, and you decide how it impacts your emotions and behaviors. Recognize that while it is human to feel fear and anxiety in the face of uncertainty, it is also possible to approach the unknown with a sense of openness and curiosity—and that doing so requires us to trust ourselves and tap into our inner-wisdom and creativity. Nobody can escape the unknown, but you *can* learn to embrace it as an integral part of your life—and in doing so, you will access the unknown's endless possibilities for growth, joy, and fulfillment.

EXPLORATION 26:
Reframing Your So-Called Failures as Guides on Your Learning Journey

In this exercise, we will cultivate a more nourishing relationship with the aspects of our past we might regret or feel ashamed of, liberating ourselves of self-limiting beliefs as we move into the future.

To begin, find a quiet place where you can sit comfortably, close your eyes, and take a few deep breaths to center yourself. Now, call to mind a significant moment in your life that was particularly challenging. Consider examples such as facing a career setback, struggling in a relationship, or dealing with a health issue.

Think about this difficult experience in detail. What happened? How did it make you feel? Allow yourself to fully acknowledge the emotions that arise, be they sadness, anger, fear, or frustration.

Next, consider the steps you took to get through this tough time. As hard as it was, how did you take action to overcome the obstacles you faced—spiritually, physically, and emotionally? Which internal resources did you draw upon? Did you develop new skills, create new friendships, or find strengths that you didn't know you had?

Take five minutes to journal about the ways you got to know yourself through this experience, and the transformative empowerment that came from surviving the challenge. Perhaps you became more resilient or autonomous, or learned to trust your instincts or connect to a deeper sense of self-love and self-connection. How has this challenging time helped you to know yourself better?

Having reflected on this experience, step back and look at your life path and the growth that has come from this challenge. Understand that your so-called "failure" was actually a stepping stone toward greater self-awareness and inner-strength. Now, see that you can reframe every "failed" moment from your past in this same way, embracing self-compassion and humility and recognizing that these experiences gave you insight, which you can lovingly carry forward as you continue to navigate life's uncertainties. By redefining our so-called failures, we let go of the shame of outdated self-limiting beliefs, and truly embrace and nurture all we are now.

EXPLORATION 27:
Shifting from Forcing Willpower to Inviting Resonance

When we define Nourish on our own terms, we get to connect to a more sustainable energy in which we approach our lives as true creators. Rather than forcing regimented structures on ourselves, we learn to drop in, listen, and let passion and connection lead the way. We get to feel resonance with ourselves, with others, and with our environment, and use this resonance to activate our lives, our drive, and our vision.

Let's explore how we can shift out of restrictive "shoulds" and the forced external protocols we call "willpower," and instead access true well-being from a heart-based internal energy we call resonance.

Find a quiet place where you can sit comfortably, close your eyes, and take a few deep breaths.

Call on a familiar situation where you feel overwhelmed, pressured, or stressed. For instance, you might imagine yourself trying to get through a project, preparing for a meeting or performance, planning for an event, or traveling.

See how this situation might activate your external "shoulds." Perhaps you believe that in order to succeed, you need to eat a certain way, or exercise every day, or stay on top of specific work tasks. While these activities may very well be healthy for your body, mind, and soul, it's important to consider how you address these "shoulds" to yourself. How do you exert your willpower? Can you feel how much pressure you put on yourself to live up to set ideas that come from the external world, or from your intellect? In which ways and to what extent do you use internal pressure to drive your achievements forward, to achieve some idealized benchmark of value or worthiness?

Now feel into your heart and your sense of self-connection when you're in this state. What happens to them? How flexible and open to life and its creative and mysterious energy do you feel when you're regimentally enforcing behaviors on yourself?

Now, let's see what happens when we bring the energy of "resonance" into this space. Bring your awareness to this stressful situation, and notice whether your mind and body start to get revved up and accumulate a list of "shoulds." Notice any internal pressure you feel in your body, and how its presence likely creates more stress.

Remaining tapped into your stress state, place your hand on your heart. Take a deep breath and ask yourself, "What am I fearing right now?" Even if you aren't fearing anything, per se, take a moment to see what surfaces. Perhaps you get a simple answer, like, "I'm fearing that I won't be organized for my meeting." Look further, beneath this immediate response. What's the fear that's driving this fear? What will happen if you arrive at your meeting unprepared? "I fear that I'll be mocked by my colleagues." Keep investigating. What's beneath *this* fear? "I fear that I'm not taken seriously enough." And then, even under that? "I fear I'll always have to work too hard just to prove I'm enough." Keep digging until you locate what feels like the root feeling beneath this fear. It might be something like, "I don't think I'll get to where I need to be in this lifetime." Whatever it is for you, this exercise is an opportunity to uncover the energy and secret beliefs we use to keep ourselves moving forward faster and further—an opportunity to see what's really fueling us. Are we fueled by the story

284

that we're not enough? Or by our connection to life and desire to honor all that we are?

Now, we'll begin to bring in the energy of resonance. With your hand on your heart, take a few breaths without any agenda, and slowly tap into your inner-self. When you feel settled, ask yourself, "What do my body, mind, and spirit truly need right now?" Let the "shoulds" take a back seat and give yourself time to listen to your inner-desires and needs. Feel the resonance of your own hand on your heart. Bring your awareness to the space around you and then let it keep expanding, into the town or city you're in, and all the people in it. Recognize that your greatest dreams are in closer reach when you connect with self-love, with the energy of joy, and with the spirit of curiosity, and when you really respond to what you need.

As you practice bringing more resonance into your life, you'll notice that you naturally begin to work with the creative energy of life itself—and from here, you'll create more peace and satisfaction in your life as a whole. You will also find a growing ability to navigate uncertainty with grace and confidence. By embracing resonance, you will step into harmony with yourself and the world around you, creating a more nourishing and fulfilling life.

EXPLORATION 28:
Redefining Boundaries to Reinforce Self-Love and a Nourishing Experience of the World
What's really happening when we do not value our own needs, when we speak aggressively to ourselves, or when we continually visualize worst-case scenarios, failing to make the positive changes we know are possible? I believe that whenever we cling to patterns or behaviors that don't serve us, we are suffering from not having clear

boundaries. In this exploration, we will put in place the conditions we need to start setting healthier boundaries, from a place of self-love.

Think of a parent and a child in a harmonious relationship. As the child grows, the parent teaches them how to take care of themselves independently. The more supportive, clear, and approachable the directions are, the better the child typically does at finding their autonomy. It can be the case that when we are encouraged to recognize ourselves as individuals or express our needs, we learn to build healthy boundaries rather than take on self-limiting behaviors as a means of self-protection.

Central to the Path of Nourish is the process of learning where you end and others begin, so that you can stay in your lane and take care of your own energy. When we learn to do this, we can feel peaceful in our own skin—and the more at peace we are with ourselves, the more we can respect other people's boundaries.

In this exploration, you are invited to write down your physical, mental, spiritual, and soulful needs—everything you need on each of these levels in order to grow a sense of safety in yourself. For when we feel safe, connected, and confident enough to listen to and value our own needs, we know how to respect ourselves and inherently practice healthy boundaries.

Find a journal and a pen, then create a quiet and comfortable environment, connecting to your breath and settling into your body to find focus. Now set your timer for ten minutes and resolve to totally relax into this exercise.

First, ask yourself what your *body* needs from you, in order to feel safe, energized, nourished, respected, and cared for.

Consider the way you speak to yourself and the way you move in your environment. Does your body need more opportunities to express itself freely, or more time in nature? Drop in deep and ask your whole felt sense what you need to feel nourished from the inside out. See what your body needs, and even how these needs may relate to your earliest unmet needs as a little girl.

Now, ask this same question to your mind and your cognitive processes. Which behaviors, which actions does your mind need from you in order to fully tend to its needs? What does your mind need to feel healthy, safe, strong, vital, secure, and able to access joy? For example, would your mind like less stimulation, less time looking at a computer screen? Would it appreciate listening to a symphony, or time in quiet nature? Again, investigate how your mind's needs might relate to any unmet need you had as a little girl. Ask yourself, "What will nourish my mind from the inside out?" Listen, and note your inner-self's responses in your journal.

Now, pose this same question to your spirit—the energy of life moving through you, which can connect you to all existence and allow you to feel included in your own life. What do you need to open up to your spiritual energy? Since our hearts are so often connected to our spiritual energy, ask your heart, "What do you long for to feel part of the world?" Again, investigate whether your spirit's needs connect to your earliest hopes and dreams as a little girl. As you listen, note down what you need to feel connected to spirit.

Finally, ask yourself what your soul needs to express itself in this lifetime. Does it need more proper attention? Does it need your mind and body to take it seriously? Does it need to trust that your body is a safe space for it, and that it won't be shut down? See what your soul needs now and how this need relates to your earliest unmet needs as a little girl.

Now that you've recognized what your body, mind, soul, and spirit need from you, you have a perfect blueprint for your boundaries. We often think of our boundaries as something that other people need to respect—but the first place we practice boundaries is in our relationship with ourselves. Ultimately, boundaries are a pact we make with ourselves to protect our own energy, respect our bodies, minds, spirits, and souls, and care for our reality and those within it. If, for example, you are letting yourself say horrible words or express hateful things to yourself all day long, you are disrespecting your own boundaries and trampling all over yourself. The more we know what we really need, the better we can take care of ourselves. And the more we practice caring for ourselves, the more we model to others how to interact with us—and the better we get at respecting others' needs, too. We become resourceful, connected, and committed to listening to ourselves from the inside out.

To finish, write the heading "I need" in your journal, and underneath it, list the self-respecting boundaries and energetic qualities you wish to create or cultivate in your life now. Put this list somewhere you can see daily, as a reminder that boundaries don't divide us from others or from life itself—they allow us to be integrated, to feel whole, and to connect.

EXPLORATION 29:
Learning to Love the Most Tender Part of Yourself
Let's take a moment to access our tenderness.

To prepare for this exploration, create a space that feels really cozy, taking some time to do so if necessary. You'll need a candle and a journal, in case you wish to write down your discoveries.

Light your candle and place it somewhere you'll see its illuminating flicker. Sit or lie down in the cozy space you've created, then settle in and let go of the day's or night's events.

Now, place your hand on your heart and bring your awareness to your breath. Notice where your breath is moving in your body, then invite it to lengthen and slow down. By slowing down, you can begin to welcome in all parts of yourself. Slowing down enables us to open, let go, and more fully occupy ourselves and the space around us.

Take ten full breaths in this way, concentrating on letting go, accepting however you feel right now, and exploring. Imagine that you are being with yourself in the same way you would be with a child, just staying with her as she breathes, in and out.

Now, feel the part of yourself that is always ready to go; the part that always has her to-do list on hand, a pen behind her ear, and her keys out, ready to get from A to B. Feel her and the way she occupies your body, and then let her know that she can take a little break now. She likes timeframes, so give her one. Tell her you need ten minutes, then allow her to let you go while you relax further.

Next, access a part of yourself that still feels like a little child. Drop in and seek to connect with any part of yourself that feels tender, vulnerable, and in need of love or reassurance. Picture this child version of yourself clearly. How does she look? How does she feel? Gently invite this child self to come forward, letting her know she is safe.

As you connect with this tender part of yourself, offer her compassion and kindness. What does she need to hear right now? Perhaps she needs to know that she is loved, that she is safe, that she is enough just as she is. Speak to her gently and with love, either silently or aloud.

Take a few moments to hold space for this tender part of yourself. Feel the warmth of your hand on your heart and the steady rhythm of your breath. Allow yourself to be fully present with your inner-child, offering her the love and care she deserves.

When you feel ready, gently bring your awareness back to the present moment. Open your eyes, and if you wish, take a few moments to journal about this experience. Reflect on what it felt like to connect with your most tender self and how you can continue to nurture this part of you in your daily life.

By taking the time to love and care for our tender selves, we build a deeper connection with our true essence. This practice helps us cultivate self-compassion, resilience, and a profound sense of inner-peace. And that is what the Path of Nourish is all about.

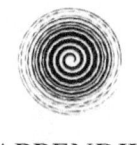

APPENDIX

The Insta-Nourish Self-Study Checklist

The following questions are offered as a nourishing resource that can fit into even the most fast-paced of lives. I invite you to regularly review these thirty questions and create a little ritual around them. Sit with these questions for ten minutes every morning or night, or any time in the day you feel a need for replenishment. Don't try to tackle all of the questions at once; start with just one or two, and allow yourself time to sink into it. Instead of answering with your head, listen inwardly, meditating deeply on the question, feeling your inmost physiological response, and letting your breath support you to feel safe and secure. In time, this practice will make you more self-confident, reminding you that the wise insight your soul is seeking can ultimately come from within.

1. How are you responding to real or perceived conflict right now? As you navigate these challenges and conflicts, is there anything you need to nourish your respect for yourself, for others, and for life itself?

2. What does your heart want? Can you locate it? And is there anything you need to nourish your connection to your heart's desire?

3. Do you feel like you are enough right now? If not, what does your inner-world need in order to feel that you are absolutely enough?

4. Are you speaking to yourself kindly, or thinking kind thoughts about yourself right now? What would support you in bringing more empathy and compassion to your inner-dialogue?

5. Is there a small, achievable choice you can make today that will help you thrive? If so, how can you commit to making one or more nourishing self-care choices today?

6. What free source of joy can you access right now? And how might nourishing your sense of joy benefit your body, mind, soul, and spirit?

7. What would it take for you to generate the energy of safety and security in your nervous system right now? And how might generating this energy of safety and security help you to receive life's nourishing gifts?

8. How are you choosing to experience reality right now? And which small shifts (that have nothing to do with food) would help you feel more nourished in this moment?

9. Do you believe you have the creative power to shift your destiny? And what kind of nourishing mindset do you need in order to feel in charge of your creative power?

10. How are you practicing self-accountability today? And what will help you nourish your sense of presence so that you can show up responsibly for yourself?

11. How are you currently relating to the sensations in your body? And what energy is your body calling for to help it feel more nourished in this moment?

12. Do you feel overwhelmed or unable to interpret what's happening inside you? And what is one small step you can take right now to calmly nourish your sense of self-connection?

13. Do you notice how foods impact your general energy or mood? And what energy would your body most like to call in today in order to feel truly nourished?

14. Are you overriding your body's cues in order to get stuff done? If so, what nourishing choice could you make today in order to allow yourself the space to relax and feel less pressured?

15. When experiencing conflict, do you check in with your body before reacting? If not, what might you need to nourish this practice? And how might taking a pause before responding benefit you and your relationships?

16. Do you think with your whole body? If not, what might you need to nourish a more holistic, integrative way of thinking?

17. Do you feel like your body is working for you, under the command of your cognitive mind and its orders, or do you work together as one? How could you better nourish this partnership? And what might be the benefit of doing so?

18. Are there feelings you are resisting feeling right now? Can you give yourself permission to feel more, and to nourish your emotional awareness?

19. Are you giving up on yourself in any way right now? If so, which nourishing words can you direct to your whole being, so that the entirety of you feels deeply valued?

20. How does recognizing your feelings help you grow self-compassion? And what might you need to nourish more self-recognition?

21. Are you craving anything right now, be it food, something material, time with somebody special, or another external energy? Are you able to respond to your energetic cravings internally, rather than reaching outside of yourself to "fix" your sense of being? Is your hunger authentic, or are you calling for something else, such as reassurance that you are okay and enough, just as you are? What might you need to nourish your sense of secure self-attachment?

22. What do you need right now, in whatever situation you are in, to take truly supportive care of yourself? How proactive can you be about nourishing your well-being in this moment?

23. What supports you to feel aligned with yourself in order to manifest your vision? And what might you need today in order to nourish this internal sense of alignment?

24. How available are you to let the energy of love into your heart? And what gift can you give yourself from within in order to nourish your heart's openness?

25. Are you able to run the energy of self-compassion through your system to soothe your state of being? And what might help you to nourish your ability to be compassionate toward yourself?

26. Do you have physiologically supportive ways to access joy, or does reaching for joy usually entail debauchery or something unhealthy for you? What might you need to become more intimate with the art of joyful healthy living? How could a healthy practice for accessing

thrills, deliciousness, and joyous experiences nourish your life?

27. Do you ever let go of the pressure you put on yourself to take care of your external appearance and allow yourself to feel beautiful just as you are? What would you need to nourish your sense that you are beautiful and enough, just as you are, right now, from the inside out?

28. Are you exhausted from trying to be perfect? What could you do or give to yourself in order to feel that you are already perfect as you are? How can you nourish this perfect, true self that already exists?

29. Do you feel that you use food to deal with your emotions or energetic upset, rather than honoring, delighting in, and receiving food as nourishment? What could help you nourish a healthier relationship with food? And what would it mean to be in grace—defined on your own terms—with the art of eating?

30. What is valuable about you? Why are you worthy of creating the life you want? And what might you need to nourish this self-confidence and belief all the more?

*T*HE TIME TO *N*OURISH IS NOW!!!

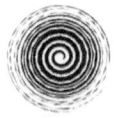

About the Author

I sabel Chiara is the author of the acclaimed books *Eat Your Words* and *Bod Behavior*, which dive deeply into the world of eating behaviors and the journey of creating true personal transformation. Having honed her expertise through more than thirty years of extensive study and practice of transformational energy modalities, Isabel is the creator of The Life Actualization Process, providing her clients with powerful tools to activate their unlimited potential. Whether through her books, sessions, public talks, or in her customizable app Nourish, Isabel's core mission as a holistic educator and intuitive guide is to help others follow their most liberated, passionate, and empowered life paths, full of prosperity, miracles, and magic.

Learn more about Isabel's many offerings at
www.isabel-chiara.com

www.ingramcontent.com/pod-product-compliance
Lightning Source LLC
Chambersburg PA
CBHW021707120626
46545CB00004B/1439